FAMILY LAW (DIVORCE)

AUSTRALIA

LBC Information Services
Sydney

CANADA AND THE USA

Carswell

NEW ZEALAND
Brooker's
Auckland

SINGAPORE AND MALAYSIA
Thompson Information (S.E. Asia)
Singapore

FAMILY LAW (DIVORCE) ACT 1996

Nuala Jackson

B.A. (Mod.) LL.M., B.L.

and

Stephanie Coggans

B.A. (Mod.), Solicitor

ROUND HALL

Sweet & Maxwell

Published in 1998 by
Round Hall Sweet & Maxwell
Brehon House, 4 Upper Ormond Quay,
Dublin 7.

Typeset by
Gilbert Gough Typesetting, Dublin.

Printed by
Colourbooks, Dublin.

ISBN 1–85800–125–0

A catalogue record for this book
is available from the British Library.

FAMILY LAW (DIVORCE) ACT, 1996

(1996 No. 33)

An Act to make provision for the exercise by the courts of the jurisdiction conferred by the constitution to grant decrees of divorce, to enable the courts to make certain preliminary and ancillary orders in or after proceedings for divorce, to provide, as respects transfers of property of divorced spouses, for their exemption from, or for the abatement of, certain taxes (including stamp duty) and to provide for related matters. [27th November, 1996]

INTRODUCTION AND GENERAL NOTE

> "The family is the basic building block of society. The nuclear family is a naturally
> occurring phenomenon. It was ordained by God and so on. I have been surrounded
> by this since the day I was born. There are occasions . . . when I ask why, if it is so
> natural and was decided upon by God and if it is a big building block of society and
> is the primary element of the Constitution, it cannot look after itself?"

> David Norris (148 *Seanad Debates* Col. 1680)

The introduction of domestic divorce in Ireland required the amendment of Article 41 of Bunreacht na hÉireann. The history of divorce in Ireland is well known but will be repeated herein briefly for the sake of completeness. The legislation providing for the granting of divorce by judicial decree, which was introduced in England by the Matrimonial Causes Act 1857 (20 & 21 Vict., c.85) did not extend in its application to this jurisdiction. Therefore, in the post-1857, pre-Independence period Irish couples could continue to obtain a dissolution of marriage by Private Act of parliament only. This procedure continued in existence until the early to mid-1920s, when the parliamentarians of the new Free State made it clear that divorce was not a concept compatible with Ireland's new found independent identity. Any Private Members' Bills in the course of passage through the Dáil during that period eventually fell into abeyance, due to a dearth of statutory instruments or political desire to deal with them.

Although, theoretically, it is to be assumed that parliamentary divorce remained available in Ireland until 1937; there being no divorce prohibition in the Constitution of the Irish Free State and no legislative prohibition in place; the gate was firmly bolted upon legislative change by the 1937 Constitution. Article 41 of Bunreacht na hÉireann, as originally introduced and as it continued until November, 1995, stated:

> "1. The State pledges itself to guard with special care the institution of Marriage on which the Family is founded and to protect it against attack.

> 2. No law shall be enacted providing for the grant of a dissolution of marriage.

> 3. No person whose marriage has been dissolved under the civil law of any other State but is a subsisting valid marriage under the law for the time being in force within the jurisdiction of the Government and Parliament established by this Constitution shall be capable of contracting a valid marriage within that jurisdiction during the lifetime of the other party to the marriage so dissolved."

The first in-road into these provisions came in the form of judicial interpretation regarding the circumstances in which a divorce granted in a foreign jurisdiction might be recognised as valid in Ireland. Definitive Supreme Court decisions, most notably *W. v. W.* [1993] 2 I.R. 376, as well as legislation in the form of the Domicile and Recognition of Foreign Divorces Act 1986 (No. 24), have provided for substantial certainty in the area of divorce recognition. A foreign decree is recognised if either of the parties was, at the time the decree was granted, domiciled in the jurisdiction which granted the decree. The recognition rules presently applicable will be considered hereinafter in the context of the jurisdictional basis for the grant of a decree of divorce domestically introduced in this statute. As the principle of reciprocity clearly does not operate as between the jurisdictional basis upon which a divorce will be granted and Ireland's recognition rules, there are strong arguments to be made for more extensive recognition rules to apply in the context of having introduced divorce legislation with a broad jurisdictional base.

The circumstances of recognition must also be considered in the light of Part III of the Family Law Act 1995 (No. 26). In practical terms, at present there is often a close link between domestic divorce proceedings and the recognition of foreign decrees. Due to the absence of divorce relief in Ireland for many years, many Irish people or people connected with Ireland, have obtained foreign decrees and have subsequently remarried on the basis of the decree. In a substantial proportion of these cases, the foreign divorce is not and never was recognised in Ireland, as the divorcing parties' link with the jurisdiction of grant was merely transitory. However, in other instances, one of the parties may arguably have been

3

domiciled in the foreign jurisdiction and thus the parties may now wish to seek alternative reliefs; being a declaration of marital status under section 29 of the Family Law Act 1995 (the 1995 Act) or, in the alternative, a decree of divorce under section 5 of the Family Law (Divorce) Act 1996 (No. 33) (the 1996 Act). It is, perhaps, worthy of comment, as there would appear to be a popular misconception on the point, that remarrying abroad having obtained a foreign decree does not lead to a valid second marriage under Irish law. The conflict of laws rule on this point is that capacity to marry is governed by the law of the domicile; with lesser support for applying the law of the intended matrimonial home; not by the *lex fori* of the marriage. Only formalities or procedural aspects of marriage are governed by the *lex fori*.

The second attempt to modify the provisions of Article 41 was more direct and came in 1986 when the first referendum seeking to alter Article 41.2 was held. The proposed amendment was in the following terms:

> "Where, and only where, such court established under this Constitution as may be prescribed by law is satisfied that:
> (i) a marriage has failed,
> (ii) the failure has continued for a period of, or periods amounting to, at least five years,
> (iii) that there is no reasonable possibility of reconciliation between the parties to the marriage, and
> (iv) any other condition prescribed by law has been complied with,
>
> the court may in accordance with law grant a dissolution of the marriage provided that the court is satisfied that adequate and proper provision having regard to the circumstances will be made for any dependent spouse and for any child who is dependent on either spouse."

The people of Ireland rejected the proposed amendment and it was to be in excess of 10 years later before judicial divorce was first to become available in Ireland. However, legal developments continued during this intervening period spurred on by the social demand for legal remedies to deal with the reality and consequences of marriage breakdown.

The first major change in this regard came with the Judicial Separation and Family Law Reform Act 1989 (No. 6), legislation which was undoubtedly a considerable success. It introduced much needed remedies and arguably, paved the way for the introduction of divorce by allowing emphasis to be placed, during the 1995 campaign, upon the issue of remarriage which significantly lessened the emphasis on marriage breakdown; as had been the case in 1985, as marriage breakdown had in the interim been legislated for in a comprehensive manner. The 1989 Act was later supplemented by the 1995 Act, but the basic structures and remedies of the 1989 Act remained, albeit supplemented by specialist remedies. It is necessary to refer to the 1989 and the 1995 Acts in the divorce context as their shadows pervade the divorce legislation particularly in terms of the ancillary reliefs which a court may grant, consequent upon a decree of divorce being granted. Minister Taylor T.D. stated:

> "If we were to single out measures which laid foundations for divorce legislation it was the 1989 Judicial Separation Legislation, the 1992 White Paper on Marital Breakdown and the Family Law Act, 1995." (467 *Dáil Debates* Col 1757)

An analysis and understanding of the 1996 Act involves a consideration of the terms of the Constitutional amendment in which the introduction of divorce was endorsed by the Irish people. Article 41.3.2° now reads:

> "1. The State pledges itself to guard with special care the institution of Marriage on which the Family is founded and to protect it against attack.
>
> 2. A Court designated by law may grant a dissolution of marriage where, but only where, it is satisfied that:
> (i) at the date of the institution of the proceedings, the spouses have lived apart from one another for a period of, or periods amounting to, at least four years during the previous five years,

    (ii) there is no reasonable prospect of reconciliation between the spouses,

    (iii) such provision as the Court considers proper having regard to the circumstances exists, or will be made for the spouses, any children of either or both of them and any other person prescribed by law,

    (iv) any further conditions prescribed by law are complied with.

3. No person whose marriage has been dissolved under the civil law of any other State but is a subsisting valid marriage under the law for the time being in force within the jurisdiction of the Government and Parliament established by this Constitution shall be capable of contracting a valid marriage within that jurisdiction during the lifetime of the other party to the marriage so dissolved."

Thus, the Constitution demands that four requirements be complied with before a divorce may be granted and these are reflected in the statutory provisions of the Family Law (Divorce) Act 1996:

    (a) The marital partners must have lived apart from one another for a period or periods of not less than four years in the five years preceding the application for divorce (a reduction from the 1986 proposal);

    (b) There must be no reasonable prospect of reconciliation (in most circumstances, compliance with (a) means that (b) is almost *res ipsa loquitur*);

    (c) The court must ensure that proper provision has been made or will be made for spouses and children and any other persons prescribed by law (it is noteworthy that the 1986 proposal referred only to children who were dependent upon either spouse);

    (d) Any other provisions prescribed by law are complied with.

Such is the level of constitutional protection and safeguarding that the 1996 Act does not, in fact, have any substantive prerequisites to the granting of a decree of divorce over and above (a) to (c) above.

The 1996 Act comprises a comprehensive code for the introduction of divorce in Ireland. It deals with the granting of decrees of divorce and the proofs to be complied with before a decree is to be granted; preliminary and ancillary orders, in the course of and consequent upon, the granting of decrees, as well as a variety of amendments to other statutory provisions some of which arose as a result of divorce and some of which are unrelated. There are certain provisions in the statute which are unexpected and novel. Of particular note are certain evidential exclusionary rules relating to communications in the course of marriage counselling or mediation and the shortening to six months of the limitation period for section 117 applications, under the Succession Act 1965 (No. 27).

In addition, certain familiar provisions are utilised in the divorce context, including the obligation on solicitors acting for the parties to advise in relation to counselling, mediation, separation agreements and other matrimonial remedies falling short of divorce, *e.g.* judicial separation and the existence at section 37 of the *Mareva* type relief, first made available in section 29 of the 1989 Act and continued in section 35 of the 1995 Act. Furthermore, there are certain amendments of other statutory provisions, not directly related to divorce, which are of considerable importance, notably the addition of section 15A to the 1995 Act, which introduces the remedy of a claim against the estate of a deceased spouse, following the granting of a decree of judicial separation under the 1989 Act. A similar provision was in existence in the post-divorce context pursuant to section 18 of the 1996 Act. The definition of "spouse" under the Domestic Violence Act 1996 (No. 1), has been extended to include divorced persons.

A useful analysis of the extent of the problem of marriage breakdown in Ireland was provided by Deputy Michael Woods T.D. at the Second Stage of the Family Law (Divorce) Bill 1996 (467 *Dáil Debates* Col. 1773):

"... the rate of breakdown and separation has accelerated here. The breakdown of new marriages in 1994 reached the alarming rate of one in six. The problem has been growing at an accelerating pace in recent years. In the 1986 census it was revealed that the marriages of 38,600 had broken down. By 1993 that figure had grown to 75,000. Allowing for the fact that breakdowns appear to be occurring at the rate of about 2,700 per annum there are by now some 45,000 broken marriages here. Of those it is fair to assume that at least 30,000 have been broken down for four years or more."

The flood of applications envisaged has not materialised. Deputy Woods (467 *Dáil Debates* Col. 1773) indicated that between 10,000 and 15,000 of those coming within the divorce criteria would wish to obtain a divorce as soon as possible. The rate of application to the courts for relief has not reflected this perceived wish. However, it is probably not due to any lack of desire on the part of such persons to obtain the relief, but rather due to a fear of the unknown in relation to ancillary reliefs which may be granted.

The Family Law (Divorce) Bill 1996 (No. 32) was presented to Dáil Éireann on June 17, 1996. Commencing the debate for the Second Stage of the Bill, the Minister for Equality and Law Reform Mervyn Taylor T.D. stated:

> ". . . this Bill will remedy a deficiency in our Law, and to some extent in our recognition of social reality, that has been persistent and visible for many years." (467 *Dáil Debates* Col. 1754)

He went on to say:

> "There will be no easy or quick divorce. There will be no divorce for marriages in difficulty. There will be divorce only for marriages that are irretrievably at an end." (467 *Dáil Debates* Cols. 1755–1756)

It is noteworthy that the Government reiterated the fact that the Family Law (Divorce) Bill 1996 which was before the Oireachtas was very similar in its terms to the draft Bill published in advance of the referendum and which was contained in the Government paper, "The Right to Re-Marry". Therefore, a strong argument was made by the Government in presenting the Bill that its terms had received the imprimatur of the people in the constitutional referendum. Fianna Fáil also expressed satisfaction that the Bill was:

> "faithful to the draft Bill published in advance of the divorce referendum . . ." (467 *Dáil Debates* Col. 1770)

The 1996 Act comprises five parts. Part I concerns commencement, interpretation, repeals and expenses. Part II deals with obtaining a decree of divorce and it is this part which sets down the necessary legal requirements to be proved in an application for a decree of divorce, satisfying not only the Act itself but also the constitutional requirements. Part III concerns preliminary and ancillary reliefs and is arguably the most important part of the Act containing the legal reliefs which empower the courts to ensure that proper provision has been made for spouses, dependent children and others. Modelled very significantly on the Judicial Separation and Family Law Reform Act 1989, it is a testament to the success of the 1989 Act that these ancillary reliefs remain largely unchanged since that first pioneering legislation, with some significant additions to make the range of reliefs available more comprehensive. Part III, in so far as it provides for preliminary reliefs, makes available, in that context, remedies under the Family Home Protection Act 1976, the Guardianship of Infants Act 1964, the Domestic Violence Act 1996 as well as providing for the granting of a maintenance pending suit. It is noteworthy that certain of the "usual" ancillary reliefs following a decree of judicial separation are not required in the post-divorce context, as the parties are no longer "spouses" in the normal legal meaning of that term and consequently not included. In particular:

(a) Spousal consent to the sale of a family home is no longer required as the parties are no longer "spouses" and therefore reliefs concerning the dispensing with spousal consent pursuant to section 4 of the Family Home Protection Act 1976, or section 54(3) of the Family Law Act 1995 are not included;

(b) Spousal succession rights under the Succession Act 1965 will not persist post-divorce and therefore their extinguishment is not required, thus there is no equivalent to section 14 of the Family Law Act 1995. Although the provisions of section 18 of the 1996 Act must be considered in evaluating claims post-death against the estate of a former spouse in the post-divorce context;

(c) The cessation/dissolution of the marital relationship and the loss of spousal status has made an equivalent to section 13 of the Family Law Act 1995 unnecessary in the context of pension rights.

However the 1996 Act contains a special extended definition of "spouse" for its own purposes, effectively extending the term to include former spouses divorced under the provisions of the Act in order to enable such persons to avail of the reliefs contained in the Act post-divorce. This is somewhat confusing and it might have been preferable to use the term "former-spouse" or "divorced spouse" in the Act, thereby leaving the legal meaning of the term "spouse" uncorrupted and uniform in content.

Part IV introduces the necessary taxation reforms for the purposes of divorce and deals with income and capital taxes as well as probate tax and stamp duty. Part V contains certain miscellaneous provisions.

Citation

Family Law (Divorce) Act, 1996

Commencement

The Act was passed on November 27, 1996. Section 1 provides that it would become operative three months after the date of its passing. The Act, therefore, commenced on February 27, 1997. It is noteworthy that there was a very significant delay between the approval of the constitutional amendment in November 1995 and the eventual coming into operation of the implementing legislation. This delay was due to the unsuccessful challenge to the validity of the constitutional referendum (*Hanafin v. Minister for the Environment* [1996] 2 I.L.R.M. 161).

A further incident upon the turbulent road to the introduction of divorce is also deserving of mention in the context of commencement. Although the Act had become operative on February 27, 1997, the constitutional entitlement to seek a divorce was enshrined in Irish law from the date of the confirmation by the Supreme Court of the validity of the Referendum and consequently the Amendment to Bunreacht na hÉireann, or at the latest from the date of signing into law of the legislation upon which the Referendum was based. The former occurred on June 12, 1996 and the President signed the Fifteenth Amendment to the Constitution Bill 1995 into law on June 17, 1996. However, this Constitutional entitlement was without legislative implementation for some time. In the intervening period, the High Court had confirmed that the substantive entitlement to apply for a divorce under the provisions of Article 41.3.2° was operative. The High Court granted a decree of divorce, based upon compliance with the requirements contained in the Constitution, prior to the 1996 Act coming into operation (*C.(R.) v. C.(C.)* [1997] I.F.L.R. 1, Barron J.)

Statutory Instruments

Circuit Court Rules (No. 1) 1997 (S.I. No. 84 of 1997)
Rules of the Superior Courts (No. 3) 1997 (S.I. No. 343 of 1997)

Acts Referred to

Adoption Acts, 1952 to 1991	
Capital Acquisitions Tax Act, 1976	1976 (No. 8)
Capital Gains Tax Acts	
Censorship of Publications Act, 1929	1929 (No. 21)
Criminal Damage Act, 1991	1991 (No. 31)
Criminal Evidence Act, 1992	1992 (No. 12)
Defence Act, 1954	1954 (No. 18)

Domestic Violence Act, 1996	1996 (No. 1)
Enforcement of Court Orders Act, 1940	1940 (No. 23)
Family Home Protection Act, 1976	1976 (No. 27)
Family Law Act, 1995	1995 (No. 26)
Family Law (Maintenance of Spouses and Children) Act, 1976	1976 (No. 11)
Finance (1909–10) Act, 1910	(10 Edward 7 & 1 Geo. 5, c. 8)
Finance Act, 1972	1972 (No. 19)
Finance Act, 1983	1983 (No. 15)
Finance Act, 1993	1993 (No. 13)
Finance Act, 1994	1994 (No. 13)
Guardianship of Infants Act, 1964	1964 (No. 7)
Income Tax Act, 1967	1967 (No. 6)
Income Tax Acts	
Insurance Act, 1989	1989 (No. 3)
Judicial Separation and Family Law Reform Act, 1989	1989 (No. 6)
Maintenance Act, 1994	1994 (No. 28)
Partition Act, 1868	(31 & 32 Vict., c. 40)
Partition Act, 1876	(39 & 40 Vict., c. 17)
Pensions Act, 1990	1990 (No. 25)
Pensions (Amendment) Act, 1996	1996 (No. 18)
Powers of Attorney Act, 1996	1996 (No. 12)
Registration of Title Act, 1964	1964 (No. 16)
Social Welfare Acts	
Status of Children Act, 1987	1987 (No. 26)
Succession Act, 1965	1965 (No. 27)

Be it enacted by the Oireachtas as follows:

PART I

PRELIMINARY AND GENERAL

Short title and commencement

1.—(1) This Act may be cited as the Family Law (Divorce) Act, 1996.

(2) This Act shall come into operation on the day that is 3 months after the date of its passing.

GENERAL NOTE

The Act was passed on the November 27, 1996 and section 1 provides that it would become operative three months after the date of its passing. The Act, therefore, commenced on the February 27, 1997 (see also Commencement section above).

Interpretation

2.—(1) In this Act, save where the context otherwise requires—
"the Act of 1964" means the Guardianship of Infants Act, 1964;
"the Act of 1965" means the Succession Act, 1965;
"the Act of 1976" means the Family Law (Maintenance of Spouses and Children) Act, 1976;
"the Act of 1989" means the Judicial Separation and Family Law Reform Act, 1989;

"the Act of 1995" means the Family Law Act, 1995;

"the Act of 1996" means the Domestic Violence Act, 1996;

"conveyance" includes a mortgage, lease, assent, transfer, disclaimer, release and any other disposition of property otherwise than by a will or a *donatio mortis causa* and also includes an enforceable agreement (whether conditional or unconditional) to make any such disposition;

"the court" shall be construed in accordance with section 38;

"decree of divorce" means a decree under section 5;

"decree of judicial separation" means a decree under section 3 of the Act of 1989;

"decree of nullity" means a decree granted by a court declaring a marriage to be null and void;

"dependent member of the family", in relation to a spouse, or the spouses, concerned, means any child—

    (a) of both spouses or adopted by both spouses under the Adoption Acts, 1952 to 1991, or in relation to whom both spouses are *in loco parentis*, or

    (b) of either spouse or adopted by either spouse under those Acts, or in relation to whom either spouse is in loco parentis, where the other spouse, being aware that he or she is not the parent of the child, has treated the child as a member of the family,

who is under the age of 18 years or if the child has attained that age—

    (i) is or will be or, if an order were made under this Act providing for periodical payments for the benefit of the child or for the provision of a lump sum for the child, would be receiving full-time education or instruction at any university, college, school or other educational establishment and is under the age of 23 years, or

    (ii) has a mental or physical disability to such extent that it is not reasonably possible for the child to maintain himself or herself fully;

"family home" has the meaning assigned to it by section 2 of the Family Home Protection Act, 1976, with the modification that the references to a spouse in that section shall be construed as references to a spouse within the meaning of this Act;

"financial compensation order" has the meaning assigned to it by section 16;

"Land Registry" and "Registry of Deeds" have the meanings assigned to them by the Registration of Title Act, 1964;

"lump sum order" means an order under section 13(1)(c);

"maintenance pending suit order" means an order under section 12;

"member", in relation to a pension scheme, means any person who, having been admitted to membership of the scheme under its rules, remains entitled to any benefit under the scheme;

"pension adjustment order" means an order under section 17;

"pension scheme" means—

    (a) an occupational pension scheme (within the meaning of the Pensions Act, 1990), or

    (b) (i) an annuity contract approved by the Revenue Commissioners

under section 235 of the Income Tax Act, 1967, or a contract
so approved under section 235A of that Act,

   (ii) a trust scheme, or part of a trust scheme, so approved under
subsection (4) of the said section 235 or subsection (5) of the
said section 235A, or

   (iii) a policy or contract of assurance approved by the Revenue Commissioners under Chapter II of Part I of the Finance Act, 1972,

or

  (c) any other scheme or arrangement (including a personal pension
plan and a scheme or arrangement established by or pursuant to
statute or instrument made under statute other than under the Social Welfare Acts) that provides or is intended to provide either or
both of the following, that is to say:

   (i) benefits for a person who is a member of the scheme or arrangement ("the member") upon retirement at normal pensionable age or upon earlier or later retirement or upon leaving, or
upon the ceasing of, the relevant employment,

   (ii) benefits for the widow, widower or dependants of the member,
or for any other persons, on the death of the member;

"periodical payments order" and "secured periodical payments order" have
the meanings assigned to them by section 13;

"property adjustment order" has the meaning assigned to it by section 14;

"trustees", in relation to a scheme that is established under a trust, means the
trustees of the scheme and, in relation to a pension scheme not so established,
means the persons who administer the scheme.

   (2) In this Act, where the context so requires—

  (a) a reference to a marriage includes a reference to a marriage that has
been dissolved under this Act,

  (b) a reference to a remarriage includes a reference to a marriage that
takes place after a marriage that has been dissolved under this Act,

  (c) a reference to a spouse includes a reference to a person who is a
party to a marriage that has been dissolved under this Act,

  (d) a reference to a family includes a reference to a family as respects
which the marriage of the spouses concerned has been dissolved
under this Act,

  (e) a reference to an application to a court by a person on behalf of a
dependent member of the family includes a reference to such an
application by such a member and a reference to a payment, the
securing of a payment, or the assignment of an interest, to a person
for the benefit of a dependent member of the family includes a
reference to a payment, the securing of a payment, or the assignment of an interest, to such a member,

and cognate words shall be construed accordingly.

   (3) In this Act—

  (a) a reference to any enactment shall, unless the context otherwise
requires, be construed as a reference to that enactment as amended

or extended by or under any subsequent enactment including this Act,

(b) a reference to a Part or section is a reference to a Part or section of this Act unless it is indicated that reference to some other enactment is intended,

(c) a reference to a subsection, paragraph, subparagraph or clause is a reference to the subsection, paragraph, subparagraph or clause of the provision in which the reference occurs unless it is indicated that reference to some other provision is intended.

GENERAL NOTE

This section contains a number of important definitions and contains some replications of definitions which are well-known in family law statutes while there are some significant, albeit minor, alterations. Many of the terms set out here are discussed, where relevant, in the context of the sections in which they arise. Some of the more important terms are specifically discussed immediately hereinafter, particularly where they are worthy of independent consideration. The reference to the shortened references of a number of statutes indicates the large volume of legislative activity in the family law area in recent years.

The definition of "conveyance" corresponds precisely with that contained in the Family Home Protection Act 1976 (No. 27), the F.H.P.A 1976, save that the 1976 Act refers to the definition as including "an enforceable agreement (whether conditional or unconditional) to make any such conveyance"; while the Family Law (Divorce) Act 1996 refers to "an enforceable agreement (whether conditional or unconditional) to make any such disposition". It is unlikely that there is any real substantive difference between these definitions, but it should be remembered that while the definition of "conveyance" is very wide and would include a sale of property, a more specific term such as "mortgage" would be limited in its effect to that type of transaction only and would not include other forms of transfer, *e.g.* a sale. The involuntary transfer of real property, *e.g.* judgment mortgages, remains outside the scope of the definition. The impact of this was considered in the context of the F.H.P.A. 1976 in *Containercare (Ireland) Ltd v. Wycherley* [1982] I.R. 143 and *Murray v. Diamond* [1982] 2 I.L.R.M. 113.

A reference to a "decree of judicial separation" means a decree under section 3 of the Judicial Separation and Family Law Reform Act 1989 (No. 6), the 1989 Act. While decrees are granted under section 3 of that Act, the grounds upon which a decree may be granted are set out in section 2. These encompass a range of fault and no-fault grounds and the constitutionality of the provision contained in section 2(1)(f), allowing for the granting of a decree, where no normal marital relationship has existed between the parties for in excess of one year prior to the date of the institution of the proceedings, was upheld by the High Court and affirmed on appeal by the Supreme Court in *T.F. v. Ireland* [1995] I.R. 321. The legislation providing for judicial separation remains extremely relevant and pertinent in Irish family law as arrangements for marriage breakdown may have to be made in the intermediate four-year period post-separation during which period a divorce decree may not be sought. In addition, many Irish people have moral objections to divorce, as was evidenced by the referendum results and thus prefer to regulate their affairs in the context of judicial separation.

The definition of a "decree of nullity" is a judicial declaration that a marriage is null and void. This definition recognises the extension of jurisdiction to grant decrees of nullity which was given to the Circuit Court under the section 38 of the Family Law Act 1995 (No. 26 of 1995), the 1995 Act.

The term "dependent member of the family" is defined in precisely the same manner as in the 1995 Act. This represents a substantial change from the definition of "dependent child of the family", which was contained in the Family Law (Maintenance of Spouses and Children) Act 1976 (No. 11) (the Family Law Act 1976), and in the 1989 Act.

Undoubtedly reflecting social, educational and economic factors, the age limits for dependency have been changed, the normal age of dependency has been increased from 16 years to 18 years and the extended period of dependency in cases where the dependent remains in full-time education has been extended from 21 years to 23 years. The unlimited maintenance obligation in terms of age in the case of physical or mental disability remains unchanged since 1976. It is submitted that the first of these extensions is perfectly understandable and desirable, the age of majority has been 18 years since the introduction of the Age of Majority Act 1985 (No. 2). It would appear to be in order that parents have an obligation to maintain their children during their dependency. Obviously, the court is empowered to have regard to any means of the children in question, including the fact that a child under 18 years might be in full or part-time employment. However, the continued obligation past the age of majority might arguably be seen as an interference in the constitutional property rights of parents. In the constitutional context however, it must be reiterated that Art. 41.3.2°.2(iii) requires proper provision to have been made for "any children" and does not restrict the enquiry into the sufficiency of provision to minor children only. Such consideration of the position of adult children was undertaken by Barron J. in *C.(R.) v. C.(C.)* [1997] I.F.L.R. 1.

The provisions dictate that a parent may be obliged to fund the educational plans of their adult children in circumstances in which they do not choose to do so, therefore the consequential financial burden is placed upon the parents. However, regard should be had to the wording of the constitutional provision dealing with divorce, referred to previously, wherein there is a requirement not only of due provision for minor children being a prerequisite to divorce, but the requirement refers to due provision being made for all children.

The definition of dependent family members at section 2(1) of the 1996 Act extends substantially beyond simply the children of the marriage, whether natural or adopted. Children in relation to whom both spouses are in *loco parentis* are also included. However, section 2(1)(b) is deserving of particular comment. It purports to include within the definition a number of other children being natural or adopted children of *either* spouse or children in relation to whom *either* spouse is in *loco parentis* (emphasis added), but is subject to an important caveat:

> "... where the other spouse, being aware that he or she is not the parent of the child, has treated the child as a member of the family".

This provision has not been judicially interpreted but would appear to indicate that where a spouse has maintained a child, believing that it is his child and it subsequently transpires that this is not the position, such a child would not come within the definition. A question arises as to the level of awareness required. Can a spouse, having believed it to be possible that a child of his spouse is not his child, but making no investigation into the matter and not having raised the issue and having treated the child as a child of the marriage, thereafter refuse to maintain that child on the basis that only at a later date (possibly following blood testing in the course of proceedings) he became actually and definitively aware that the child was not his?

There is a wide definition of "pension scheme" included in section 2 of the Act. This will be discussed in the context of section 17 of the Act (see page 58). Section 2(2), it is submitted, is confusing. It endorses the use of the term "spouse" to describe divorced persons and the use of the term "marriage" to describe a dissolved marriage. The scope of these definitions is limited, applying only "in this Act". Therefore, a divorced person remains a spouse for the purposes of the 1996 Act, but will not continue to come within the definition of "spouse" as contained in other enactments, *e.g.* Succession Act 1965 (No. 27) and F.H.P.A. 1976, nor will such person continue to be a spouse for the purposes of other benefits, *e.g.* spousal pension schemes and taxation, subject to Part IV of the 1996 Act. This has been considered earlier herein. However, it is submitted that, in the context of post-divorce reliefs and activities; including the granting of ancillary reliefs which must, of necessity post-date the granting of a decree of divorce; the use of the terms "former spouse" or "divorced spouse" and "former marriage" or "dissolved marriage" would have been preferable.

Repeal

3.—Section 14(2) of the Censorship of Publications Act, 1929, is hereby repealed.

GENERAL NOTE

The repeal section now contained in section 3 of the Act was not included in the Bill as initiated. The provision recognises that section 14(2) of the Censorship of Publications Act 1929 (No. 21), which restrained publication of information arising in the context of various matrimonial proceedings, is now obsolete due to the *in camera* protection which has been given to proceedings under the Family Law (Divorce) Act 1996. Section 34 of the Judicial Separation and Family Law Reform Act 1989 indicated that proceedings under that Act were to be determined otherwise than in public and section 38(5) of the 1996 Act extends the application of section 34 to proceedings for divorce. The scope of *in camera* protection would appear to be wide as discussed in the judgment of Laffoy J. in *P. v. P.* [1996] 1 I.R. 144. Interpreting section 34 of the 1989 Act, the court referred to:

> "confidential matters which arose in the proceedings and which section 34 requires should be kept confidential and private to the parties to the proceedings and the Court. . ."

During the course of the Oireachtas debates upon the Bill, Minister Taylor also gave some indication of the scope of protection which the *in camera* rule affords such proceedings:

> "Because the in camera rule applies to those proceedings they cannot, in any event, The be reported. The printing of law reports is, of course, not prohibited. In practice the names of the parties or addresses and other distinguishing features are erased from all reports as well as unreported judgments. Publication of the details of a case which has been heard in camera constitutes contempt." (469 *Dáil Debates* Col. 521)

No specific offence is created for breach of statutory entitlement to privacy and confidentiality in these types of proceedings. Infringements are left to be dealt with in the context of contempt of court proceedings. In most instances contempt proceedings will be instigated by the innocent party whose rights of privacy and confidentiality are being or have been violated, although obviously a court would have a contempt jurisdiction of its own motion. The former scenario is more common, placing a heavy financial and emotional burden upon the innocent party. The creation of a criminal offence might have had a more probative effect and would also support investigation and action being taken by the State authorities.

Expenses

4.—The expenses incurred by the Minister for Equality and Law Reform, the Minister for Health or the Minister for Justice in the administration of this Act shall, to such extent as may be sanctioned by the Minister for Finance, be paid out of moneys provided by the Oireachtas.

PART II

THE OBTAINING OF A DECREE OF DIVORCE

Grant of decree of divorce and custody etc., of children

5.—(1) Subject to the provisions of this Act, where, on application to it in that behalf by either of the spouses concerned, the court is satisfied that—

(a) at the date of the institution of the proceedings, the spouses have lived apart from one another for a period of, or periods amounting to, at least four years during the previous five years,

(b) there is no reasonable prospect of a reconciliation between the spouses, and

(c) such provision as the court considers proper having regard to the circumstances ex ists or will be made for the spouses and any dependent members of the family,

the court may, in exercise of the jurisdiction conferred by Article 41.3.2 of the Constitution, grant a decree of divorce in respect of the marriage concerned.

(2) Upon the grant of a decree of divorce, the court may, where appropriate, give such directions under section 11 of the Act of 1964 as it considers proper regarding the welfare (within the meaning of that Act), custody of, or right of access to, any dependent member of the family concerned who is an infant (within the meaning of that Act) as if an application had been made to it in that behalf under that section.

GENERAL NOTE

    Dealing with section 5(1) of the 1996 Act, Minister Taylor referred to the fact that the Act replicates the terms of the constitutional amendment. He went on to state:

> "These conditions have already been the subject of long and detailed debate in the House on the 15th Amendment of the Constitution Bill. They have been voted on by the people. They are enshrined as Article 41.3.2° of the Constitution and cannot, of course, be the subject of change other than on the basis of an amendment of the Constitution." (467 *Dáil Debates* Col. 1760)

Undoubtedly one of the most ambiguous parts of the Act concerns the legal definition of "lived apart" as contained in section 5(1)(a). There is no definition contained in the Act and this is regrettable. Minister Taylor in the Dáil debate at the Second Stage of the Bill to amend the Constitution, on September 27, 1995 indicated that parties could live apart while still residing under the same roof. The Minister stated:

> "The term "living apart" is used in the Judicial Separation and Family Law Reform Act, 1989, and it is also a familiar term in many other jurisdictions where it has been held that this phrase will clearly cover where the spouses have physically separated and are living in different places. The case law also states that where domestic life is not shared, it is possible for there to be two households under the one roof."

A useful analysis is provided by Shatter in *Family Law* (4th ed., 1997), p. 361:

> "For such circumstances to arise, all normal interaction between them as a married couple must have practically ended. They must be sleeping apart, eating apart, not communicating to any substantial degree and effectively leading entirely separate lives. For some, there may be a narrow dividing line between the determination that they are living apart or still living together. For example, a couple sharing the same home not talking to each other, sleeping in separate bedrooms, not co-operating in the day-to-day running of the household and the making of family arrangements, never eating a common (shared) meal may be regarded as living apart."

However, this analysis is in the context of the Judicial Separation and Family Law Reform Act 1989 and section 2(3)(a) of that Act contains a partial definition of "living apart" which said definition, in turn, seems to depend upon how one interprets the term "household":

> "(a) In this section spouses shall be treated as living apart from each other unless they are living with each other in the same household . . . "

The Family Law (Divorce) Act 1996 does not provide any definition and therefore the matter remains moot. This creates considerable uncertainty for couples where their marital/familial relationship has ceased, but they continue to cohabit for financial or other reasons. Decrees have been granted in circumstances in which parties have lived apart albeit under the same roof. The standard of proof required in such circumstances would appear to be quite high.

The corollary, arguably, also applies and there are situations, *e.g.* foreign employment, hospitalisation, imprisonment, where parties might have lived in separate places but yet should not be considered to have "lived apart" for the purposes of this Act. The additional requirement of a mental element in relation to living apart, such as an intention not to cohabit, is not specified in the Act but arguably is consistent with the ethos and rationale of the Act. Shatter, p.361 is instructive in this regard, in the context of the 1989 Act:

> "The Act does not require anything more than proof of the fact of separation. There is no reference to any required intention as an additional element. However, in other jurisdictions it has been held that similar "living apart" provisions require some mental element and only start when one spouse regards the marriage as at an end. Thus, being forced by circumstances to work abroad or by ill health to be hospitalised, or serving a prison sentence, or being on service with the army abroad does not, of itself, on the basis of these authorities automatically trigger the commencement of a period of living apart for the purpose of the subsection. Such a period of living apart may, however, be regarded as having commenced the date upon which it is established that one of the spouses regarded cohabitation or consortium as having ended."

So far as the term "living apart" is concerned within the context of the 1989 Act, this has not yet been the subject of indepth judicial interpretation. The vast majority of judicial separation decrees are granted on the basis that no normal marital relationship has existed between the parties for in excess of 12 months, prior to the institution of proceedings. The "living apart" grounds, *i.e.* those contained in section 2(1)(d) and 2(1)(e) of the 1989 Act, are very rarely used and if used, it is almost invariably in the context of parties who have lived apart by residing in separate places. If the evidence is such as to support the proposition that the parties have lived entirely separate lives, albeit under the same roof, it is easier to use this evidence to support the lack of any normal marital relationship, rather than go the extra step of proving that the lifestyles experienced amounted to "living apart". It is a complex issue and one upon which there is a body of foreign precedent.

It is difficult not to share the concerns voiced by Deputy Helen Keogh T.D. in the Dáil debates (467 *Dáil Debates* Cols. 1786–1787) where she doubted that the term had a clear and settled meaning in law. In summary, the difficulties in interpreting the term include:

(a)   Whether and in what circumstances, couples may be considered to be living apart, while residing under the same roof;

(b)   Whether the term encompasses an element of intention which would be relevant in the context of couples whose separation commenced otherwise than in the context of marital breakdown, but evolved into such a context;

(c)   The extent to which reliance may be placed upon foreign authorities in circumstances in which the Act appears to envisage that parties may be living apart, but not separated. This difficulty arises from attempts to rationalise the terms of section 5(1)(a) with those of sections 6(2)(b) and 7(2)(b), discussed hereinafter.

Final resolution will only come with a Supreme Court determination of the point, but it is noteworthy that this difficulty has constitutional and not merely legislative origins, as the phrase was inserted in the constitutional amendment. Thus, Deputy Keogh stated (467 *Dáil Debates* Col. 1787):

> "We would ordinarily clarify this issue by amending this Bill and including a similar definition of "living apart", but that is not an option here because the entitlement of this House to legislate for divorce for couples who have lived apart derives from

15

the constitutional amendment and the function of interpreting the Constitution belongs to the Judiciary, not to this House."

Section 5(1) of the 1996 Act also sets out the two other constitutional imperatives to be satisfied before a divorce is granted. At subsection (1)(b), the lack of any reasonable prospect of reconciliation is referred to. During the course of the debates, some support was voiced for mandatory counselling requirements. This is considered in the context of section 6 of the Act, but concerns must be expressed as to the constitutionality of any such obligatory requirement and also as to the reality of such an obligation bearing in mind the duration of living apart required by section 5(1)(a). At section 5(1)(c), the court is mandated to ensure that proper provision in all of the circumstances exists, or will be made for the spouses and the dependent children.

A number of points arise. First, there is a distinction in this regard between the wording of the 1996 Act and the wording of the Constitution. The latter requires the court to be satisfied that proper provision has been made for "any children of either or both of [the spouses]". The Act refers to such provision in relation to "any dependent members of the family". The 1996 Act includes in section 2, a comprehensive definition of "dependent member of the family", which has been considered previously. However, suffice it to say at this point that the definition excludes independent children over 23. The constitutional requirement would appear to be more extensive in ambit.

In *C.(R.) v. C.(C.)* [1997] I.F.L.R. 1. a divorce was sought under the provisions of the Constitution, prior to the coming into operation of the 1996 Act. There were three adult children, all of whom were in employment and there was no evidence of any special requirements for their welfare. Therefore, it is submitted that they would not come within the definition of "dependent member of the family" as defined in section 2. While the applicant was proposing to make specific provision for the adult children and the situation was not, therefore, one in which the court was compelling him to do so, the observations of Barron J. are of interest:

> "Since the jurisdiction invoked is that contained in the Constitution and not that amplified by the Act, it is necessary for the Court to consider the position of the children. While I do not purport to determine that non-dependent children should necessarily have provision made for them, I am satisfied that in the particular circumstances of the present case it is proper that certainly the two daughters of the marriage should have provision made for them in the interests of the family as a whole."

Therefore, based upon the supremacy of the Constitution under Irish law, the court must presumably extend its investigation of proper provision beyond dependent members of the family to all children of either party of whatever age. The discussion of section 2 is instructive, although it is unlikely that extensive provision for non-dependant family members would or ought to be ordered to be made save in extremely unusual circumstances.

Secondly, this is a proof which must be satisfied before the decree is made. It is not open to the court to grant the decree and then advert its mind to the issue of ancillary reliefs as being an issue consequential upon the divorce decree. The standard of proper provision is subjective dependent upon the circumstances of the individual litigants. The court does not have to be satisfied that such provision presently exists, it is sufficient that it will be made in the future. In practice, presently existing provision is likely to have come about through the previous and continuing implementation by the parties of the terms of a previous deed of separation or orders made in the context of judicial separation or other matrimonial proceedings. However, such previous arrangements may be re-opened and their propriety re-assessed by the court in the divorce proceedings although section 20(3) of the 1996 Act states that the terms of previous separation agreements which are still in force should be taken in to account by the court in determining ancillary reliefs.

Although the section 20 criteria to be taken into account in determining issues of ancillary reliefs do not specifically apply to a consideration of section 5(1)(c), undoubtedly the factors listed therein are equivalent to those which the court will consider in determining the issue of proper provision for the purposes of section 5(1)(c). If proper provision does not presently exist, the court is required to ensure that such provision will be made. The most obvious manner in which such provision is likely to be made is through the use of the ancillary relief mechanisms. However, it is submitted that an anomaly exists between section 5(1)(c) and section 18.

Section 18 permits a court to make orders for provision for a spouse out of the estate of the other spouse. Section 18(1) requires the court, in making such an order, to specify that "it is satisfied that proper provision in the circumstances was not made for the applicant during the lifetime of the deceased spouse". Section 5(1)(c) would indicate that if such a proof is satisfied, the decree should not have been granted in the first place. It is arguable that the court in determining future proper provision, might take the possibility of section 18 orders into account. The possibility of such relief being sought and obtained in the future would appear to be somewhat tenuous to satisfy the strict constitutionally based requirements of section 5(1)(c). Section 18 does not envisage the application thereunder being made until after death and therefore the Act does not appear to provide for the making of an order equivalent to section 18 at the time of granting the decree. Thus leaving the potentially valuable asset of succession rights out of the reach of the court in determining proper provision at the time of the granting of the decree or thereafter pre-death. This point was raised in the Second Stage Dáil debate by Deputy Willie O'Dea T.D.:

> "It is extraordinary that [section 18] states that this right will only be granted 'if it was not possible to make proper provision for the applicant during the lifetime of the deceased spouse.' If it was not possible to do so, why was the divorce granted in the first place? Surely, [section 5(1)(c)] makes it clear that a divorce cannot be granted unless the court is satisfied that proper provision is being made." (467 *Dáil Debates* Col. 1806)

During the Committee Stage of the Bill, considerable anxiety was expressed regarding the possibility of collusion by the parties to a divorce application in relation to the matters required by section 5(1) and in particular, in relation to section 5(1)(a). Concerns were expressed as to the amount of independent research which would be undertaken by the court. An inquisitorial procedure was advocated, but rejected by the Minister who pointed out that the risk of collusion and perjury were a concern in all litigation and that the assessment of the quality of evidence received remained a matter for determination by the judge.

It remains beyond doubt, however, that the court must be satisfied that the proofs set down in section 5 have been complied with. There is no indication in the 1996 Act that any standard of proof higher than the usual civil standard of the balance of probabilities is to apply. Nevertheless, the court is charged not only with guarding the Act but also with guarding the Constitution. While it is unlikely that the court would often be obliged to go behind the consistent evidence of both parties, or the uncontradicted evidence of one party in the case of an uncontested divorce. Clearly the court would have jurisdiction and a duty to do so where dissatisfied with the evidence provided. The pracice to date has, in general, been non-interventionist but instances do exist of courts refusing to grant a decree when not satisfied as to the sufficiency of the provision made as between the parties notwithstanding the agreement of the parties in this regard. The protective role of the court is thus evident. The requirements of the Rules of Court, that affidavits of means (where financial reliefs are being sought) and affidavits of welfare (where there are dependent children) should be filed, should serve to assist the court in considering whether or not the requirements of section 5(1)(c) have been complied with and whether orders pursuant to section 5(2) are required.

Dealing with section 5(2) at the Second Stage of the Bill, Minister Taylor did not elaborate upon why it was necessary to have a duplication in the powers of the court to make orders in relation to children, save that it would appear to have been envisaged that the court could give directions under section 11 of the Guardianship of Infants Act 1964 (No. 7), the 1964 Act, even where these were not specifically sought by the parties, of its own motion. However, in addition to replicating section 15(1)(f), it is obviously the case that the court would, in any event, have had the ability to give such directions in relation to children in accordance with the provisions of section 5(1)(c).

Deputy Woods (467 *Dáil Debates* Cols. 1780–1781) and before the Select Committee on Legislation and Security (July 17, 1996, L6 No. 12), proposed the appointment of a commissioner for children who would be attached to the courts:

"who would be responsible for highlighting to parents the needs of children in marriage breakdown and divorce and for pressing the needs of children in court where necessary."

At later stages, formal amendments were proposed in relation to the appointment of guardians *ad litem* to argue the case of the children before the court but such proposals were not adopted.

During the course of the Bill's passage through both the Dáil and the Seanad, considerable debate took place relating to the importance of continued contact with relatives other than parents in the post-divorce context. Particular concern was placed upon continued contact with grandparents. When the Bill came before the Select Committee on Legislation and Security (July 17, 1996, L6 No. 12) Deputy Woods attempted to insert an amendment providing for access applications being made by grandparents.

The need for such a provision to be expressly legislated for derives from the wording of section 11 of the 1964 Act. This section indicates that the only exception to guardian's applications for access and custody, is in the case of a natural father who is unmarried to the natural mother of the infant and who has not been appointed a guardian under the provisions of the Status of Children Act 1987 (No. 26) the 1987 Act, such father being entitled to apply either for access or custody of the infant in question. It was, of course, open to a court to direct access with a third party in the course of an application, which was commenced by a parent/guardian, but this route required the co-operation of the parent/guardian to "get the ball rolling". In the case of *D. (H.) v. D. (G.)*, unreported, High Court, July 30, 1972 Carroll J. referred, at p.11, to the fact that the welfare of the infant was the paramount consideration and access to persons other than the natural parents of a child should be allowed if this standard of proof of welfare was achieved. The learned judge expressly referred to the desirability of access by grandparents in certain circumstances.

The legislators were desirous of a limited form of relief in the case of more remote relatives. It was proposed that parents of the non-custodial parent or, if such parents were dead, or residing out of the jurisdiction, the brother or sister of the non-custodial parent would be entitled to apply for an access order in relation to a child. Undoubtedly, the proposals were well-motivated, attempting to ensure that the security of the extended family unit would be preserved post-marital breakdown.

However, a number of comments must be made. First, the proposal did not extend to the parents/family of the custodial parent with whom contact might also have been severed by the custodial parent. Secondly, the proposal was to apply in a marriage breakdown situation only, ignoring the difficulties which might arise prior to any marriage breakdown. Presumably if the preservation of extended family relationships is important in post-divorce/judicial separation, it is likewise important during the marriage itself. It is submitted that it would be somewhat anomalous that a grandparent who was not permitted by a parent(s) to see a child would have to wait until the marriage ceased prior to enlisting the assistance of the courts. Finally the entitlement was to apply for access only, not custody, although clearly the latter would have constitutional implications. Arguably, even the granting of rights to apply for access would have constitutional implications bearing in mind the strong parental protections enshrined in Article 41 of the Constitution.

It was on the basis of the constitutional uncertainties that the proposed amendments were not accepted. Minister Taylor stated that:

> "The difficulty is that situations could arise whereby third parties would have the right to interfere in the affairs of a family unit recognised and protected by the Constitution. However, where what is proposed is a relatively narrow right to apply for access only, a right that would not extend to other aspects of a child's welfare, such as custody, schooling and so on, the difficulties may be diminished." (469 *Dáil Debates* Col. 539)

Attempts have been made to resolve the issue in the Children Act 1997 (No. 40). Section 9 of the 1997 Act, amending section 11 of the 1964 Act, permits any relative of a child or a person who has acted *in loco parentis* to apply for access to the child. This provision eliminates the concerns expressed above.

Safeguards to ensure applicant's awareness of alternatives to divorce proceedings and to assist attempts at reconciliation

6.—(1) In this section "the applicant" means a person who has applied, is applying or proposes to apply to the court for the grant of a decree of divorce.

(2) If a solicitor is acting for the applicant, the solicitor shall, prior to the institution of the proceedings concerned under section 5—

- (a) discuss with the applicant the possibility of a reconciliation and give to him or her the names and addresses of persons qualified to help to effect a reconciliation between spouses who have become estranged,

- (b) discuss with the applicant the possibility of engaging in mediation to help to effect a separation (if the spouses are not separated) or a divorce on a basis agreed between the applicant and the other spouse and give to the applicant the names and addresses of persons qualified to provide a mediation service for spouses who have become estranged, and

- (c) discuss with the applicant the possibility (where appropriate) of effecting a separation by means of a deed or agreement in writing executed or made by the applicant and the other spouse and providing for their separation.

(3) Such a solicitor shall also ensure that the applicant is aware of judicial separation as an alternative to divorce where a decree of judicial separation in relation to the applicant and the other spouse is not in force.

(4) If a solicitor is acting for the applicant—

- (a) the originating document by which the proceedings under section 5 are instituted shall be accompanied by a certificate signed by the solicitor indicating, if it be the case, that he or she has complied with subsection (2) and, if appropriate, subsection (3) in relation to the matter and, if the document is not so accompanied, the court may adjourn the proceedings for such period as it considers reasonable to enable the solicitor to engage in the discussions specified in subsection (2), and, if appropriate, to make the applicant aware of judicial separation,

- (b) if the solicitor has complied with paragraph (a), any copy of the originating document aforesaid served on any person or left in an office of the court shall be accompanied by a copy of the certificate aforesaid.

(5) A certificate under subsection (4)(a) shall be in a form prescribed by rules of court or a form to the like effect.

(6) The Minister may make regulations to allow for the establishment of a Register of Professional Organisations whose members are qualified to assist the parties involved in effecting a reconciliation, such register to show the names of members of those organisations and procedures to be put in place for the organisations involved to regularly update the membership lists.

Safeguards to ensure respondent's awareness of alternatives to divorce proceedings and to assist attempts at reconciliation

7.—(1) In this section "the respondent" means a person who is the respondent in proceedings in the court under section 5.

(2) If a solicitor is acting for the respondent, the solicitor shall, as soon as may be after receiving instructions from the respondent in relation to the proceedings concerned under section 5—

    (a) discuss with the respondent the possibility of a reconciliation and give to him or her the names and addresses of persons qualified to effect a reconciliation between spouses who have become estranged,

    (b) discuss with the respondent the possibility of engaging in mediation to help to effect a separation (if the spouses are not separated) or a divorce on a basis agreed between the respondent and the other spouse and give to the respondent the names and addresses of persons qualified to provide a mediation service for spouses who have become estranged, and

    (c) discuss with the respondent the possibility (where appropriate) of effecting a separation by means of a deed or agreement in writing executed or made by the applicant and the other spouse and providing for their separation.

(3) Such a solicitor shall also ensure that the respondent is aware of judicial separation as an alternative to divorce where a decree of judicial separation is not in force in relation to the respondent and the other spouse.

(4) If a solicitor is acting for the respondent—

    (a) the memorandum or other document delivered to the appropriate officer of the court for the purpose of the entry of an appearance by the respondent in proceedings under section 5 shall be accompanied by a certificate signed by the solicitor indicating, if it be the case, that the solicitor has complied with subsection (2) and, if appropriate, subsection (3) in relation to the matter and, if the document is not so accompanied, the court may adjourn the proceedings for such period as it considers reasonable to enable the solicitor to engage in the discussions specified in subsection (2) and, if appropriate, to make the applicant aware of judicial separation,

    (b) if paragraph (a) is complied with, any copy of the document aforesaid given or sent to the other party to the proceedings or his or her solicitor shall be accompanied by a copy of the relevant certificate aforesaid.

(5) A certificate under subsection (4)(a) shall be in a form prescribed by rules of court or a form to the like effect.

Adjournment of proceedings to assist reconciliation or agreements on the terms of the divorce

8.—(1) Where an application is made to the court for the grant of a decree of divorce, the court shall give consideration to the possibility of a reconciliation between the spouses concerned and, accordingly, may adjourn the proceedings at any time for the purpose of enabling attempts to be made by the spouses, if they both so wish, to effect such a reconciliation with or without the assistance of a third party.

(2) Where, in proceedings under section 5, it appears to the court that a reconciliation between the spouses cannot be effected, it may adjourn or further adjourn the proceedings for the purpose of enabling attempts to be made by the spouses, if they both so wish, to reach agreement, with or without the assistance of a third party, on some or all of the terms of the proposed divorce.

(3) If proceedings are adjourned pursuant to subsection (1) or (2), either or both of the spouses may at any time request that the hearing of the proceedings be resumed as soon as may be and, if such a request is made, the court shall, subject to any other power of the court to adjourn proceedings, resume the hearing.

(4) The powers conferred by this section are additional to any other power of the court to adjourn proceedings.

(5) Where the court adjourns proceedings under this section, it may, at its discretion, advise the spouses concerned to seek the assistance of a third party in relation to the effecting of a reconciliation between the spouses or the reaching of agreement between them on some or all of the terms of the proposed divorce.

GENERAL NOTE

Sections 6 and 7 of the Family Law (Divorce) Act 1996 replicate the provisions contained in sections 5 and 6 of the Judicial Separation and Family Law Reform Act 1989, requiring solicitors for the parties to certify that the parties have been advised by their legal representatives of alternative remedies available to them. These alternatives include marriage guidance counselling, mediation services, the conclusion of deeds of separation or separation agreements and decrees of judicial separation.

With the absence of judicial separation, the alternative remedies in relation to which advice must be given are the same as in the case of judicial separation. The precise manner in which the advice is to be given is not specified and this would appear to be left to the discretion of the individual solicitor. Proposals were made during the course of the Oireachtas debates, that solicitors would be obliged to provide lists of qualified persons in relation to reconciliation, counselling and mediation, but no specific guidelines have been included in the Act, although in practice such lists are regularly prepared by solicitors and given to their clients for consultation.

The certificate of the applicant's solicitor, that advices as to alternative remedies have been given to their clients, is required to be filed with the initiating documentation; the civil bill in the case of the Circuit Court and the special summons in the case of the High Court. The certificate of the respondent's solicitor is required to be filed at the same time as entering an appearance, thus the certification process takes place at the earliest possible opportunity. The provisions require that certification is signed by the solicitor concerned. A proposal was made during the passage of the Bill through the Seanad that the certificate would be signed by the solicitor and also by the client, but it was rejected (149 *Seanad Debates* Col. 19).

In relation to sections 6 and 7 Minister Taylor in commenting on the Bill did not deal with the situation where a party was not legally represented. The purpose of sections 6 and 7 was to make the parties aware of the alternatives to divorce. However, no mention was made of how lay litigants were to be made so aware. Arguably, section 8 of the Act would enable the court to adjourn proceedings involving a lay litigant, if it felt that reconciliation or amicable settlement could be thereby achieved. But it would place too heavy an onus on the court and would be outside the terms of section 8 to read into it any obligation on the court to advise the parties in relation to alternative remedies available.

The court is empowered by section 8 to consider the possibility of reconciliation and amicable settlement and to adjourn the proceedings for this purpose, but is not obliged to enter into a process of advising the parties in relation to these matters. It is admitted that it would be entirely inappropriate for the court to do so. Amendments were proposed before the Select Committee on Legislation and Security by Deputy Woods, (July 16, 1996, L6 No. 11, Cols. 641–642) which aimed to deal with the situation of the lay litigant by requiring certification by appropriate marriage guidance counsellors and mediators in such circumstances. These proposals were rejected.

Before the Select Committee on Legislation and Security, Deputy Woods proposed that in addition to a certificate being provided by a solicitor for the applicant for divorce under section 6, indicating that advice had been given relating to alternative remedies/reliefs, certification by "a person qualified to help effect a reconciliation between the spouses" would also be required indicating that "the applicant has attended that person and has discussed the possibility of a reconciliation". Similar certification requirements were also proposed in relation to mediation. Responding to and rejecting such proposals, the Minister stated before the Seanad, that this would merely add an unnecessary process of certification.

Reference should also be made to the proposal of obligatory counselling made by Deputy Woods (467 *Dáil Debates* Col. 1778) at the Second Stage of the Bill:

> "The Bill should contain a provision placing an obligation on the spouses initiating a separation or divorce process to participate in counselling, proof of which could take the form of a certificate from the counselling service, or other similar document."

Deputy Woods recognised that exceptions to mandatory counselling would be required and that it might not be appropriate after long-term separation or desertion/abandonment. He continued:

> "However, we must seek to develop supportive counselling structures to ensure every possible opportunity is provided to avert marriage breakdown and divorce."

While the desirability of this latter objective cannot be doubted, it is arguable that there might be certain constitutional difficulties in imposing a system of mandatory counselling. The notion of mandatory mediation was also advanced. In this regard, reference should be made to the decision of Budd J. in *S.(J.) v. S.(C.)(Orse. T.(C.)* [1997] I.F.L.R. 140, where the High Court in the context of nullity and the direction of medical/psychiatric inspections for the purposes of such proceedings indicated that while a party might be directed to attend for such examination and the court could subsequently take notice of a failure to attend, both sides in the case were doubtful as to whether it would be constitutional to compel attendance. The precise point was not argued but issues relating to the right to bodily integrity clearly arise.

The dictum of Budd J., at 155, albeit in a different context is instructive:

> "It is clear that the Court will not lightly order an examination which is unpleasant, painful or potentially dangerous. . . . However, there is no evidence that the appellant would be put at risk by attending an interview. In any event the petitioner's submission is the Order sought is for the appointment of the psychiatric inspector and that there is no mandatory requirement on a party to attend. Obviously, the adverse comment may be made if a party refuses to attend, but this may well be subject to a reasonable explanation. . . . While I accept that a psychiatric examination may pry into a person's inner mind, I do not think that this necessarily constitutes an interference with a right to bodily integrity."

This dictum would support the view that a requirement of mandatory counselling might not be subject to constitutional censure. However, policing such a requirement would, it is submitted be extremely difficult. It is desirable that parties attempt to resolve their difficulties through the use of such methods but to punish for failure to participate or to participate fully would run counter to the objective sought to be achieved.

In the context of adequate counselling services, it is interesting to note that Deputy Woods (467 *Dáil Debates* Col. 1779) also discussed the notion of counselling leave, which would appear to have been envisaged as being similar to maternity or adoptive leave. This concept has not been approved or advanced in the legislation although it is clearly a meritorious idea.

It is arguable that the terms of sections 6 to 8 of the 1996 Act, although admirable in their underlying objectives, are somewhat unrealistic. Minister Taylor indicated:

> "The purpose is to inform and encourage parties of options to settle disputes in Court over matters which could, perhaps, be settled for the most part out of Court with less cost, acrimony, resentment and bitterness and for the good of the parties concerned and their children." (467 *Dáil Debates* Col. 1761)

Advice as to reconciliation is clearly desirable, but it must be recognised that having lived apart for at least four years, the likelihood is that one or both of the marital partners will have developed completely different lifestyles. Four years is a considerable period of time in any context and equally so in the life of a family, or in terms of the continuity of a relationship. The scenario set out by Deputy Woods before the Select Committee on Legislation and Security would appear to be entirely removed from the reality of marriage breakdown:

> "The point of the four year waiting period is to allow for a lengthy gap between the origins of the conflict and the final resolution, if that is possible. The idea is to allow the dust to settle and to ensure partners who decide to break up and apply for a divorce have given due consideration to all the implications and aspects which arise. In the four year delay period there is time and space for much of the anger which surrounds the conflict at the point of the breakdown to subside. It makes sense, therefore, to re-evaluate the position at or near the end of the four year period. Feelings may have altered and some people may be willing to reconcile."

It is submitted that in a four year period not only will the dust have settled if the parties have stood still contemplating their relationship and their future, they will undoubtedly have choked upon the dust which will have accumulated around them. While reconciliation will sometimes take place and should be encouraged, it is submitted that in practice reconciliation is an option for very few couples satisfying the criteria for divorce set down in section 5 of the 1996 Act.

The objectives of sections 6 and 7, as enumerated by Minister Taylor, ignore the fundamental fact that most parties who apply for relief under the 1996 Act, or who would seek advice in relation to divorce, are doing so because they wish to obtain a decree of divorce, encompassing as it does the dissolution of the marriage, thus leaving the parties free to marry again. Most parties are well aware that if their sole objective is to separate, it is not necessary for them to proceed pursuant to the 1996 Act. Bearing in mind that none of the alternative reliefs which must be discussed with the parties pursuant to sections 6 and 7 of the Act are in any way comparable to a decree of divorce, insofar as they do not offer the option of remarriage, there would appear to be a lack of realism in sections 6 and 7.

In addition, the requirement in section 5(1)(a), *i.e.* that the parties must have lived apart for a period of at least four years during the previous five years, would appear to be particularly unrealistic when considering the requirement in section 6(2)(b) and section 7(2)(b), that the parties should be advised in relation to the possibility of engaging in mediation "to help effect separation (if the spouses are not separated)".

This envisages the possibility that parties may have "lived apart" for the purposes of section 5(1)(a), without being "separated" for the purposes of sections 6 and 7. While it is clearly possible, and has been previously discussed herein, parties may live apart although still residing under the same roof, the authorities from other jurisdictions indicate that the lifestyle of the parties, albeit residing in close proximity to each other, would be required to amount to a *de facto* separation of their lives, if the "living apart" criterion is to be satisfied. Perhaps this gives rise to the possibility that the interpretation of "lived apart" under the 1996 Act should be interpreted more liberally than is the case elsewhere. It is normal in other jurisdictions to talk in terms of the living apart and separation going hand in hand, it is often the case that parties are referred to as "living separately and apart". However, the Irish Act would appear to indicate that parties sometimes may not be separated, while at the same time living apart. Undoubtedly, such circumstances would be rare.

Section 6(6) provides that the Minister may by regulation provide for the establishment of a register of professional organisations whose members are qualified to assist in reconciliation procedures. During the course of its passage through the Houses of the Oireachtas, amendments were proposed by the opposition parties, which would have likewise provided for such a register in relation to mediation services. Deputy Keogh stated:

> "We need to establish a regulatory regime involving accreditation and recognition of training qualifications if we are sincere about shifting family disputes from the courts to mediators." (467 *Dáil Debates* Col. 1790)

It is difficult to appreciate why such limited regulation of reconciliation services was accepted by the Government, but was rejected in relation to mediation facilities. No provision equivalent to section 6(6) was included in the Bill as initiated. Before the Dáil, Minister Taylor indicated that he remained of the view:

> "that the question of who is or who is not qualified to act as a counsellor or as a mediator is best answered by the organisations which engage those persons." (469 *Dáil Debates* Col. 550)

However, when the matter came before the Seanad, the Minister accepted a proposed amendment, albeit in its limited scope, relating to reconciliation services only. (149 *Seanad Debates* Cols. 284–287)

Non-admissibility as evidence of certain communications relating to reconciliation, separation or divorce

9.—An oral or written communication between either of the spouses concerned and a third party for the purpose of seeking assistance to effect a reconciliation or to reach agreement between them on some or all of the terms of a separation or a divorce (whether or not made in the presence or with the knowledge of the other spouse), and any record of such a communication, made or caused to be made by either of the spouses concerned or such a third party, shall not be admissible as evidence in any court.

GENERAL NOTE

Section 9 of the Family Law (Divorce) Act 1996 was originally not included in the Bill as initiated, but was inserted at the Committee Stage in the Seanad. It confers, in the context of divorce proceedings, evidential privilege upon communications made in the course of reconciliation counselling or mediation. The 1996 Act, at section 45, introduces a similar privilege in relation to such communications, to operate in the context of judicial separation proceedings. The desirability of such a rule is unquestionable. Parties who attempt to settle their differences other than by the litigation route must be afforded the opportunity of complete openness and frankness in the course of such discussions and should not commence same overshadowed by the possibility that what they say may be used in evidence against them in the future, if the process being engaged in is unsuccessful.

It is surprising that the legislature has sought to introduce such a privilege in a piecemeal fashion related to particular categories of proceedings. It is submitted that it would have been preferable if such a privilege had been introduced in blanket form for all matrimonial/family law proceedings. The provisions of sections 9 and 45 possibly do not, in any event, represent a change in the law, but rather serve to clarify it. In *E.R. v. J.R.* [1981] 1 I.L.R.M. 125, Carroll J. held that a privilege attached to communications with a marriage guidance counsellor, although it remained uncertain as to whether this was limited to a priest or minister acting as a counsellor, being an extension of sacredotal privilege. It was and remains possible for parties to agree that communications are made "without prejudice" and are therefore inadmissible in evidence and such a condition may likewise be imposed by the parties themselves in relation to reconciliation or mediation counselling. An interesting point arises where the counsellor has played a dual role. One of the parties may have attended for individual counselling prior to joint marriage counselling commencing or, following joint marriage counselling, the counsellor may have sought to embark upon individual counselling of one of the parties. It is presumably a question of fact as to when marriage counselling started and ended and communications prior to or after such counselling remain admissible.

Effect of decree of divorce

10.—(1) Where the court grants a decree of divorce, the marriage, the subject of the decree, is thereby dissolved and a party to that marriage may marry again.

(2) For the avoidance of doubt, it is hereby declared that the grant of a decree of divorce shall not affect the right of the father and mother of an infant, under section 6 of the Act of 1964, to be guardians of the infant jointly.

GENERAL NOTE

The provisions of section 10 of the Family Law (Divorce) Act 1996 (the 1996 Act) were altered during the course of the passage of the Bill through the Oireachtas and in particular, section 10(2) was added confirming the joint guardianship rights of parents subsequent to the granting of a decree of divorce. Section 10(1) deals with the effect of a decree of divorce and is quite minimalist in its terms reflecting only the fact that the marriage is thereby dissolved and that the parties are thereby rendered free to remarry. However, section 10(1) must be considered in the light of section 2(2) of the Act dealing with the definition of a spouse. It states that:

> "*In this Act*, where the context so requires—
> (c)   a reference to a spouse includes a reference to a person who is a party to a marriage that has been dissolved under this Act . . ." (emphasis added)

This indicates that the term "spouse" continues to be used in the 1996 Act to describe a party who has been previously married to another party whose marriage has been dissolved pursuant to the terms of section 5 of the Act. It is important to note that section 2(2) limits this enlarged definition to the context of the 1996 Act. It is submitted that this does not mean that the parties may remain "spouses" for the purposes of other Acts, although this is not clearly stated in the 1996 Act. Logic would dictate that following the dissolution of a marriage, the parties cease to be spouses in the general sense.

It is clear from a consideration of Irish decisions concerning the recognition of foreign divorces, that following such recognition the parties cease to be entitled to apply for a variety of spousal reliefs and cease to be entitled to a number of spousal rights, otherwise available to them under the family law and succession statutes. It is submitted that, following the granting of a decree of divorce pursuant to the 1996 Act, that the parties cease to be "spouses" for the purposes of spousal rights and remedies contained in other Acts, but that the term spouse continues to operate for the purposes only of the 1996 Act in relation to reliefs and remedies thereunder. However, it would have been preferable if this was categorically stated and indeed clarity would have been assisted had the 1996 Act used vocabulary to distinguish between spouses who remain married and divorced "spouses". That such a general cessation of spousal rights occurs post-divorce was made clear by the Minister when he stated:

> "Where a couple divorce, the parties being no longer spouses will no longer have rights of succession." (467 *Dáil Debates* Col. 1765)

PART III

PRELIMINARY AND ANCILLARY ORDERS IN OR AFTER PROCEEDINGS FOR DIVORCE

GENERAL NOTE

Part III of the Family Law (Divorce) Act 1996 (the 1996 Act) empowers the court to make comprehensive preliminary and ancillary orders in proceedings for divorce instituted after the coming into operation of the Act on February 27, 1997. These powers originate in the context of judicial separation, as set out in Part II of the Judicial Separation and Family Law Reform Act 1989 (the 1989 Act), as repealed and amended by Part II of the Family Law Act 1995 (the 1995 Act), and indeed most of the contents of Part III of the 1996 Act replicate existing provisions of these Acts. Thus, for practitioners, Part III of the 1996 Act will be familiar. Clearly the biggest difference between divorce and judicial separation is that on divorce, the status of "spouse" terminates, and the inheritance rights, and in some cases, pension rights of the former spouses are automatically terminated. In examining Part III, reference must be made to section 5(1)(c) which provides that the decree cannot be granted unless the court is satisfied that "proper provision" exists or will be made for the spouses and any dependent members of the family. If proper provision already so exists, it may be enshrined as part of the court order granting the decree by way of ancillary orders.

There is no definition in the legislation of what comprises proper provision and in relation to divorce the only reported Irish case on the point *C. v. C.* [1997] 1 I.L.R.M. 401, is of no assistance. In this case the provisions ultimately agreed by both parties for the future support of the wife and children of the marriage, prior to the court hearing, left the respondent wife and children in a superior financial position to the applicant husband. There was in effect no assistance required from the court as to what comprised proper provision, although Barron J. clearly distinguished the case in so far as he did not:

> "purport to determine that non-dependent children should necessarily have provision made for them. I am satisfied that in the particular circumstances of the present case, it is proper that certainly the two daughters of the marriage should have provision made for them in the interests of the family as a whole."

It remains to be seen whether there will be future judicial clarification of what comprises "proper provision", and for the moment the only assistance available is to consider the principles set out in section 20 of the 1996 Act.

In taking into account agreements arrived at between the parties by way of separation agreement, the court is directed by the terms of section 20(3) of the 1996 Act to have regard to the terms of any separation agreement which was signed by both spouses, which is still in force. In practice, the courts are also likely to take into account terms of orders previously made in the context of judicial separation proceedings, especially if those orders have operated to the satisfaction of both parties, although the Act does not specify that the terms of any judicial separation order must be taken into account. If proper provision does not already exist as outlined above, then as already stated, such provision is likely to be made through the use of ancillary reliefs.

The provisions in the 1996 Act for ancillary and preliminary reliefs clearly allow for a complete re-examination and assessment of arrangements previously governing the breakdown of a marriage. It would appear that part of the reason why the expected flood of applications for divorce decrees has not materialised is because most of the applications processed to date are in respect of situations where most matters the subject of ancillary reliefs have been agreed by the parties before hand, and the orders are made on consent between the parties subject to court approval which is usually forthcoming. It would appear that some potential applicants have a fear of the manner in which Part III of the 1996 Act allows for such a comprehensive re-examination of the basic arrangements for the marriage breakdown, leading to a situation where there is no hope of finality or certainty for the parties.

Such judicial pronouncements as have been made do not serve to ease such fears. Some degree of initial encouragement seemed to emerge from the endorsement by the Supreme

Court in *F. v. F.* [1995] 2 I.R. 354 of the desirability of finality in matrimonial litigation. However, this desire has not been endorsed by the legislature in the 1996 Act. Denham J. stated in *F. v. F.*, at 369 that:

> "certainty and finality of litigation are important. Some issues in family law are not capable of a final order, *e.g.* maintenance. However, the fact that some issues in family law courts are not capable of finality does not deprive this area of law of the important concepts of certainty and finality. Whereas care for dependants requires that there be no finality in some areas the general law regarding certainty should apply unless excluded by law or justice."

In the case of *J.D. v. D.D.*, unreported, High Court, May 14, 1997, McGuinness J., in the course of determining an application for judicial separation with ancillary reliefs, commented on the fact that:

> "By (the enactment of) the Family Law (Divorce) Act 1996, the Oireachtas has made it clear that a 'clean break' situation is not to be sought and that, if anything, financial finality is virtually to be prevented . . . The Court, in making virtually any order in regard to finance and property on the breakdown of a marriage, is faced with the situation where finality is not and never can be achieved. . . . The statutory policy is, therefore, totally opposed to the concept of the 'clean break'."

While the judgment of the Supreme Court on appeal in *J.D. v. D.D.* offers a greater degree of comfort repeating the court's support of the notion that there would be a substantial degree of certainty and finality in the area of marriage breakdown reliefs and family law generally, the decided cases in relation to the granting of ancillary reliefs in the context of the 1996 Act are not encouraging. The wording of the 1996 Act does not inspire confidence. Arguably there has been an abdication of responsibility in this regard by the legislature to the judiciary. By and large, repeated applications for a wide range of reliefs remain possible and it is for the court to determine the issue of "proper provision" and through the application of the section 20 principles to decide if further relief is merited. This serves to place a heavy burden upon the judiciary, renders certainty unachievable and most importantly increases legal costs for the litigants with the potential for nuisance litigation.

In circumstances where parties to a separation agreement or judicial separation negotiate agreements, with the benefit of legal advice, which contain a term limiting or waiving their rights to apply in the future for reliefs available under the 1996 Act, it will be interesting to see how such terms are viewed by the courts. Certainly McGuinness J. in *J.D. v. D.D.* was clear that "no agreement on property between the parties can be completely final, since such finality would be contrary to the policy and provisions of the legislation", and she rightly feared such policy would create "considerable difficulties" for parties and legal advisors in attempting to reach settlements. It appears, therefore, that such limiting terms, or waivers, would not be effective, and the impossibility of obtaining a clean break should be clearly advised by practitioners to their clients.

Deputies in the course of the Second Stage of the Dáil debates confined themselves mainly to the substantive provisions of the Bill. Very little overall comment was made in relation to the preliminary and ancillary reliefs, which is hardly surprising given the fact that this had been discussed thoroughly in the context of previous legislation. Also, given the fact that the terms of the proposed divorce legislation had been made available to the public prior to the constitutional referendum. The legislature was substantially guided by the fact that the public had voted for the constitutional reforms on the basis of the terms of legislation, of which they had been made aware prior to the referendum.

Preliminary orders in proceedings for divorce

11.—Where an application is made to the court for the grant of a decree of divorce, the court, before deciding whether to grant or refuse to grant the decree, may, in the same proceedings and without the institution of proceedings under the Act concerned, if it appears to the court to be proper to do so, make one or more of the following orders—

    (a) a safety order, a barring order, an interim barring order or a protection order under the Act of 1996,

    (b) an order under section 11 of the Act of 1964,

    (c) an order under section 5 or 9 of the Family Home Protection Act, 1976.

GENERAL NOTE

This provides a mechanism whereby applications for interim relief can be made, and is a very necessary provision in areas where the full hearing is unlikely to come on before the court for some time. When divorce proceedings have been instituted, but before the court decides whether or not to grant a decree, the court may grant to either spouse preliminary orders under the following legislation, without the institution of proceedings under those specific Acts. Such applications include:

    (a) A safety order, barring order, interim barring order or a protection order under the Domestic Violence Act 1996;

    (b) An order under section 11 of the Guardianship of Infants Act 1964;

    (c) An order under sections 5 or 9 of the Family Home Protection 1976.

Section 11 of the 1996 Act is specific as to the powers of the court to make these preliminary orders before deciding whether to grant, or refuse to grant a decree of divorce. Therefore, it is possible to envisage a situation where the court would ultimately refuse to grant a decree of divorce, but would have already granted, for example, orders relating to the welfare of the children, which orders would obviously lapse after the refusal of the divorce decree.

However, in these circumstances, if the decree of divorce itself had been refused (presumably on the basis that the proofs required by section 5 of the 1996 Act had not been complied with) equivalent reliefs could be sought and probably obtained in the context of an application for judicial separation, or pursuant to the terms of the individual statutes providing for the reliefs set out in sections 11 and 12 on a substantive basis, *e.g.* the Family Law Act 1976, the Domestic Violence Act 1996, the Guardianship of Infants Act 1964 or the Family Home Protection Act 1976.

The section is essentially designed to afford immediate protection to a spouse or to dependent family members, when necessary. It is an exact replica of section 6 of the 1995 Family Law Act, with the exception of the reference in section 11(a) to the Domestic Violence Act 1996, which repealed/replaced the provisions of the Family Law (Protection of Spouses and Children) Act 1981, as referred to in the Family Law Act 1995. The extent of such interim applications is dictated by court lists and the likely hearing date to be assigned for the full hearing. Significant reductions in such waiting periods have been achieved at Circuit Court level in recent years, particularly before the Dublin Circuit Court, with a consequent decrease in the number of interim applications brought pursuant to sections 11 or 12 of the 1996 Act.

Maintenance pending suit orders

12.—(1) Where an application is made to the court for the grant of a decree of divorce, the court may make an order for maintenance pending suit, that is to say, an order requiring either of the spouses concerned to make to the other spouse such periodical payments or lump sum payments for his or her support and, where appropriate, to make to such person as may be specified in the order such periodical payments for the benefit of such (if any) dependent member of the family and, as respects periodical payments, for such period beginning not earlier than the date of the application and ending not later than the date of its determination, as the court considers proper and specifies in the order.

(2) The court may provide that payments under an order under this section shall be subject to such terms and conditions as it considers appropriate and specifies in the order.

GENERAL NOTE

Section 12 mirrors section 7 of the Family Law Act 1995 (the 1995 Act), which itself was largely similar to section 13 of the Judicial Separation and Family Law Reform Act 1989 (the 1989 Act). All three sections allow the court to make interim maintenance orders, *i.e.* orders during the period between the date of issuing proceedings seeking a decree, and the ultimate determination by the court of the application. The section does not provide for retrospective maintenance prior to the date of the institution of proceedings. This section allows for the granting of interim periodical payments or lump sum payments and Minister Taylor, during the Second Stage of the Dáil debates, referring to the availability of interim lump sum maintenance, stated:

> "Provision for Interim Lump Sum Payments is intended to cover cases where there may be hardship, or where immediate bills have to be paid by a spouse". (467 *Dáil Debates* Col. 1761).

The criteria for making orders under section 12, are set out in section 20, which designates the matters to which the courts shall have regard in deciding whether or not to make an order. Although section 20 essentially replicates the provisions of section 16 of the 1995 Act, certain parts of section 20(1) are new. The court is directed to have regard to the rights of any person, other than the spouse, but including a person to whom either spouse has remarried. The provisions of section 22 of the 1996 Act permit a variation of orders made under section 12, although presumably a very long delay in the ultimate hearing date would have to exist to justify an interim application and a later application to vary same. It is assumed that the usual material change of circumstances would have to arise to justify such a variation. The provisions of section 22(3) should be noted insofar as it applies to section 12. It directs that a maintenance pending suit; which is paid for the support of a dependent member of the family, will stand automatically discharged when the dependent member reaches the age of 18 or 23 years during the currency of the order, as appropriate, or may be ordered discharged by the court, if any application in that regard is made to it. The definition of "dependent member" has already been referred to and is set out in section 2 of the Act.

It is noteworthy, as hereinbefore mentioned, that section 12 allows for interim maintenance orders to be backdated to the date the application was made, but not earlier. The order will only survive until the final determination of the court in respect of the application for the grant of a decree. Such retrospection in the case of orders for interim maintenance can be useful. For example, the enforcement of maintenance orders is considerably easier than the enforcement of maintenance provisions agreed between the parties whether informally, or in the context of a separation or maintenance agreement. The retrospective order would have the benefit of enforcement mechanisms including, attachments of earning orders and contempt proceedings.

In the case of an agreement, the only remedy for enforcement is the equitable remedy of specific performance. This relief is cumbersome and results are slowly achieved. More effective perhaps, where there is such an agreement which is not being complied with, would be to seek an order for interim maintenance to apply retrospectively to the date of the institution of the proceedings effectively in the terms of the prior agreement thus making available the enforcement remedies of attachment and committal and also attachment of earnings in relation to defaults, whether retrospective or present.

However, the extent of retrospection is limited and cannot extend further back than the date of the application for a decree of divorce. Some debate has taken place as to the meaning of "the date of the application". Clearly, the section itself envisages two distinct points between which the interim payments may be ordered to be made, *i.e.* between "the date of the application" and "the date of its determination".

The "application" being addressed is the application for the primary relief of the decree of divorce itself. This is evident from the wording of the section itself. It is submitted that one applies to court for a divorce on the day that proceedings are instituted seeking such relief. This is somewhat supported by the fact that formerly the relevant document for the institution of family law proceedings was referred to as an application. The attempt at uniformity of pleading throughout the civil law at Circuit Court level has led to the use of civil bills in family law proceedings. Nevertheless, it is submitted that the application for relief is made upon the date of issuing of the civil bill.

Section 12(2) allows the court to impose such terms and conditions on the making of payments under an order as it considers appropriate, but these terms and conditions must be specified in the order. For example, the court could direct that a lump sum order be paid by a spouse to be used specifically for the discharge of the entire mortgage, or to be used to discharge the children's school fees and expenses. Practitioners should note that orders made under this section will almost invariably be made without any proper/adequate financial information or details, at least relating to the respondent, let alone discovery. Accordingly, amounts might be ordered which will sometimes not accurately reflect what is proper, had full disclosure been made. The interpretation of "proper" must be viewed in the context of the nature of the application and, in practice the courts would appear to support this approach. Concerns are sometimes expressed that interim awards set a benchmark and may have an influence on final maintenance payments.

As against this, financial circumstances usually compel such an application if adequate financial provision is not be made and failure to seek interim maintenance might lead a court to the view that there was an absence of financial need on the part of the applicant. While it is presently common to seek discovery at the earliest possible stage in the proceedings, it is unlikely that full discovery will have been made prior to any interim application for maintenance.

Periodical Payments and Lump Sum Orders

13.—(1) On granting a decree of divorce or at any time thereafter, the court, on application to it in that behalf by either of the spouses concerned or by a person on behalf of a dependent member of the family, may, during the lifetime of the other spouse, or, as the case may be, the spouse concerned, make one or more of the following orders, that is to say—

(a) a periodical payments order, that is to say—

  (i) an order that either of the spouses shall make to the other spouse such periodical payments of such amount, during such period and at such times as may be specified in the order, or

  (ii) an order that either of the spouses shall make to such person as may be so specified for the benefit of such (if any) dependent member of the family such periodical payments of such amount, during such period and at such times as may be so specified,

(b) a secured periodical payments order, that is to say—

  (i) an order that either of the spouses shall secure, to the satisfaction of the court, to the other spouse such periodical payments of such amounts, during such period and at such times as may be so specified, or

  (ii) an order that either of the spouses shall secure, to the satisfaction of the court, to such person as may be so specified for the benefit of such (if any) dependent member of the family such periodical payments of such amounts, during such period and at such times as may be so specified,

(c) (i) an order that either of the spouses shall make to the other spouse a lump sum payment or lump sum payments of such amount or amounts and at such time or times as may be so specified, or

(ii) an order that either of the spouses shall make to such person as may be so specified for the benefit of such (if any) dependent member of the family a lump sum payment or lump sum payments of such amount or amounts and at such time or times as may be so specified.

(2) The court may—

(a) order a spouse to pay a lump sum to the other spouse to meet any liabilities or expenses reasonably incurred by that other spouse before the making of an application by that other spouse for an order under subsection (1) in maintaining himself or herself or any dependent member of the family, or

(b) order a spouse to pay a lump sum to such person as may be specified to meet any liabilities or expenses reasonably incurred by or for the benefit of a dependent member of the family before the making of an application on behalf of the member for an order under subsection (1).

(3) An order under this section for the payment of a lump sum may provide for the payment of the lump sum by instalments of such amounts as may be specified in the order and may require the payment of the instalments to be secured to the satisfaction of the court.

(4) The period specified in an order under paragraph (a) or (b) of subsection (1) shall begin not earlier than the date of the application for the order and shall end not later than the death of the spouse, or any dependent member of the family, in whose favour the order is made or the other spouse concerned.

(5) (a) Upon the remarriage of the spouse in whose favour an order is made under paragraph (a) or (b) of subsection (1), the order shall, to the extent that it applies to that spouse, cease to have effect, except as respects payments due under it on the date of the remarriage.

(b) If, after the grant of a decree of divorce, either of the spouses concerned remarries, the court shall not, by reference to that decree, make an order under subsection (1) in favour of that spouse.

(6) (a) Where a court makes an order under subsection (1)(a), it shall in the same proceedings, subject to paragraph (b), make an attachment of earnings order (within the meaning of the Act of 1976) to secure payments under the first mentioned order if it is satisfied that the person against whom the order is made is a person to whom earnings (within the meaning aforesaid) fall to be paid.

(b) Before deciding whether to make or refuse to make an attachment of earnings order by virtue of paragraph (a), the court shall give the spouse concerned an opportunity to make the representations specified in paragraph (c) in relation to the matter and shall have regard to any such representations made by that spouse.

(c) The representations referred to in paragraph (b) are representations relating to the questions—

  (i) whether the spouse concerned is a person to whom such earnings as aforesaid fall to be paid, and

  (ii) whether he or she would make the payments to which the relevant order under subsection (1)(a) relates.

 (d) References in this subsection to an order under subsection (1)(a) include references to such an order as varied or affirmed on appeal from the court concerned or varied under section 22.

GENERAL NOTE

The requirement for post-divorce financial support has increased in Ireland, due to the economic conditions which prevail. Deputy Woods stated that Ireland, with a rate of 30 per cent, still has the lowest rate of women working outside the home in the OECD. This compares with Denmark at 74 per cent, and 64 per cent in the United Kingdom (467 *Dáil Debates* Col. 1775).

Clearly this figure does not paint an encouraging picture for an applicant wife and financial arrangements remain one of the most contentious areas for both applicant and respondent spouses, as the economic realities of judicial separation and divorce are that both spouses rarely find themselves in positions of financial strength after the decree has been granted.

The payments outlined in section 13 can be ordered by the court, either at the time of granting the decree of divorce, or any time thereafter, on application to it by either of the spouses, or by a person acting on behalf of a dependent family member. This is the first section which firmly sets out the intention of the legislature, that post-divorce, the legal rights and responsibilities of spouses towards one another will continue. In circumstances where a spouse remarries, he or she could conceivably have financial responsibility towards more than one spouse and more than one set of dependent family members. Remarriage of the recipient spouse implies the cessation of maintenance payable in respect of that spouse, but maintenance continues of course in respect of dependant members of the family pursuant to section 13(5).

It remains to be seen whether or not agreements properly negotiated and reached between parties before asking the court for a decree of divorce; which stipulate that both parties have waived their rights to apply for review or variation of maintenance orders in the future or acknowledge that future maintenance applications, would be binding. The well-known provisions of the section 27 of the Family Law (Maintenance of Spouses and Children) Act 1976 (No. 11) provided that an agreement whereby a spouse contracted out of the right to apply for maintenance was void. The Supreme Court endorsed this in *H.D. v. P.D.*, unreported, Supreme Court, May 8, 1978. While the 1996 Act has no equivalent to section 27 and post-divorce, section 27 ought not to apply as the parties are no longer "spouses" for the purposes of the 1976 Act, the underlying principle is that of public policy. The dictates of public policy probably still imply that a clause denying a right to apply would not be enforced but such a clause or an acknowledgement of respective future financial intentions could be examined by the court in the context of the overall circumstances of the case. Practitioners should therefore ensure that such settlements should set out specifically in writing the spouse's requirements in this regard. There is no provision for the exclusion or restriction of the applicability of section 22 to orders made pursuant to section 13.

The reliefs set out in section 13 mirror those set out in section 8 of the Family Law Act 1995. Section 13(1)(a) provides for a preliminary payments order, similar to a usual maintenance order for either a spouse or a dependent family member. Section 13(1)(b) provides for the making of a secured periodical payments order, which must be secured to the satisfaction of the court, *e.g.* by an attachment of earnings condition, or a payment order secured on a particular bank account or bond. There is no indication given as to when such an order should be made and in practice, they would appear to be rare. Section 13(1)(c) provides for a lump sum payment or payments to be made to either the spouse or dependent family member, which payments can be directed to be made either in one lump or in instalments, or again secured to the satisfaction of the court.

Section 13(2)(a) contains a provision directing that a lump sum payment can be ordered to be paid to the other spouse for any liabilities or expenses which they may have been reasonably incurred before any application pursuant to subsection (1) has been made, *e.g.* to reimburse them for money spent, as a result of loans taken by the spouse or debts subsequently incurred, because maintenance was not being paid. What is reasonable in each case will depend on all the circumstances of same. For example, a court may consider that monies borrowed for necessary house maintenance are reasonably incurred, but monies spent on interior decorator's fees might be considered unreasonable.

Section 13(2)(6) allows a lump sum to be paid in similar circumstances to a "specified person" on behalf of a dependent member of the family, *e.g.* monies to be paid directly to a school for school fees. Applicants should be encouraged by practitioners to keep detailed financial records and to reconstruct such records where necessary in respect of past expenses. Generally, when an application for divorce comes before the court, it will consider all financial issues before the court at the time of hearing and will probably only in a small number of cases make specific orders in respect of past expenses incurred.

If a lump sum order is made in favour of a spouse at the hearing of the application, there is nothing, apart from the provisions of section 13(5), to stop that spouse making an application for another lump sum order in the future. This subsection directs that remarriage is a bar to such applications provided all responsibilities under the original order have been discharged. However once paid, a lump sum cannot be reviewed by the court even with the assistance of section 22.

It is unlikely, however, that a court would not take into account all financial circumstances surrounding an application for a further lump sum, particularly if the applicant is financially secure. Lump sums may be ordered to cover, *e.g.* arrears of maintenance or maintenance into the future, if it is feared that a respondent spouse may leave the jurisdiction. Lump sum orders could also cover a sum equivalent to the value of the interest of the applicant spouse in the family home or cover debts which must be discharged on the breakdown of the marriage.

In the case of *J.D. v. D.D.*, unreported, High Court, May 14, 1997, McGuinness J. dealt with an application by a wife for a judicial separation, together with ancillary orders. The financial resources of the marriage in question were considerable. The applicant wife made a very strong case for the payment by the respondent husband of a large lump sum which would provide the wife with not only a satisfactory income for her lifetime, but also with security and ease of financial management for the wife to have her own income and run her own life. It was argued on behalf of the respondent husband however that payment of so large a lump sum would deprive him of virtually all the disposable capital he had accumulated over his working life.

In considering this aspect the High Court referred to the Family Law (Maintenance of Spouses and Children) Act 1976, section 27 of which forbids the making of an order which purports to cut-off the right of a spouse to apply for maintenance:

> "Just as the payment of a large capital sum for an annuity could not prevent the wife, in certain circumstances, from applying for maintenance in the future, so also it could not prevent the husband, if he fell on hard times, from applying for maintenance to be paid to him by the wife, thus reducing her annuity income."

Having assessed the circumstances of the marriage, and taken into account the provisions of section 16 of the 1995 Act, section 20 of the 1996 Act, the court ordered that a lump sum payment be made together with periodic maintenance payments.

Section 13(5) provides that when a spouse remarries, in whose favour a periodical payments order or lump sum payments order has been made, the orders will no longer have any effect and no future payments will be made thereunder other than payments which were due on the date of the remarriage. Section 13(5)(b) provides for the future in such circumstances where a decree of divorce has been granted, and recipient/prospective recipient remarries, then the court may not make any new orders under section 13(1) in favour of the remarried spouse. Section 13(4) provides that apart from remarriage, periodical payment orders will also cease on the death of either spouse. Review may also take place in accordance with general legal principles when there has been a fundamental change of circumstances.

Section 13(5)(a) is concerned with cessation of orders and is limited in its application to periodic and secured periodic orders; lump sum orders, under section 13(1)(c) do not appear within the ambit of section 13(5)(a). There is an underlying logic as the lump sum obligation has already accrued and in most instances, if not already paid will represent a default. However, lump sum orders may be payable by instalments and at the date of remarriage certain of these instalments may remain outstanding. These obligations would not appear to cease automatically. Alternatively, section 22(1)(d) expressly provides for applications to vary instalment maintenance lump sums. It envisages the remarriage of the parties or either of them as a circumstance in which variation of such orders might occur, providing for such an application for a new spouse, section 22(2)(c), in the case of a remarriage.

Section 13(6) deals with attachment of earnings orders and directs that such orders may be so secured at the same time as a periodical payments order, without having to wait for default in respect of the payments. This applies only to those who are employed by another person or body, and not to those who are self-employed or by implication to those who work in the "black economy". Section 13(6) would seem to suggest that these orders would be made in almost all cases where a periodical payments order is being made and, indeed that they should be the norm.

This contrasts sharply with the original attachment of earnings relief introduced in section 10 of the Family Law (Maintenance of Spouses and Children) Act 1976 which provided that such orders would be available on default or on consent. The present provisions are in mandatory terms and place the onus of proving that such order should not be made upon the proposed paying spouse. It is submitted that this provision goes too far in this regard and that it would have been sufficient merely to remove the default requirement. The provision assumes a disrespect for court orders and, if applied to its full strength, would impose upon many maintenance debtors the negative aspects of attachment of earning orders.

The paying spouse, under section 13(6), however, must be given an opportunity to make representations to the court as to why such attachment orders should not be made. These representations include confirming to the court whether or not the paying spouse is an employed person and further confirming whether or not the person "would make" the payments. This allows for evidence to be given, *e.g.* in relation to a previous good record of maintenance paying, and if appropriate, the history of the financial aspects of the marriage; particularly with reference to the financial irresponsibility or otherwise of one of the spouses. This major change in the law came about by way of section 8 of the 1995 Act and practitioners should note that sections 10 to 20 of the Family Law (Maintenance of Spouses and Children) Act 1976 continue to apply.

During the course of the Oireachtas debates upon the Family Law (Divorce) Bill 1996, the enforcement difficulties which often arise in relation to maintenance were noted. The value of the attachment of earnings order in the case of employed persons who default on their maintenance obligations is well established. The extremely broad provisions of section 8(6) of the 1995 Act have not been widely used in practice, but the broad enforcement support is repeated in the Family Law Act 1996. It is not expected to be utilised in the divorce context any differently than in the case of judicial separation applications. Section 13(6) supports the granting of attachment of earnings orders in respect of maintenance orders but nevertheless the courts remain reluctant in this regard. It would appear that there is some degree of conflict between judicial interpretation and legislative intent. Minister Taylor stated:

> "The purpose of the subsection is to reduce, where possible, the need for a dependent spouse to engage in subsequent court proceedings for enforcement of maintenance." (467 *Dáil Debates* Col. 1762)

But despite this, the position remains that it is unlikely that an attachment of earnings order will be made in the absence of some degree of default history. In many ways, the practical application of the provision, being considerably more liberal than the draconian terms in which the subsection is written, is to the overall advantage of the family as undoubtedly employment prospects may be impacted upon by the existence of an attachment of earnings order.

Enforcement difficulties persist and have persisted for a considerable period, both in relation to lump sum orders and periodic maintenance payments, in the case of self-employed persons. In these situations, the maintenance creditor normally must have resort to an attachment and committal procedure in an effort to have the previous orders of the court complied with. A number of points arise in relation to the suitability of such procedures in the family law context:

(a) Such an application involves a return to court with the consequent implications in terms of legal costs;

(b) Courts are reluctant to commit to prison in a family law context;

(c) the time spent in prison does not assist in the accumulation of the required funds;

(d) Parties themselves are reluctant to embark upon a route which may end up in the imprisonment of their former partner and the father/mother of their children;

(e) It does not necessarily result in the monies due being paid and additional arrears may be caused to accrue; and

(f) The court has a discretion in deciding whether or not to grant the reliefs sought.

In effect, the usefulness of the attachment and committal procedure is primarily *in terrorem*.

An interesting amendment was proposed by Deputy Woods before the Select Committee on Legislation and Security which aimed to impose interest penalties upon lump sum and periodic maintenance orders in cases of default. The rate of interest was to be fixed by ministerial order from time to time (July 17, 1996, L6 No. 12, Col. 669). The Minister indicated that an amendment in such terms was not necessary due to the provisions of the Courts (No. 2) Act 1981 (No. 31), which empowered the courts "to order payment of interest in respect of money that is the subject to a court order." (149 *Seanad Debates* Col. 32)

It is submitted, however, that maintenance awards are only partly assisted by existing legislation and that its application in this context is cumbersome. Pursuant to the provisions of section 27 of the Debtors (Ireland) Act 1840 (3 & 4 Vict., c. 105), interest accrues in relation to judgment debts. A judgment for lump sum maintenance or for accrued arrears of maintenance presumably attracts the application of the provisions of section 27 of the 1840 Act from the date of the judgment.

The Courts Act 1981 considers court interest in sections 21 and 22. The former simply provides for the accrual of interest in relation to Circuit Court costs, while the latter section gives the court a discretion to award interest for the period between the date the cause of action accrued and the date of the judgment. Post-judgment, section 27 of the 1840 Act once again applies.

Therefore, the position relating to interest on periodic maintenance payments is somewhat complex. Such payments would not appear to automatically attract interest in cases of default as each individual periodic obligation would not appear to constitute a separate judgment debt. In the case of default, the "cause of action" in respect of arrears would presumably accrue as of the date of default. Therefore, presumably the discretionary powers contained in section 22 of the Courts Act 1981 would appear applicable. Once judgment in respect of the arrears is recovered, presumably section 27 of the 1840 Act applies in the normal way.

Further proposals advocated during the Oireachtas debates involved enabling the court to order that payments be secured by establishing a direct debit payment system (Select Committee on Legislation and Security, July 17, 1996, L6 No. 12, Col. 692). The value of the latter is that the payment occurs without the requirement of regular steps being taken by the maintenance debtor to provide payment. However, a direct debit is only useful to the extent that there are funds available to fulfil it.

Perhaps a regrettable omission is that there is no provision in this section or in section 8 of the Family Law Act 1995, for automatic increases in the amount payable by way of periodical payments order. Practitioners should be careful to note that any increases required should be sought by way of agreement and negotiation before the order is made, or by application to the court during the hearing of the case. One disadvantage of the absence of an automatic in-built provision for increase in court maintenance awards is that awards can quickly become outdated. The normal standard applied for bringing a maintenance variation application is that there has been a material change of circumstances and it is not usually possible to say that simply the passage of time is such a material change, save, perhaps where an extremely long period of time has elapsed such that the original order is entirely obsolete.

However, maintenance variation applications are made pursuant to section 22 of the 1996 Act and section 20 makes it clear that the wide range of factors which it lists should likewise be taken into account by the court in section 22 applications. These factors clearly extend further than a necessity of showing a material change of circumstances since the making of the original order of the last variation thereof. However, the position remains that a variation in maintenance requires a return to court with the consequent financial and emotional costs entailed in each such application.

In assessing whether any order should be made pursuant to section 13, the court is directed by the provisions of section 20 to take various matters into consideration. In *J.D. v. D.D.*, unreported, High Court, May 14, 1997, McGuinness J. commented that, "In making the necessary (financial) calculations, full regard must be paid to the guidelines set out in section 16 of the 1995 Act", which guidelines are almost identical to those of section 20 of the 1996 Act.

Property adjustment orders

14.—(1) On granting a decree of divorce or at any time thereafter, the court, on application to it in that behalf by either of the spouses concerned or by a person on behalf of a dependent member of the family, may, during the lifetime of the other spouse or, as the case may be, the spouse concerned, make a property adjustment order, that is to say, an order providing for one or more of the following matters:

(a) the transfer by either of the spouses to the other spouse, to any dependent member of the family or to any other specified person for the benefit of such a member of specified property, being property to which the first-mentioned spouse is entitled either in possession or reversion,

(b) the settlement to the satisfaction of the court of specified property, being property to which either of the spouses is so entitled as aforesaid, for the benefit of the other spouse and of any dependent member of the family or of any or all of those persons,

(c) the variation for the benefit of either of the spouses and of any dependent member of the family or of any or all of those persons of any ante-nuptial or post-nuptial settlement (including such a settlement made by will or codicil) made on the spouses,

(d) the extinguishment or reduction of the interest of either of the spouses under any such settlement.

(2) An order under paragraph (b), (c) or (d) may restrict to a specified extent or exclude the application of section 22 in relation to the order.

(3) If, after the grant of a decree of divorce, either of the spouses concerned remarries, the court shall not, by reference to that decree, make a property adjustment order in favour of that spouse.

(4) Where a property adjustment order is made in relation to land, a copy of the order certified to be a true copy by the registrar or clerk of the court concerned shall, as appropriate, be lodged by him or her in the Land Registry for registration pursuant to section 69(1)(h) of the Registration of Title Act,

1964, in a register maintained under that Act or be registered in the Registry of Deeds.

(5) Where—

(a) a person is directed by an order under this section to execute a deed or other instrument in relation to land, and

(b) the person refuses or neglects to comply with the direction or, for any other reason, the court considers it necessary to do so,

the court may order another person to execute the deed or instrument in the name of the first-mentioned person; and a deed or other instrument executed by a person in the name of another person pursuant to an order under this subsection shall be as valid as if it had been executed by that other person.

(6) Any costs incurred in complying with a property adjustment order shall be borne, as the court may determine, by either of the spouses concerned, or by both of them in such proportions as the court may determine, and shall be so borne in such manner as the court may determine.

(7) This section shall not apply in relation to a family home in which, following the grant of a decree of divorce, either of the spouses concerned, having remarried, ordinarily resides with his or her spouse.

GENERAL NOTE

The position of the property adjustment order in matrimonial situations is firmly enshrined in Irish law, beginning with section 15 of the Judicial Separation and Family Law Reform Act 1989, as amended by section 9 of the Family Law Act 1995. Section 15 is identical to the provisions of this section. The amendments to the 1995 Act, inserted by section 52 of the 1996 Act, provide that section 9(1) property adjustment order applications may be made at the time of the decree of judicial separation *or at anytime thereafter* (emphasis added).

The court can make a property adjustment order on granting a decree of divorce or by application to the court at any time thereafter during the lifetime of the other spouse pursuant to section 14. The order can be made in favour of a dependent family member or to a specified person to be held by them for the benefit of a family member. Section 14(3) provides that a property adjustment order cannot be made in favour of a spouse who has remarried. Section 14(7) contains a further restriction precluding the operation of the section in the context of the family home in which a remarried spouse ordinarily resides with his or her new spouse.

Clearly, this provision can only apply in the context of a post-divorce application and not to an application made at the time of the granting of the decree, as prior to the decree there was no recognisable marriage. There is nothing to prevent the operation of the section in relation to the premises in which a spouse resides with a permanent partner, even if marriage to that partner is envisaged post-divorce.

Applications may be made for a property adjustment order against the other spouse on more than one occasion, unless the first such order made specifically excludes or restricts any further applications in accordance with section 14(2). In practice orders under section 14 are most frequently made by way of a simple transfer of the property, usually the family home and contents, from one spouse to the other in consideration of a lump sum payment by the other spouse to the value of their interest in the property, or a portion thereof depending on the transferee's ability to pay. In this regard the decisions in *R.F. v. J.F.* [1995] 3 F.L.J. 90 and *M.M. v. C.M.* [1996] I.F.L.R. 214 are instructive. In the former case McGuinness J. ordered the transfer of a family home held in the joint names of the spouses into the sole name of the husband subject to the payment of £25,000 by the husband to the wife. The court was influenced by the fact that the husband required the stability of staying in the family home in order to re-establish his livelihood, while the wife also required financial assistance towards acquiring accommodation suitable to her needs and those of the dependent children. It should be noted that in this case the wife did not wish to reside in the family home having moved to live in a different part of the country.

In *M.M. v. C.M.* a transfer of a husband's interest in the family home was ordered by Morris J. to the wife in exchange for the discharge of maintenance arrears accrued by the husband. The family home was held in the spouses' joint names and while the arrears accrued were substantial, they did not represent the full value of his share in the property. A property adjustment order may direct a transfer of the whole or part only of property and where property is held in the sole name of a spouse, a transfer into joint names may also be ordered. This occurred in relation to a family home in the case of *J.C. v. C.C.* [1994] 1 F.L.J. 22., per Barr J.

As with most other ancillary reliefs available under the 1996 Act, the basic approach to be adopted by the court in deciding whether to make such orders is to attempt to ensure that proper provision exists or will be made for each spouse and for any dependent family member having regard to the circumstances of the case. In deciding whether or not to make a property adjustment order, the court must have regard to the matters set out in section 20 of the 1996 Act. This section differs from the provisions of section 16 of the 1995 Act in that section 20(3) directs the court in the context of divorce to have regard to the terms of any separation agreement entered into by the parties which is still in force. The role of separation agreements will be further considered hereinafter with reference to section 14(1)(c) of the 1996 Act. Although there have been a number of written decisions and numerous oral judgments granting property transfer orders, there is little guidance to be gleaned as to the principles applicable to the circumstances in which such orders will be granted which goes further than the generalised section 20 guidelines. This absence consequently makes it difficult to predict results.

Partial assistance may be derived from the decision of McGuinness J. in *J.D. v. D.D.*, unreported, High Court, May 14, 1997 in which the principles applicable to the granting of financial reliefs were discussed. Although the dicta therein is of general application it is instructive in the specific context of property adjustment orders. The "one-third rule", endorsed by the English courts, *i.e.* that the financially dependent spouse should be granted approximately one-third of the capital assets which was rejected by the High Court. The court discussed the "subsistence level approach" in the case of less-well-off couples and awards consistent with lifestyle in the case of wealthier couples. It is submitted that such approaches are of little guidance, as they are imprecise, difficult to predict and encapsulate a high degree of subjectivity, however no definitive guidelines for its application in the Irish context were given. Principles of justice, equity and fairness will apply and courts will usually consider it unwarranted to transfer the bulk of assets to one spouse.

In *A.O'L v. B.O'L* [1996] 2 F.L.J. 63, McGuinness J., as she then was, considered it be inequitable to transfer a family home entirely to a wife where the husband had owned the property prior to the marriage and had made all of the mortgage repayments. A sale of the property was ordered and the proceeds of sale were to be divided among the parties, notwithstanding the ownership by the husband of other assets. In summary, the general focus of the legislation allowing for multiple applications and review/variability of previous orders applies in the context of property adjustment orders with some limitations:

(1) The section provides that orders can be sought either at the time of granting the decree, or at any time thereafter, which would appear to indicate that there is no limit on the number of occasions a spouse can seek and a court can grant a property adjustment order under section 14(a) to (d) provided these applications are made during the lifetime of the other spouse. Such orders cannot be granted to a spouse who has remarried pursuant to section 14(3) and they do not constitute a variation of a previous property adjustment order under section 14(1)(a);

(2) The provisions of section 14 of the 1996 Act must be contrasted with the provisions of section 15 of the Judicial Separation and Family Law Reform Act 1989 which originally introduced this relief. Section 15(2) stated:

"(2) The court may, following the granting of a decree of judicial separation consider and determine whether an order or orders should be made by it in favour of a spouse under this section on *one occasion only unless on that occasion a spouse wilfully conceals information of a material nature relevant to the making of any such order or orders.*" (emphasis added)

There is no equivalent provision in the 1996 Act;

(3)   Section 22 of the 1996 Act in listing the types of orders which may be subject to variation excludes orders made under section 14(l)(a) of the 1996 Act, but envisages that variations may be sought and made in relation to orders under section 14(l)(b) to (d), subject to (4) hereinafter. The court has no power to vary a property adjustment order under section 14(l)(a) which prevents any interference in a straightforward property adjustment order once it has been made. There is no restriction, however, on further applications being made in respect of other property;

(4)   Section 14(2) provides that the court may restrict or completely exclude the provisions of section 22 in relation to a property adjustment order made under section 14(l)(b), (c) or (d). Accordingly, if a practitioner is acting on behalf of a spouse who requires, so far as legally possible that all property matters be finalised without recourse to review, then specific applications should be made to the court for a section 14(2) exclusion order;

(5)   Other restrictions on the grant or extent of a property adjustment order are set out under section 14(3) which provides that remarriage is a bar to further property adjustment orders in favour of the remarried spouse;

(6)   Further, under section 14(7) a property adjustment order cannot be made in relation to specifically, a family home, if after the decree has been granted, one of the spouses having remarried ordinarily resides there with his/her new spouse. It is possible therefore that an order could be made leaving the family home in the spouses' joint names; allowing one of the spouses to reside in it to the exclusion of the other and allowing the non-residing spouse liberty to apply for an order for sale, or a property adjustment order in the future. If the spouse residing in the family home remarries and brings the new party to live there, then clearly relief previously granted to the non-residing spouse will be defeated. Conversely, the spouse who lives in the family home but who does not remarry can be put out by a subsequent property adjustment order obtained by the other spouse;

(7)   A determination of the respective interests of spouses in a property under section 36 of the Family Law Act, 1995 will not prevent the making of a property adjustment order in relation to that or another property, no issue of *res judicata* arises. It was so held in *E.M. v. W.M.* [1994] 3 F.L.J. 93.

Section 14(l)(a) gives the court extensive powers to provide for a property transfer order by one spouse to the other spouse to a dependent family member, or to another person to hold such a property for the benefit of a dependent family member. The term "property" refers not only to the family home, but also to any property in which either spouse has an interest either in possession or reversion. For example, a spouse due to benefit from property held by their parents for life and thereafter in reversion by that spouse could be deprived of that benefit if a property adjustment order is made directing that such property will be transferred to their spouse or a dependent family member. The mode and time of acquisition will not per se preclude the making of such an order and property may have been inherited by the transferor spouse or acquired by that spouse prior to marriage.

Similarly, property adjustment orders may be made in relation to legal or beneficial interests in property and in relation to property the subject of co-ownership, whether between the spouses *inter se* or as between the spouses and third parties. Property adjustment orders may be made in respect of local authority, as well as other housing. These orders are granted by transferring the tenancy from joint to sole names. It is important to obtain an exclusion order under section 15(l)(a) in these circumstances. The provisions of section 14 of the 1996 Act also apply to the contents of the family home or of other matrimonial property. Orders made under section 14(l)(a) cannot be varied and are specifically excluded from the remit of section 22 by section 22 (1)(e).

Section 14(1)(b) allows the court to make a property adjustment order settling property owned by a spouse in possession or reversion for the benefit of the other spouse and/or dependent family member. There does not appear to have been very many applications made under the 1995 Act and the term "settlement" in this context has not been defined in any of the Family Law Acts. In the context of section 14(1)(b) it would seem to include property which is vested in trustees for the benefit of either a spouse or dependent family member, which settlement yields income for the beneficiaries of the trust.

Under section 14(1)(c) and (d), the court has power to vary, extinguish or reduce any ante-nuptial or post-nuptial settlements made on the spouses, whether by will or codicil or otherwise and the variation made by the court can benefit either of the spouses or a dependent family member. In the case of an extinguishment or reduction of an interest under such settlement, only the interests of the spouses or either of them may be interfered with. A broader power of variation would appear to be provided for in section 14(1)(c) where the court is not limited to varying only the interests of the spouses or either of them under the settlement. An ante-nuptial settlement is an agreement made for the benefit of a couple who subsequently marry, which regulates certain matters between them in anticipation of marriage or bestows a benefit upon them based on such anticipation. The definition of what can be termed a "post-nuptial settlement" causes more difficulty.

In the case of *Brooks v. Brooks* [1995] 3 All E.R. 257 the court considered the equivalent English provision, section 24(1)(c) of the Matrimonial Causes Act 1973 and attempted to define the term "settlement" within the meaning of the section. Referring to "ante-nuptial" and "post-nuptial" settlements, the court stated that:

> "these expressions are apt to embrace all settlements in respect of the particular marriage, whether made before or after marriage."

It was held in that case that the court had power to vary the scheme in that case "so far as it constitutes a settlement made by the husband", although it also clearly stated that "not every pension scheme constitutes a marriage settlement."

There has been some controversy as to whether or not a separation agreement entered into between the parties constitutes a "post-nuptial" settlement. In the case of *C.N. v. R.N.* [1995] 1 F.L.J. 14, McGuinness J., as she then was considered the term "post nuptial" settlement and held that the term as used in section 15(1)(c) of the 1989 Act included separation agreements "which come squarely within the established definition of post nuptial settlements". She stated that had the intention of the legislature not been to give in section 15(1)(c) a specific power to vary separation agreements that one would have expected "a specific provision to exclude separation agreements from the operation of the subsection". This case was determined in the context of an application for reliefs ancillary to the granting of a decree of judicial separation. Therefore the broader issue was whether or not a decree of judicial separation, and in consequence, the reliefs ancillary thereto could be granted where a separation agreement was in place. The court in the *C.N. v. R.N.* decision was of the view that the prior agreement did not preclude a later application for judicial separation.

The issue was considered by the Supreme Court in the case of *O'D. v. O'D.*, unreported, Supreme Court, December 18, 1997 on foot of a case stated by McGuinness J., as she then was. In *O'D. v. O'D.* Keane J. stated that:

> "A separation agreement is not a post nuptial settlement. It may . . . incorporate a settlement of property. In the English cases . . . referred to by Judge McGuinness in her decision in *N.(C.) v. N.(R.)* it was held that the court had power to vary a post nuptial settlement so contained in a deed of separation but that was in the context of divorce a vinculo matrimonii and decrees of nullity. Under section 15(1)(c) of the 1989 Act a property transfer order may take the form of an order varying a post-nuptial settlement. But such a property transfer order may only be made where a decree of judicial separation is granted and it is clear, for the reasons already set out, that no such decree may be granted where the parties have already entered into a separation agreement."

Clearly both cases can be distinguished on their facts. The distinguishing feature relates primarily to the nature of the primary relief being sought in judicial separation proceedings.

In circumstances where the relief sought is a release from the common law duty to cohabit, *i.e.* judicial separation, the foregoing cases represent different viewpoints as to whether an application for relief might be made judicially when the parties have already released themselves contractually from the common law duty. The Supreme Court's view would appear to be that the contractual release precludes a subsequent application for a judicial separation, however, similar constraints do not apply in the case of divorce. Therefore it appears that as a property transfer order can be made when a decree of divorce is granted, this may take the form of a variation of a post-nuptial settlement made in the context of an agreement to separation.

The power of the court under section 14(1)(c) and (d) to vary or review the terms of a separation agreement entered into by the parties is a most useful provision. It allows a possible escape route to a party who concluded a separation agreement under pressure and who is now seeking a review of its terms. The provisions of section 20(3) which directs the court in making an order pursuant to, *inter alia*, section 14 to have regard to the terms of any separation agreement entered into between the spouses, the provisions of which are still operative, must also be recalled.

Settlements which may be varied or otherwise altered under section 14(1)(c) and (d) include those made by will or codicil. This reflects the fact that entitlements under such settlements constitute a benefit in the hands of a beneficiary. These entitlements may be redistributed by the court for the benefit of either of the spouses, or for the other family members. There could be substantial implications in such orders as far as the intentions of the settlor are concerned, as he may specifically have wished to control benefits under the settlement in order that they would not accrue to other family members. To this extent the 1996 Act enables the intention of settlor to be defeated. During the Second Stage of the Dáil debate on the Bill, Deputy Helen Keogh T.D. remarked:

> "Does the Minister agree that a Court will be able to vary the terms of such a will, and if so, is he satisfied this will not represent an unconstitutional interference in the property rights of the testator?" (467 *Dáil Debates* Col. 1792)

Testamentary freedom is a constitutionally protected property right. Issues of the constitutional hierarchy of rights arise and it is undoubtedly the case that making proper provision for one's family is also a constitutional requirement and one which public policy undoubtedly supports. If it were otherwise, the entitlement of a spouse to a legal right share under the Succession Act 1965 would be suspect in the context of interference with property rights of individuals. However, there is a difference between such a provision and the powers contained in section 14(1)(c) and (d). The interference envisaged in the 1965 Act is between spouses, *i.e.* the interference with the testamentary freedom of one party *in favour* of their spouse. Whereas in section 14 the courts are empowered to interfere with the testamentary intention of a third party in favour of the spouse of an intended beneficiary.

The circumstances in which settlement variation orders may be made were discussed in *R.F. v. J.F.*, unreported, Circuit Court, August 23, 1995. Directions were made by the court to the husband *in personam* that the wife would be paid money from a trust fund, notwithstanding that the wife was not a beneficiary thereunder and the husband was not a trustee. He was described in the trust deed as a "Protector" of the trust, a role which the court determined to be "a decisive and powerful" one. Section 14(4) provides for the lodgment in either the Land Registry or the Registry of Deeds of a certified copy of a property adjustment order, thus ensuring that any prospective purchaser is on notice of the order made before the final transfer has been registered.

Section 14(5) is the same as section 9(5) of the 1995 Act, allowing a court to order that another person can execute all necessary deeds and instruments to give effect to a property adjustment order in circumstances where the spouse directed to do so by the order, fails, refuses or neglects to so do. Prior to the enactment of section 9(5) of the 1995 Act practical difficulties frequently arose in circumstances where the last refuge of a spouse against whom a property adjustment orders was made was to wilfully refuse to sign the necessary documents to give effect to the order. Section 14(5) is designed to circumvent such problems and while anybody can be designated to sign the documents in these circumstances, it is in practice the County Registrar or clerk of the court who is appointed to do so.

Under section 14(6), the costs incurred in complying with the provisions of a property adjustment order can be apportioned by the court to be paid by both spouses, or by either of them. If a property adjustment order is made in respect of a property which is mortgaged, usually the consent of the mortgagor must be obtained before the transfer will actually be completed. Usually the mortgage document will contain a covenant against assignment of the mortgage, but in practice most institutions will consent to the assignment of a mortgaged property once there is evidence that the transferee will be in a position to finance mortgage payments previously paid by both parties. Lending institutions are, however, frequently reluctant to permit maintenance payments to be taken into account in calculating the ability to repay. If possible, practitioners should ascertain the requirements of the mortgagor in advance of the hearing as it will be of assistance to the court to know in advance whether or not a property adjustment order can be implemented.

The provisions of section 22(l), which directs a court to take into account the rights of a person to whom either of the spouses is remarried. Clearly, a person who marries one of the original spouses will acquire rights in respect of what is now their family home.

Section 33 grants an exemption to the payment of stamp duty by a spouse who is awarded property by way of a property adjustment order, notwithstanding the fact that when the decree is granted the parties are no longer spouses. The exception is granted specifically to orders made under Part III of the Act and does not apply to orders made in respect of anyone other than the spouse concerned. A property adjustment order made in favour of a dependent family member therefore will not attract the exemption from stamp duty. Similarly, pursuant to the provisions of section 35 the Act, no order made under Part III of the Act shall attract a liability to capital gains tax, provided that the asset being disposed of by one spouse to another did not form part of the trading stock of a trade carried on by the disposing spouse. The date of acquisition for the purposes of a subsequent disposal is backdated to the date of acquisition by the transferor spouse. There is a similar exemption contained in section 34 of the Act in respect of capital acquisitions tax which would have been payable by virtue of a gift or inheritance taken pursuant to an order made under Part III of the Act.

It can be concluded from the provisions of section 20 that a wide range of factors must be taken into consideration by the court in deciding whether or not to make a property adjustment order, but this still appears to leave the court with a huge degree of flexibility and very wide discretion in deciding whether or not to make such orders. While such flexibility is commendable, it is difficult for practitioners to predict to a client what might happen to the marital assets by way of a property adjustment order. Therefore where possible, all options open to the court should be outlined to the client, in advance of the hearing.

Certainty and finality in the area of distribution of marital assets is at a minimum, particularly with the spectre of a section 22 application hovering. This contrasts with the view of the Supreme Court expressed in *F. v. F.* [1995] 2 I.R. 354, in which the desirability of finality in family law was endorsed. However, the absence of a finality ethos in family law legislation was acknowledged by McGuinness J. in *J.D. v. D.D.*, unreported, High Court, May 14, 1997. The paucity of reported case law in this area makes it impossible to gain an overview of how courts have arrived at decisions to make property adjustment orders since their introduction in 1989. It would be of enormous benefit to practitioners and to clients to have access to case law which would demonstrate judicial thinking in relation to the applicability of property adjustment orders to, for example, agricultural land and, mostly importantly, the family home.

Miscellaneous ancillary orders

15.—(1) On granting a decree of divorce or at any time thereafter, the court, on application to it in that behalf by either of the spouses concerned or by a person on behalf of a dependent member of the family, may, during the lifetime of the other spouse or, as the case may be, the spouse concerned, make one or more of the following orders:

(a) an order—

(i) providing for the conferral on one spouse either for life or for such other period (whether definite or contingent) as the court may specify of the right to occupy the family home to the exclusion of the other spouse, or

    (ii) directing the sale of the family home subject to such conditions (if any) as the court considers proper and providing for the disposal of the proceeds of the sale between the spouses and any other person having an interest therein,

(b) an order under section 36 of the Act of 1995,

(c) an order under section 5, 7 or 9 of the Family Home Protection Act, 1976,

(d) an order under section 2, 3, 4 or 5 of the Act of 1996,

(e) an order for the partition of property or under the Partition Act, 1868, and the Partition Act, 1876,

(f) an order under section 11 of the Act of 1964,

and, for the purposes of this section, in paragraphs (b), (c) and (d), a reference to a spouse in a statute referred to in paragraph (b), (c) or (d) shall be construed as including a reference to a person who is a party to a marriage that has been dissolved under this Act.

(2) The court, in exercising its jurisdiction under subsection (1)(a), shall have regard to the welfare of the spouses and any dependent member of the family and, in particular, shall take into consideration—

(a) that, where a decree of divorce is granted, it is not possible for the spouses concerned to reside together, and

(b) that proper and secure accommodation should, where practicable, be provided for a spouse who is wholly or mainly dependent on the other spouse and for any dependent member of the family.

(3) Subsection (1)(a) shall not apply in relation to a family home in which, following the grant of a decree of divorce, either of the spouses concerned, having remarried, ordinarily resides with his or her spouse.

General Note

This section empowers the court to make a variety of orders under existing Acts, including the Family Law Act 1995, the Family Home Protection Act 1976, and the Domestic Violence Act 1996. The court on granting a decree of divorce, or at any time during the lifetime of the other spouse may also, pursuant to section 15(1)(a) make specific orders relating to the occupation or sale of a family home. The court is also empowered to make orders pursuant to the Guardianship of Infants Act 1964 by way of ancillary relief. It is pursuant to this section that applicants seek orders for custody, access and other matters in the interests of and welfare of children.

Section 15 is largely similar to section 10 of the 1995 Act, which in turn mirrored section 16 of the Judicial Separation and Family Law Reform Act 1989. The purpose of the section insofar as it relates to the other pieces of legislation, set out in section 15(a) to (f) is to avoid the necessity of instituting separate proceedings under those Acts, which clearly has an impact on efficiency and costs. In effect, this section is a form of "one-stop-shop" for multiplicity of matrimonial reliefs.

Section 15(1) directs that these miscellaneous ancillary orders will be granted by the court at the time of the granting of decree of divorce or any time thereafter once again leaving open the possibility of several applications being made in respect of these matters. Once again the clean break principal is not endorsed. Applications under this section must be made by either of the spouses concerned or by a person on behalf of a dependent family member, and must be made during the lifetime of either spouse.

Section 15(1)(a)(i) allows the court to grant an exclusion order, allowing one spouse to remain in the family home to the exclusion of the other. Such orders regularly go hand in hand with a property adjustment order. An order under section 15(1)(a)(i) may be made notwithstanding the refusal of a property adjustment order. Typically a family home might be left in joint names with one spouse having an exclusive right to reside therein thus allowing the non-occupying spouse to retain an interest therein and if held as joint tenants, the right of survivorship. The duration of the order may be specified by the court to be a right to occupy the property for life, or for another specified term. For example, a spouse may be permitted to remain in the family home for a period of five years or until such time as the youngest child completes full-time education. Section 15(1)(a)(ii) allows the court to direct that the family home may be sold and the proceeds disposed of between the spouses and any one else having an interest in the property, subject to any conditions which the court may wish to attach. This general power of sale may be granted by the court in addition to or instead of a property adjustment order.

Exclusion orders can be made regardless of whether the family home is held in the sole name of one of the spouses or in their joint names. Clearly, an exclusion order made for life in respect of a property owned by the excluded spouse, can have severe implications for that spouse. For example, he may be unable to use the family home to raise a mortgage to purchase a new home, if the first family home is already mortgaged, nor can the property be sold to raise cash. It is yet another example of how divorced spouses continued to be tied to one another, notwithstanding the so-called end of the marriage. In addition, the provisions of section 15(3) must be carefully noted. These are considered below.

In practice, of course it is always open to the applicant to seek an order from the court that an exclusion order would automatically expire either on the remarriage of the first spouse, or upon cohabitation with a third party as husband and wife for a specified period of time. There are often evidential difficulties in proving the latter proviso both in relation to cohabitation and the fact that such cohabitation is in a manner akin to husband and wife. Examples of such difficulties include a co-habitee suspected to be a partner but claiming to be a tenant or co-habitee who maintains another residence also. If the right of occupation is conditional, the condition must be clear and unambiguous, if it is to be effective. It is open to either spouse to make an application for variation under section 22 of any exclusion order made, and there is no provision under section 15 to exclude or block the other spouse's entitlement to make such an application. Section 15(3) curtails the right to seek section 15(1)(a) relief, whether in relation to occupation or sale of premises where a spouse has remarried and ordinarily resides therein with their new spouse using the premises as the family home. This provision envisages a situation in which an application for relief is made at a time after the application for the decree of divorce. No similar protection exists for long-term co-habitees, including those who have not married consequent upon the decree of divorce being obtained. Clients should be advised that an application to vary an exclusion order under section 22 may not be made in respect of a family home in which a spouse resides, who, having previously obtained an exclusion order allowing them to reside in that family home, remarries and ordinarily resides there with their new spouse. In effect, the residing spouse's remarriage can automatically provide them with relief which may have been denied to them in the course of the initial proceedings, *i.e.* a secure right to reside for life without fear of an application for variation.

Applications may also be made to vary orders made under section 15(1)(a)(ii), although once the proceeds of the sale are disposed of, they are often lost forever. A sale under this subsection has the advantage of releasing the spouses from any further ties in respect of the family home and the court may direct the proportions into which the proceeds should be divided between the parties, usually after the deduction of encumbrances. A case which dealt with the equivalent power of sale under the 1995 Act was *A.O'L. v. B. O'L.* [1996] 2 F.L.J. 67. An order was made directing that both the family home and an apartment belonging to the husband be sold and that after the deduction of the mortgages on both properties the sum of £80,000 be paid to the wife to enable her provide alternative accommodation for herself and the infant child of the marriage. The balance of the proceeds of sale were to be paid to the husband to enable him acquire an alternative property for himself. Similarly, in *J.D. v. P.D.,* High Court, August, 1994, Lynch J. directed a sale of the family home and that the proceeds were to be divided 83 per cent to the wife and 17 per cent to the husband.

Practitioners should be aware that it is possible to use the power contained in section 15(1)(a)(ii) to give effect to more complex orders than appears to be envisaged by the section at first glance. The decision in *C.N v. R.N (No. 2)* [1996] 1 I.F.L.R. 1 is instructive in this regard. In a hearing before the Circuit Court, McGuinness J., as she then was, ordered that the family home be sold and that 70 per cent of the net proceeds of sale be used to purchase a house in the joint names of the parties, in which the wife would be granted an exclusive right to reside. The joint tenancy thereby created could not be severed unless by further order of the court. The balance of 30 per cent was to be used or invested to create an income for the wife in her later years.

This decision is of interest as it illustrates the scope of the reliefs which may be granted under section 15(1)(a)(ii) and it is particularly worthy of consideration as a right to reside was given in the premises to be acquired. The jurisdiction to grant the right to reside to the wife must have had its foundation in the power of the court to attach conditions to orders for sale under section 15(1)(a)(ii). Clearly the new premises, yet to be acquired, would not have come within the definition of a "family home" and therefore the jurisdiction to grant a right of residence/occupation could not have derived from section 15(1)(a)(i), which is expressly limited in its scope to rights of occupation of the family home.

Practitioners should also be aware that a myriad of conditions can be sought to be attached to the sale of the family home, ranging from a direction that the home should not be sold until the conclusion of children's school exams, to a specification as to which auctioneer should have carriage of sale. Most importantly, in exercising its jurisdiction under section 15(1)(a), the court shall have regard to a number of factors, including the welfare of spouses and dependent family members. The court must specifically take into account the fact that a decree of divorce renders it impossible for the spouses to live together, although in the context of a divorce the spouses will usually not have been living together for four out of the previous five years, save in exceptional circumstances. The court must also consider the practicability of ensuring that proper and secure accommodation should be provided for a spouse who is wholly/mainly dependent on the other spouse and for any dependent member of the family. The court is expressly directed by section 15(2) to have regard to these matters. These criteria would appear to establish a bias in favour the financially dependent spouses, usually the wife. Arguably this merely serves to consolidate social stereotypes. Finally, the provisions of section 20 apply to this section and further proscribe the thinking of the court in arriving at a decision in this regard.

In the course of the Second Stage debate on the Bill, Deputy Keogh (467 *Dáil Debates* Col.1792) adverted to the fact that the provisions of section 15(1)(a)(i) and (ii) where expressed to be in the alternative:

> "This subsection seems to be open to the interpretation, because of the use of the word 'or', that a court will be able to make one or other of these orders but not both. In other words, it will not be able to order the sale of the family home and confer the right on one spouse to occupy it until such time as it has been sold."

This concern was re-iterated by Deputy O'Donnell before the Select Committee on Legislation and Security (July 17, 1996, L6 No. 12) but was rejected by the Minister who replied:

> "It is difficult to conceive of a situation where the court would give a life or other interest in the home to one spouse and at the same time make an order directing the sale of that home. Also, it is inconceivable that the court at the time it directs the sale of the home would give a life or other interest to a spouse."

It is submitted, however, that that which was inconceivable to the Minister may regularly occur. Where there are children of the marriage, the court may wish to protect their occupation of the family home with the custodial parent during their dependency and provide for the sale of the premises, thereafter allowing for the realisation by both spouses of a valuable asset towards which they have both contributed. Arguably, even in these circumstances, the non-custodial parent may feel aggrieved by having been without the benefit of his/her investment for a considerable period of time. However, the primary objective of the court will be to ensure secure and suitable accommodation for the children and the economics of the majority of cases dictate that this means that they should remain in the family home, as the proceeds from an immediate sale would not re-house the children.

In these circumstances, the most appropriate order would appear to be an order under section 15(1)(a)(i) granting the custodial parent an exclusive right of occupation during the period of dependency of the children and an order under section 15(1)(a)(ii) directing a sale at such date in the future. The expression of sections 15(1)(a)(i) and (ii) as being alternatives would appear to preclude such orders being made together. In practice, the court will often make the order pursuant to section 15(1)(a)(i) as stated above, *i.e.* of limited duration, thereby leaving the question of sale open to be determined in the future when the period of exclusive occupation ends. The realism of such an approach cannot be doubted. Where children are young, making an order for sale in the future verges towards converting the court into the role of prophet.

However, the position of a party who has to immediately vacate the premises then becomes extremely unsatisfactory as he/she cannot even be assured of realising their asset in the future. This often occurs in circumstances where they will have to discharge or assist in discharging the mortgage on the premises in the intervening time. It is submitted that finality should be the desired result to the greatest extent possible and that the parties should be put in a position to plan for their future, whether this involves a sale and division of the family home, an attempt at purchasing the interest of the other party therein, whether at full value or not, or a property transfer order.

It is submitted that the concern expressed relating to the alternatives contained in section 15(1)(a) is ill-founded and remediable. The entitlement to reside in the family home pending sale, at whatever date such sale is due to take place may if necessary, be included in the conditions which section 15(1)(a)(ii) envisages. The judgment of McGuinness J. in *C.N. v. R.N. (No. 2)* [1996] 1 I.F.L.R 1., supports this view.

However, orders made under section 15(1)(c) to (f) will influence the court in arriving at decisions in respect of other ancillary reliefs relating to the occupation of the family home. For example, an order directing that custody of small children be given to a wife will have an impact on deciding to whom the family home should be transferred or who should reside therein. The provisions of section 15(1)(b) to (f) enable the court to make a number of ancillary orders without needing to have before it separate applications under the individual pieces of legislation. Either a spouse or a third party on behalf of a dependent member of the family can make these applications and it should be noted that the provisions of section 20 of the 1996 Act do not apply here.

Section 15(1)(b) permits the court to make orders pursuant to section 36 of the Family Law Act 1995 which repeals and replaces section 12 of the Married Women's Status Act 1957 (No. 5) (the 1957 Act) determining their respective interests in the property. Section 12 of the 1957 Act provided the court with a means to determine ownership rights of each spouse in family property "as it thinks proper", in so far as either the High Court or the Circuit Court could make an order in relation to a property dispute between spouses. The court could not make property adjustment orders and had no discretionary power pursuant to this section. Equitable principles relating to contributions, together with the presumption of advancement applied. Nonetheless, before the coming into operation of the 1989 Act, there was a considerable number of cases which invoked the provisions of section 12 of the 1957 Act, as for a long number of years this was the only mechanism available to assist in the resolution of spousal proprietary disputes.

Section 36(4) of the Family Law Act 1995 has a broader ambit than section 12 of the 1957 Act, particularly as a spouse may now obtain an order, against the other spouse, following either property or the proceeds of sale of property from an identifiable source in which the applicant spouse claims a beneficial interest. Section 36(7) of the 1995 Act also extends the powers to an applicant whose marriage has been annulled or dissolved in another jurisdiction, provided always that the application for relief is made within three years of that annulment or divorce. Similarly, section 44 of the 1996 Act extends the application of section 36 of the 1995 Act to a situation where a property dispute arises between engaged couples or couples who have formerly been engaged.

The Family Law Act 1981 had similarly extended the application of section 12 of the 1957 Act to engaged couples and the repeal of section 12 left the mode of dispute resolution between engaged couples in a form of limbo, prior to the introduction of section 44 of the 1996 Act. Clearly, section 15(1)(b) of the 1996 Act allows an applicant for divorce to seek ancillary relief by way of section 36 of the 1995 Act. Section 36(1) allows either spouse to apply to the court summarily for a determination of any disputes arising between them in relation to title to or possession of property. Section 36(2) allows the court to make any orders in that regard, that it considers proper. Section 36(3) permits either a spouse or the child of a deceased spouse to make an application to the court where it is claimed that the other spouse had in their possession or under their control:

(a) Monies to which the applicant was beneficially entitled; or
(b) Property to which, or to any interest in which, the applicant was beneficially entitled and that spouse no longer has possession or control of the money or property in question, or the applicant does not know whether or not that spouse so controls or possesses the property.

In those circumstances, the applicant may make an application for an order pursuant to section 36(2) of the 1995 Act and section 36(4) which, if granted, could direct the respondent spouse to pay to the applicant either:

(a) The monies to which the application relates or the applicant's share of same; or
(b) A sum of money in respect of the value of the property in question or the applicant's interest therein.

Section 36(4)(b) directs that for the order to be obtained, the respondent spouse must not have made the payment or disposition in question to the applicant. In circumstances where it is necessary to obtain an order for sale or an order for partition, in order to effect relief under section 36, the court can make either of these orders without the necessity of instituting separate proceedings.

The scope of section 15(1)(b) remains limited. It relates to actual beneficial interests in properties and does not involve the use of discretion or asset relocation. As the reliefs available in respect of a property dispute when seeking a decree of divorce are considerably wider, by seeking an order under section 14 or by seeking a lump sum payment order to take account of the interest held by one spouse in a particular property, the scope and rationale behind applications pursuant to section 15(1)(b) of the 1996 Act is likely to be very specific. However, in circumstances where finance may not permit the making of a lump sum payment order or where a court may wish to determine the exact ownership of each spouse in marital property, the subsection will be useful. The property owning spouse will be seeking to have his ownership confirmed.

Section 15(c) allows orders to be made under sections 5, 7 or 9 of the Family Home Protection Act 1976, but section 4, which allows an order to be made dispensing with the consent of a spouse to any conveyance of the family home, is excluded because the applicant under the divorce legislation is no longer a spouse and spousal consent under the 1976 Act is therefore no longer applicable. In circumstances where upon the granting of a decree of divorce one spouse is given the right to occupy the former family home, but the property remains in the sole legal and beneficial ownership of the non-occupying spouse. This could imply that the latter spouse could use the family home as security for borrowings or convey an interest in the family home without giving notice to or obtaining the consent of the occupying spouse.

Section 5 of the 1976 Act contains powers of a general nature which seek to protect the right of the spouse to reside in the family home in circumstances where one of the spouses is engaging in conduct that may lead to loss of any interest in the family home, or may render it unsuitable for habitation as a family home, provided always that the spouse has acted with the intention of depriving either the applicant spouse or a dependent child of their residence in the family home. An example of an action by a defaulting spouse under this section would be a failure to discharge mortgage repayments, advertising the family home for sale or cutting off the electricity or water supply to the house. Section 5(2) of the Act allows the court to compensate a spouse so deprived of their right of residence. This compensation may be paid by way of restitution of an uninhabitable home to one which is habitable, or to make an order directing that debts accumulated as a result of non-payment of mortgages be discharged. An extensive range of orders may be made under section 5, including an interim transfer of the family home or a restraint upon the registration of judgment mortgages.

The case of *M.C. v. A.C.*, unreported, High Court, July 1992, illustrates the section in operation. This involved a situation where the husband did not pay the mortgage and used the family home as security for additional bank loans. Lavan J. concluded that the husband's conduct was a "conscious and deliberate act intended to deprive his wife and children of their home."

Section 7 of the 1976 Act restricts the right of the spouse to remove household chattels from the family home with the consent of either the other spouse or the court pending the final hearing of the case. Protection is also available under section 8 of the Domestic Violence Act 1996, which directs that any restrictions granted pursuant to section 6 remain in force whilst any barring or safety order is operative.

Section 9 of the 1976 Act prevents a spouse from disposing of household chattels and provides that if matrimonial proceedings have been instituted by either spouse, then neither of them can "sell, lease, pledge, or otherwise dispose or remove any of the household chattels" in the family home, until the case has been heard. Section 9(1) includes a useful provision in that where it appears to the court that there are reasonable grounds for believing that the other spouse "intends to sell etc. a proportion of the household chattels in a family home as would be likely to make it difficult for the applicant/spouse or dependent child of the family to reside in the family home without undue hardship", then the court may by order prohibit the other spouse from making any such intended disposition or removal. While it is specified that a spouse who contravenes the provisions of section 9 is guilty of an offence and liable on summary conviction for a fine not exceeding £100 or imprisonment for up to six months, in practice this sanction is rarely imposed. Relief under sections 5, 7 and 9 of the 1976 Act is usually required in the circumstances of urgency prior to the hearing of the action in order to preserve family assets. Interlocutory applications are commonplace and jurisdiction in such matters is derived from section 11 of the 1996 Act.

Section 15(1)(d) allows for the making of orders pursuant to the provisions of the Domestic Violence Act 1996. Once again, these orders can be sought on behalf of dependent members of the family. Section 3(2) of the Domestic Violence Act 1996 concerns the making of a barring order where the court "is of the opinion that there are reasonable grounds for believing that the safety or welfare" of the applicant or any dependent child requires such order be made. Barring orders can be made in these circumstances against respondents who are or are not residing at the place where the applicant and dependent children reside. Section 3 also covers prohibitions against spouses using or threatening to use violence against the applicant or dependent children, molesting or putting in fear, or attending or watching or besetting a place where the applicant or dependent children reside.

These latter prohibitions are not confined to the family home but to any place in which the applicant may reside. A barring order can be made as an ancillary order under section 15(1)(d) of the 1996 Act and can be granted as a permanent order or as an order of limited duration. It is unlikely that in the context of divorce proceedings a barring order would be required on anything less than a permanent basis.

Section 2 of the Act allows for the making of a safety order in similar circumstances to a barring order. Clearly, in the context of proceedings for divorce a safety order will operate to prohibit specified forms of misconduct, detailed in section 2. A safety order may be used perhaps in circumstances in which, following the granting of a decree of divorce, the respondent spouse returned to the family home on a regular basis to collect the children for access and engaged in threatening behaviour. This would cover situations whereby a barring order was not required, but some form of protection was necessary.

Section 4(1) of the Act provides for the making of an interim barring order in circumstances where the court believes that there are reasonable grounds for believing that there is:

(a) An immediate risk of significant harm to the Applicant and any dependent child if the order is not made immediately,

(b) Where the granting of a protection order would not be sufficient to protect the applicant or any dependent child.

Thus it can be seen that an interim barring order can be sought by way of preliminary relief under section 11(a) or here under section 15(1)(d). It is difficult to see how an interim barring order could be made as an ancillary order as it would seem to be more appropriate that it would be made by way of preliminary order and then a final barring order made on the granting of the decree. Section 5(1) of the Domestic Violence Act 1996 provides for the making of a protection order, and again similar questions arise as to the viability of making a protection order by way of an ancillary order.

In the case of *A.K.v. J.K.* [1996] 1 F.L.J. 22, McGuinness J. granted the applicant an interim barring order, pending the determination of judicial separation proceedings, by way of preliminary relief. In that case, the applicant made the application three years after she had left the family home with the children. The delay in this regard was held not to debar her from relief due to delay and clearly, in circumstances where divorce was being sought, the parties will already have been living apart for four out of the previous five years. It is note-worthy that for the purposes of this section, as indeed for the purposes of seeking orders under section 15(1)(b) and 15(1)(c), that a reference to a spouse includes references to persons who have already been divorced under the 1996 Act. The provisions of section 51 of the 1996 Act which direct that protection under the Domestic Violence Act 1996 may be granted to persons who have obtained foreign divorces validly recognised in the State.

Section 15(1)(e) allows for the making of orders for the partition of property or for the making of orders under the Partition Acts 1868 (31 & 32 Vict., c.40) and 1876 (39 & 40 Vict., c.17). This covers circumstances where orders for the sale of property in lieu of parti-tion can be directed by the court in respect of property held by the spouses jointly or in common. The section also allows the court to give directions in circumstances where the actual physical or legal partition of a property could be the appropriate remedy.

Section 15(1)(f) allows the court to make orders relating to custody and access of chil-dren and incorporates the terms of section 11 of the Guardianship of Infants Act 1964. The applicable principle is the "welfare principle", incorporating the child's social, physical, intellectual, moral and religious welfare. Although the courts have long been making joint custody orders, the amendments to section 11 introduced by the Children Act 1997 ex-pressly provide for such orders. Rarely will children be directed to spend equal time with both parents. Rather one parent becomes the primary carer with generous access rights be-ing made available to the other. Divorced parents will remain as guardians of their children and will have an equal say in relation to important lifestyle decisions. The range of amend-ments which may be ordered under section 15(1)(f) is enormous and can be tailor made to suit the subjective needs of the family concerned. The court will often seek the assistance of an appropriate professional in determining the welfare of children.

Financial compensation orders

16.—(1) Subject to the provisions of this section, on granting a decree of divorce or at any time thereafter, the court, on application to it in that behalf by either of the spouses concerned or by a person on behalf of a dependent mem-ber of the family, may, during the lifetime of the other spouse or, as the case may be, the spouse concerned, if it considers—

(a) that the financial security of the spouse making the application ("the applicant") or the dependent member of the family ("the member") can be provided for either wholly or in part by so doing, or

(b) that the forfeiture, by reason of the decree of divorce, by the appli-cant or the member, as the case may be, of the opportunity or pos-sibility of acquiring a benefit (for example, a benefit under a pension scheme) can be compensated for wholly or in part by so doing, make a financial compensation order, that is to say, an order requiring the other spouse to do one or more of the following:

(i) to effect such a policy of life insurance for the benefit of the applicant or the member as may be specified in the order,

        (ii) to assign the whole or a specified part of the interest of the other spouse in a policy of life insurance effected by that other spouse or both of the spouses to the applicant or to such person as may be specified in the order for the benefit of the member,

      (iii) to make or to continue to make to the person by whom a policy of life insurance is or was issued the payments which that other spouse or both of the spouses is or are required to make under the terms of the policy.

(2) (a) The court may make a financial compensation order in addition to or in substitution in whole or in part for orders under section 13, 14, 15 or 17 and in deciding whether or not to make such an order it shall have regard to whether proper provision having regard to the circumstances exists or can be made for the spouse concerned or the dependent member of the family concerned by orders under those sections.

   (b) An order under this section shall cease to have effect on the remarriage or death of the applicant in so far as it relates to the applicant.

   (c) The court shall not make an order under this section in favour of a spouse who has remarried.

   (d) An order under section 22 in relation to an order under paragraph (i) or (ii) of subsection (1) may make such provision (if any) as the court considers appropriate in relation to the disposal of—

       (i) an amount representing any accumulated value of the insurance policy effected pursuant to the order under the said paragraph (i), or

      (ii) the interest or the part of the interest to which the order under the said paragraph (ii) relates.

GENERAL NOTE

The supplementary role of section 16 orders was emphasised by the Minister;

> "these Orders are designed to supplement or substitute for, where necessary, other Orders in support of a dependent spouse and children". (469 *Dáil Debates* Col. 1763).

The role of the financial compensation order was first set out in section 11 of the Family Law Act 1995, having made no appearance in the Judicial Separation and Family Law Reform Act 1989. Either spouse can apply for a financial compensation order for their benefit, or the benefit of a dependent member of the family. An application may also be made by a third party on behalf of a dependent member of the family, provided it is made during the lifetime of either spouse. Section 16(2)(a) allows the court to make financial compensation orders, either in addition to or in substitution for orders made for other ancillary reliefs. The court is specifically directed to have regard first of all to whether or not proper provision can be made for the applicant spouse and dependent members of the family, by way of other reliefs, such as maintenance orders, property adjustment orders or pension adjustment orders.

Section 16(1)(a) provides that the financial security of the applicant or the dependent family member may be provided for either wholly or in part by an application for a financial compensation order. Section 16(1)(b) provides that any loss which may have accrued to an applicant or a dependent member of the family as a result of their forfeiture, by reason of the divorce or the opportunity or of the possibility of acquiring a spousal benefit from a fund; the example of a pension fund is given in the Act itself. There is no specific reference in section 16(1)(b) to the loss of Succession Act rights, which automatically follow upon the granting of divorce. The wording of section 16(1)(b) would appear wide enough to allow a court to have regard to the loss of succession rights.

A financial compensation order will require a spouse to do one or more of the following:

(a) To effect a specific life insurance policy for the benefit of the applicant or dependent family member;

(b) To transfer either in whole or in part, the interest of the other spouse in a policy of life insurance effected by that spouse or by both spouses to the applicant spouse or to a specified person for the benefit of a dependent family member;

(c) To pay or continue to pay the premiums required to be made under the terms of a life policy.

The term life insurance is not defined in the 1996 Act, nor is any guidance given as to what kind of policies might be affected by section 16. Presumably, these would include life endowment insurance, joint life policies, term policies or single premium policies, which tend to be used as a form of investment. The court has a very wide discretion to decide the manner in which a life policy might be set up for the benefit of the applicant or dependent children. For example, it might be ordered that the applicant be permitted to choose the type and value of the policy and that the respondent be directed to pay the premiums thereunder. In the alternative, the respondent might be directed to take out a life insurance policy by way of a single premium, and to hold the consequent policy in trust for the applicant and dependent family members.

Financial compensation orders can be made by the court, pursuant to section 16(2)(c), at any time during the lifetime of a respondent spouse, save that a court shall not make a financial compensation order in favour of an applicant who has remarried. Section 16(2)(b) directs that orders made under section 16 cease to have effect on the remarriage or death of the applicant, so far as it relates to the applicant. Obligations relating to dependent family members continue. The operation of the cessation under section 16(2)(b) would appear to be automatic and there does not appear to be a need to make an application to court. An application to the court can be made by either spouse pursuant to the provisions of section 22 of the Act, to have the order varied, discharged or suspended. A court could, under section 16(2)(d)(i) or (ii), give directions in relation to the disposal of the proceeds representing the accumulated value of the insurance policy, or to the interest or part of the interest in respect of which an assignment order was made.

There are circumstances in which a court may determine that notwithstanding the desirability of making a financial compensation order, such an order will not be made. This may arise in circumstances where the cost of maintaining the premiums payable on such life insurance policies is prohibitive, *i.e.* the age of the respondent would be a relevant factor or due to the poor health of one of the spouses, which might render it difficult to obtain such life cover. In circumstances where spouses are perhaps in their forties or fifties, it may be difficult to obtain life insurance policies which are within the financial means of the parties. In practice, it is usual that the applicant spouse would be seeking some level of benefit pursuant to a life assurance policy to achieve either or both of the following considerations: to secure maintenance payments after the death of the payor and/or to compensate for a loss of her legal right share under the Succession Act 1965.

A financial compensation order could be made in contemplation of circumstances where, for example, the proceeds of the policy could be used to take over the maintenance payments in the event of the death of one of the spouses. All in all, it appears likely to be the case that financial compensation orders will be made to protect the future financial security of dependent spouses. In those circumstances it is open to the court, by way of section 16, to make provision for the dependent spouse by way of a lump sum, to be paid under a policy on the death of the former spouse, thereby providing a capital security, which would have been otherwise unavailable while at the same time not interfering with present assets.

It would also appear that a financial compensation order would be useful where an order might be made pursuant to section 18(10) of the 1996 Act, which would deny one of the parties the right to make a claim against the estate of the other. An order under this section would also be useful where one of the spouses wishes their pension to remain unaffected by a pension adjustment order. Financial compensation orders are, accordingly, more likely to be made in the course of divorce proceedings to take account of the fact that a decree of divorce automatically terminates a spouse's right under the Succession Act 1965. The power of a court to provide for a dependent member of the family by way of financial compensation order would be very important if such dependent member suffer from any physical or mental disability which would render them unlikely ever to be financially independent.

In determining whether to make a financial compensation order, the court in addition to deciding whether the financial security of the applicant spouse or dependent family member requires such an order to be made, will have regard to the provisions set out in section 20 of the Act.

Section 34 of the Act provides that if a gift or inheritance is taken in consequence of an order, such as a financial compensation order by a divorced spouse, then that gift or inheritance will be exempt for the purposes of capital acquisitions tax. In other words, the capital acquisitions tax relief applicable to inter-spousal gifts pertains notwithstanding the fact that the person is no longer "a spouse".

Practical difficulties that arise for practitioners in advising clients whether or not to seek a financial compensation order include the difficulties of quantifying loss of future benefits in respect of which an applicant may require to be compensated. In addition, practitioners will have to be familiar with the types of policies and benefits available, as not every case will finance the advice of an accountant. It is vital that the level of cover is sufficient to provide a return that will enable current maintenance levels, inflated into the future, to be achieved. This may be a complex calculation which must provide for spousal and children's maintenance during dependency and that of the maintenance creditor thereafter. If acting for an applicant seeking a financial compensation order, the possible cost of obtaining a life insurance policy under section 16 should be ascertained in advance of the court hearing, as should the practical implications of obtaining these policies. Details of existing policies which might be allocated to this purpose should also be available from the affidavits of means supplied.

Pension adjustment orders

17.—(1) In this section, save where the context otherwise requires—

"the Act of 1990" means the Pensions Act, 1990;

"active member" in relation to a scheme, means a member of the scheme who is in reckonable service;

"actuarial value" means the equivalent cash value of a benefit (including, where appropriate, provision for any revaluation of such benefit) under a scheme calculated by reference to appropriate financial assumptions and making due allowance for the probability of survival to normal pensionable age and thereafter in accordance with normal life expectancy on the assumption that the member concerned of the scheme, at the effective date of calculation, is in a normal state of health having regard to his or her age;

"approved arrangement", in relation to the trustees of a scheme, means an arrangement whereby the trustees, on behalf of the person for whom the arrangement is made, effect policies or contracts of insurance that are approved of by the Revenue Commissioners with, and make the appropriate payments under the policies or contracts to, one or more undertakings;

"contingent benefit" means a benefit payable under a scheme, other than a payment under subsection (7) to or for one or more of the following, that is to say, the widow or the widower and any dependants of the member spouse concerned and the personal representative of the member spouse, if the member spouse dies while in relevant employment and before attaining any normal pensionable age provided for under the rules of the scheme;

"defined contribution scheme" means a scheme which, under its rules, provides retirement benefit, the rate or amount of which is in total directly determined by the amount of the contributions paid by or in respect of the member of the scheme concerned and includes a scheme the contributions under which are used, directly or indirectly, to provide—

    (a) contingent benefit, and

    (b) retirement benefit the rate or amount of which is in total directly determined by the part of the contributions aforesaid that is used for the provision of the retirement benefit;

"designated benefit", in relation to a pension adjustment order, means an amount determined by the trustees of the scheme concerned, in accordance with relevant guidelines, and by reference to the period and the percentage of the retirement benefit specified in the order concerned under subsection (2);

"member spouse", in relation to a scheme, means a spouse who is a member of the scheme;

"normal pensionable age" means the earliest age at which a member of a scheme is entitled to receive benefits under the rules of the scheme on retirement from relevant employment, disregarding any such rules providing for early retirement on grounds of ill health or otherwise;

"occupational pension scheme" has the meaning assigned to it by section 2(1) of the Act of 1990;

"reckonable service" means service in relevant employment during membership of any scheme;

"relevant guidelines" means any relevant guidelines for the time being in force under paragraph (c) or (cc) of section 10(1) of the Act of 1990;

"relevant employment", in relation to a scheme, means any employment (or any period treated as employment) or any period of self-employment to which a scheme applies;

"retirement benefit", in relation to a scheme, means all benefits (other than contingent benefits) payable under the scheme;

"rules", in relation to a scheme, means the provisions of the scheme, by whatever name called;

"scheme" means a pension scheme;

"transfer amount" shall be construed in accordance with subsection (4);

"undertaking" has the meaning assigned to it by the Insurance Act, 1989.

(2) Subject to the provisions of this section, where a decree of divorce ("the decree") has been granted, the court, if it so thinks fit, may, in relation to retirement benefit under a scheme of which one of the spouses concerned is a member, on application to it in that behalf at the time of the making of the order for the decree or at any time thereafter during the lifetime of the member spouse by either of the spouses or by a person on behalf of a dependent member of the family, make an order providing for the payment, in accordance with the provisions of this section, to either of the following, as the court may determine, that is to say—

    (a) the other spouse and, in the case of the death of that spouse, his or her personal representative, and

    (b) such person as may be specified in the order for the benefit of a person who is, and for so long only as he or she remains, a dependent member of the family,of a benefit consisting, either, as the court may determine, of the whole, or such part as the court considers appropriate, of that part of the retirement benefit that is payable (or which, but for the making of the order for the decree, would have been payable) under the scheme and has accrued at the time of the making of the order for the decree and, for the purpose of determining the benefit, the order shall specify—

    (i) the period of reckonable service of the member spouse prior to the granting of the decree to be taken into account, and

    (ii) the percentage of the retirement benefit accrued during that period to be paid to the person referred to in paragraph (a) or (b), as the case may be.

(3) Subject to the provisions of this section, where a decree of divorce ("the decree") has been granted, the court, if it so thinks fit, may, in relation to a contingent benefit under a scheme of which one of the spouses concerned is a member, on application to it in that behalf not more than one year after the making of the order for the decree by either of the spouses or by a person on behalf of a dependent member of the family concerned, make an order providing for the payment, upon the death of the member spouse, to either of the following, or to both of them in such proportions as the court may determine, that is to say—

    (a) the other spouse, and

    (b) such person as may be specified in the order for the benefit of a dependent member of the family,

of, either, as the court may determine, the whole, or such part (expressed as a percentage) as the court considers appropriate, of that part of any contingent benefit that is payable (or which, but for the making of the order for the decree, would have been payable) under the scheme.

(4) Where the court makes an order under subsection (2) in favour of a spouse and payment of the designated benefit concerned has not commenced, the spouse in whose favour the order is made shall be entitled to the application in accordance with subsection (5) of an amount of money from the scheme concerned (in this section referred to as a "transfer amount") equal to the value of the designated benefit, such amount being determined by the trustees of the scheme in accordance with relevant guidelines.

(5) Subject to subsection (17), where the court makes an order under subsection (2) in favour of a spouse and payment of the designated benefit concerned has not commenced, the trustees of the scheme concerned shall, for the purpose of giving effect to the order—

    (a) on application to them in that behalf at the time of the making of the order or at any time thereafter by the spouse in whose favour the order was made ("the spouse"), and

    (b) on the furnishing to them by the spouse of such information as they may reasonably require,

apply in accordance with relevant guidelines the transfer amount calculated in accordance with those guidelines either–

    (i) if the trustees and the spouse so agree, in providing a benefit for or in respect of the spouse under the scheme aforesaid that is of the same actuarial value as the transfer amount concerned, or

  (ii) in making a payment either to—

    (I) such other occupational pension scheme, being a scheme the trustees of which agree to accept the payment, or

    (II) in the discharge of any payment falling to be made by the trustees under any such other approved arrangement,

as may be determined by the spouse.

(6) Subject to subsection (17), where the court makes an order under subsection (2) in relation to a defined contribution scheme and an application has not been brought under subsection (5), the trustees of the scheme may, for the purpose of giving effect to the order, if they so think fit, apply in accordance with relevant guidelines the transfer amount calculated in accordance with those guidelines, in making a payment to—

  (a) such other occupational pension scheme, being a scheme the trustees of which agree to accept the payment, or

  (b) in the discharge of any payment falling to be made by the trustees under such other approved arrangement,

as may be determined by the trustees.

(7) Subject to subsection (17), where—

  (a) the court makes an order under subsection (2), and

  (b) the member spouse concerned dies before payment of the designated benefit concerned has commenced,

the trustees shall, for the purpose of giving effect to the order, within 3 months of the death of the member spouse, provide for the payment to the person in whose favour the order was made of an amount that is equal to the transfer amount calculated in accordance with relevant guidelines.

(8) Subject to subsection (17), where—

  (a) the court makes an order under subsection (2), and

  (b) the member spouse concerned ceases to be a member of the scheme otherwise than on death,

the trustees may, for the purpose of giving effect to the order, if they so think fit, apply, in accordance with relevant guidelines, the transfer amount calculated in accordance with those guidelines either, as the trustees may determine—

  (i) if the trustees and the person in whose favour the order is made ("the person") so agree, in providing a benefit for or in respect of the person under the scheme aforesaid that is of the same actuarial value as the transfer amount concerned, or

  (ii) in making a payment, either to—

    (I) such other occupational pension scheme, being a scheme the trustees of which agree to accept the payment, or

    (II) in the discharge of any payment falling to be made under such other approved arrangement,

as may be determined by the trustees.

(9) Subject to subsection (17), where—

  (a) the court makes an order under subsection (2) in favour of a spouse ("the spouse"),

    (b) the spouse dies before the payment of the designated benefit has commenced, the trustees shall, within 3 months of the death of the spouse, provide for the payment to the personal representative of the spouse of an amount equal to the transfer amount calculated in accordance with relevant guidelines.

(10) Subject to subsection (17), where—

    (a) the court makes an order under subsection (2) in favour of a spouse ("the spouse"), and

    (b) the spouse dies after payment of the designated benefit has commenced,

the trustees shall, within 3 months of the death of the spouse, provide for the payment to the personal representative of the spouse of an amount equal to the actuarial value, calculated in accordance with relevant guidelines, of the part of the designated benefit which, but for the death of the spouse, would have been payable to the spouse during the lifetime of the member spouse.

(11) Where—

    (a) the court makes an order under subsection (2) for the benefit of a dependent member of the family ("the person"), and

    (b) the person dies before payment of the designated benefit has commenced,

the order shall cease to have effect in so far as it relates to that person.

(12) Where—

    (a) the court makes an order under subsection (2) or (3) in relation to an occupational pension scheme, and

    (b) the trustees of the scheme concerned have not applied the transfer amount concerned in accordance with subsection (5), (6), (7), (8) or (9), and

    (c) after the making of the order, the member spouse ceases to be an active member of the scheme,

the trustees shall, within 12 months of the cessation, notify the registrar or clerk of the court concerned and the other spouse of the cessation.

(13) Where the trustees of a scheme apply a transfer amount under subsection (6) or (8), they shall notify the spouse (not being the spouse who is the member spouse) or other person concerned and the registrar or clerk of the court concerned of the application and shall give to that spouse or other person concerned particulars of the scheme or undertaking concerned and of the transfer amount.

(14) Where the court makes an order under subsection (2) or (3) for the payment of a designated benefit or a contingent benefit, as the case may be, the benefit shall be payable or the transfer amount concerned applied out of the resources of the scheme concerned and, unless otherwise provided for in the order or relevant guidelines, shall be payable in accordance with the rules of the scheme or, as the case may be, applied in accordance with relevant guidelines.

(15) Where the court makes an order under subsection (2), the amount of the retirement benefit payable, in accordance with the rules of the scheme concerned to, or to or in respect of, the member spouse shall be reduced by the amount of the designated benefit payable pursuant to the order.

(16) (a) Where the court makes an order under subsection (3), the amount of the contingent benefit payable, in accordance with the rules of the scheme concerned in respect of the member spouse shall be reduced by an amount equal to the contingent benefit payable pursuant to the order.

(b) Where the court makes an order under subsection (2) and the member spouse concerned dies before payment of the designated benefit concerned has commenced, the amount of the contingent benefit payable in respect of the member spouse in accordance with the rules of the scheme concerned shall be reduced by the amount of the payment made under subsection (7).

(17) Where, pursuant to an order under subsection (2), the trustees of a scheme make a payment or apply a transfer amount under subsection (5), (6), (7), (8), (9) or (10), they shall be discharged from any obligation to make any further payment or apply any transfer amount under any other of those subsections in respect of the benefit payable pursuant to the order.

(18) A person who makes an application under subsection (2) or (3) or an application for an order under section 22(2) in relation to an order under subsection (2) shall give notice thereof to the trustees of the scheme concerned and, in deciding whether to make the order concerned and in determining the provisions of the order, the court shall have regard to any representations made by any person to whom notice of the application has been given under this section or section 40.

(19) An order under subsection (3) shall cease to have effect on the death or remarriage of the person in whose favour it was made in so far as it relates to that person.

(20) The court may, in a pension adjustment order or by order made under this subsection after the making of a pension adjustment order, give to the trustees of the scheme concerned such directions as it considers appropriate for the purposes of the pension adjustment order including directions compliance with which occasions non-compliance with the rules of the scheme concerned or the Act of 1990; and a trustee of a scheme shall not be liable in any court or other tribunal for any loss or damage caused by his or her non-compliance with the rules of the scheme or with the Act of 1990 if the non-compliance was occasioned by his or her compliance with a direction of the court under this subsection.

(21) The registrar or clerk of the court concerned shall cause a copy of a pension adjustment order to be served on the trustees of the scheme concerned.

(22) (a) Any costs incurred by the trustees of a scheme under subsection (18) or in complying with a pension adjustment order or a direction under subsection (20) or (25) shall be borne, as the court may determine, by the member spouse or by the other person concerned or by both of them in such proportion as the court may determine and, in the absence of such determination, those costs shall be borne by them equally.

(b) Where a person fails to pay an amount in accordance with paragraph (a) to the trustees of the scheme concerned, the court may, on application to it in that behalf by the trustees, order that the amount be deducted from the amount of any benefit payable to the person under the scheme or pursuant to an order under subsection (2) or (3) and be paid to the trustees.

(23) (a) The court shall not make a pension adjustment order in favour of a spouse who has remarried.

(b) The court may make a pension adjustment order in addition to or in substitution in whole or in part for an order or orders under section 13, 14, 15 or 16 and, in deciding whether or not to make a pension adjustment order, the court shall have regard to the question whether proper provision, having regard to the circumstances, exists or can be made for the spouse concerned or the dependent member of the family concerned by an order or orders under any of those sections.

(24) Section 54 of the Act of 1990 and any regulations under that section shall apply with any necessary modifications to a scheme if proceedings for the grant of a decree of divorce to which a member spouse is a party have been instituted and shall continue to apply notwithstanding the grant of a decree of divorce in the proceedings.

(25) For the purposes of this Act, the court may, of its own motion, and shall, if so requested by either of the spouses concerned or any other person concerned, direct the trustees of the scheme concerned to provide the spouses or that other person and the court, within a specified period of time—

(a) with a calculation of the value and the amount, determined in accordance with relevant guidelines, of the retirement benefit, or contingent benefit, concerned that is payable (or which, but for the making of the order for the decree of divorce concerned, would have been payable) under the scheme and has accrued at the time of the making of that order, and

(b) with a calculation of the amount of the contingent benefit concerned that is payable (or which, but for the making of the order for the decree of divorce concerned, would have been payable) under the scheme.

(26) An order under this section may restrict to a specified extent or exclude the application of section 22 in relation to the order.

GENERAL NOTE

A pension adjustment order may be sought under section 17 of the 1996 Act by either an applicant spouse or by a person acting on behalf of a dependant family member as one of the ancillary reliefs available under the Part III of the Act. The order may be obtained either at the time the decree of divorce is granted or in the case of an application to adjust a retirement benefit, at any time during the lifetime of a spouse who is a member of the pension scheme in question, or in the case of an application to adjust a contingent benefit, within 12 months of the granting of the decree. Section 12 of the 1995 Family Law Act introduced this relief, which allowed for the first time the potential redistribution of a family asset which heretofore the court had no power to adjust or distribute in any way. The provisions of section 17, as with section 12 of the 1995 Act, have no applicability to separation agreements.

The effect of the relief in both section 12 of the 1995 Act and section 17 of the 1996 Act is to provide the spouse and in certain circumstances a dependant family member with pension entitlements in their own right. This award is made regardless of the terms of the pension scheme in question, which were probably not drafted to take account of the fact that benefits thereunder might ultimately be paid out to a non-member spouse or other dependant family member.

Although the power to redistribute pension benefits has been available since 1995, it would appear that its use has not been widespread probably for two reasons. Firstly, the provisions set out in section 12 and section 17 are complicated, technical and unproven. Secondly, section 17(23)(6) stipulates that a pension adjustment order may be made "in addition to or in substitution in whole or in part for an order or orders under sections 13, 14, 15 or 16", and goes on to direct that the cost "shall have regard" to whether provision can be made for the applicant by making an order under the any of those sections. This appears to suggest that the court should consider a pension adjustment order as a last resort and certainly directs it to see whether proper provision can be made by adjusting non-pension benefits to leave the pension rights of the scheme member intact, *e.g.* by making a property adjustment order or lump sum order. Clearly this will be appropriate where the non-pensions assets are of substantial value in comparison to the pension rights, but the converse would not apply. One of the advantages of prioritising use of other ancillary reliefs over the pension adjustment order is to limit additional costs which arise in adjusting a pension because of the probable involvement of the trustees of the scheme (section 17(22)(a)).

Section 17 is largely similar to section 12, the main differences are referable to the fact that a divorce terminates the marriage and therefore terminates any benefits which would have been payable only to a spouse of the member of the scheme, *e.g.* a spouse's "death in service" pension.

Section 17(1) defines all relevant terms and these definitions are applied throughout the Guidance Notes issued by the Pensions Board in relation to the provisions of the Family Law Act 1995 and the Family Law (Divorce) Act 1996. Extracts of the Pensions Board Guidance Notes are reproduced at Appendix C. The definitions are also applied throughout the Pension Schemes (Family Law) Regulations 1997 (S.I. No. 107 of 1997), which came into effect on February 27, 1997. Before deciding whether to make any order under section 17, the court must apply the provisions of section 20 of the 1996 Act and in particular section 20(2)(k), which directs the court to take account of the value to each spouse of any benefit which they will lose as a result of the decree. The definition of pension scheme in section 2(1) of the 1996 Act differentiates between a *defined benefit occupational pension scheme* and a *defined contribution scheme*. Examples of schemes included are:

    (a)   Statutory pension schemes;
    (b)   Personal pension schemes;
    (c)   Exempt approved retirement benefit schemes under the Finance Act 1972;
    (d)   Overseas pension scheme benefits.

The definition of a pension scheme specifically excludes benefits payable under the Social Welfare Acts. A scheme must provide for monies to be paid on retirement or death to come within the scope of the legislation and so excludes permanent health insurance schemes or income continuance policies.

As with the 1995 Act, benefits fall into the category of either a *contingent benefit* or a *retirement benefit* and both are defined in section 17(1), but are treated differently. A contingent benefit is commonly referred to as a *death in service benefit*. It is payable to a widow or widower or dependant family member, if the member of the scheme dies while in relevant employment, prior to normal pensionable age. Examples of a death in service benefit include:

    (a)   Death in service benefits under a personal pension plan;
    (b)   Lump sum death in service benefits under an occupational pension scheme;
    (c)   Pension payable on death under an occupational pension scheme;
    (d)   Benefit payable under a scheme approved by the Revenue Commissioners.

Retirement benefits are all those payable under a pension scheme other than contingent benefits. Examples of retirement benefits include:

    (a)   Member's pension payable at normal retirement age;
    (b)   Member's pension payable on early retirement;
    (c)   Refund of member's contributions;
    (d)   Spouse or dependant family members pension which is payable on the death or retirement of the member.

The order is then served on the trustees of each scheme of which the member spouse was a member during the relevant period. On the basis of the relevant period and the relevant percentage set out in the order, the trustees then compute the "designated benefit" payable from that scheme. Examples of such computations are set out in extracts from Part 4 of the Pension Board Guidance Notes (Appendix C, pp. 184–188).

The designated benefit may eventually become payable as a "transfer amount" on the occurrence of certain specified events, such as the death of the member spouse. However, a non-member spouse may prefer to initiate a transfer amount and in so doing have an amount of money from the appropriate scheme applied for the purposes of setting up their own pension scheme as set out in section 17(5). The transfer amount will be equal to the value of the designated benefit, which value will have been calculated by the trustees of the scheme in accordance with its rules. Section 17(5) directs that the trustees shall, if an application is made to them by the spouse who has the benefit of a pension adjustment order, either at the time the order was made or at any time thereafter, provided that they have obtained all reasonable information from that spouse, set up either a separate scheme for the non-member spouse to the same actuarial value of the transfer amount, or make a payment to either another occupational pension scheme or to another approved arrangement to be chosen by the non-member spouse. The spouse who had obtained the pension adjustment order would then have their own independent pension benefit. Section 17(5) only comes into play where an application is made thereunder to the trustees of the relevant scheme. Where no such application is made section 17(6) comes into operation granting a discretion to the trustees of the scheme to either set up a new independent scheme as above, or to make the relevant payments to another occupational pension scheme, thus enabling the trustees to give effect to a pension adjustment order in the absence of specific instructions from the non-member spouse.

Section 17(2) does not impose a time limit within which an application for "earmarking" must be made other than it must be made during the lifetime of the member spouse. Applications pursuant to section 17(3), by contrast, for the splitting of a contingent benefit, must be made within one year after the decree has been granted. It is difficult to understand why the legislature chose to differentiate between retirement benefits and contingent benefits in this way.

A difficulty could clearly be envisaged, in circumstances where an applicant wife obtains a pension adjustment order in respect of a contingent benefit which is to be paid to her husband under his scheme of employment. If the husband leaves the employment and fails to transfer the contingency benefits to another scheme, or allows them to lapse or terminate; then the contingency, *i.e.* the death of the husband will not have come about and the pension adjustment order granted to the wife will [...] scribing to a new scheme [...] the course of his new [...] not entitled to make any [...] if more than a year has [...] benefits to an applicant [...] some time after the decree [...] with the passage of time. [...] will be higher.

CORR

The second and third sentences of paragr

Conversely, one of the benefits to an section 17(2) some time after the decr scheme will be frozen as of the date c to the passage of time by increasing the per value of the pension adjustment order, if adjusted, wou favour of an applicant spouse or [...] t family member, but not in favour of both. However, an applicant spouse or a person applying on behalf of a dependant family member may apply for orders in respect of retirement benefit and/or contingent benefit under a scheme of which one of the spouses is a member. The provisions of section 17(23) are notable as they provide, as do similar provisions in sections 13, 14, 15 and 16 of the Act in relation to other ancillary reliefs that no pension adjustment order will be made in favour of a spouse who has remarried.

There are various provisions of section 17 which deal with notice and information requirements and these are discussed in Part 2 of the Pensions Board Guidance Notes (Appendix C, pp.176–181). Prior to deciding whether the making of a pension adjustment order is appropriate in any case, the court will require details of the pension scheme to be put before it. Practitioners should therefore examine the pension scheme document carefully to ascertain the relevant information which must be placed before the court, in view of the fact that no pension may be adjusted in any way without a court order. If necessary, clarification on the terms of the scheme should be sought from the trustees of the scheme under section 17(25), and it would appear that the trustees of the pension schemes are anxious to facilitate the parties in making orders on a consensual basis to minimise costs and inconvenience to all parties involved. Adequate time should be given to the trustees of the scheme to supply the information to which the spouse of a member of a scheme is entitled pursuant to section 54 of the Pensions Act 1990 (No. 25). That section allows the applicant spouse access to basic information such as a copy of the pension scheme and annual reports. This information should be sought in writing from the trustees before an application is made by way of notice of motion under section 17(25). Clear information must be placed before the court to facilitate its deliberations, particularly details of the two specific elements, which must be incorporated into a pension adjustment order:

(i)   The period of reckonable service of the member prior to the granting of the decree; and

(ii) A percentage of the amount of benefit accrued during that period which is to be paid on foot of the order.

Pursuant to section 17(25) the court may of its own motion direct the trustees to provide the necessary information within a certain time limit. Note also the disclosure regulations made under the Pensions Act 1990, *i.e.* the Occupational Pension Scheme (Disclosure of Information) Regulations 1991 (S.I. No. 215 of 1991), which are applicable to the 1996 Act by virtue of section 17(24).

Information duly obtained in this regard must be set out in the affidavit of means to be sworn by the relevant party pursuant to the Rules of the Circuit Court (No. 1) 1997 (S.I. No. 84 of 1997) (see Appendix B). Pursuant to Rule 19 the following specific information is required:

(a) The nature of the pension scheme;

(b) The benefits payable thereunder;

(c) The normal pensionable age of the member's spouse; and

(d) The period of reckonable service of the member's spouse.

The information usually provided in relation to the pension scheme will include a description of the type of scheme involved and a description of benefits payable under the scheme which would outline the accumulated retirement fund which is available at normal retirement age to the members which could provide the relevant benefits. Section 17(25) also requires specific information to be provided by the trustees, *i.e.* a calculation of the value and amount of the retirement or contingent benefit which is payable or which would have been payable to the member spouse, but for the granting of a decree of divorce.

Section 17(22) refers to costs which will be incurred by the trustees, either in providing the relevant information or in complying with the pensions adjustment order. Such costs are to be borne in by either or both parties at the court's determination or by both parties equally in the absence of any ruling of the court. If these costs are not paid as outlined in section 17(22)(a), then section 17(22)(b) comes into play allowing the trustee to apply to the court for an order directing that the amount of such costs be deducted from any benefit payable under section 17(2) or 17(3), or payable under the scheme. The monies deducted are then paid over to the trustees.

The methods of calculating the designated benefit payable from a scheme after a pension adjustment order is made in respect of the member spouses' retirement benefit under that scheme or varied, depending on the circumstances. Different approaches to calculations will be required, *e.g.* where a member retires at normal pensionable age, or where a member retires at prior to reaching normal pensionable age (Appendix C).

Section 17(7) provides for circumstances in which the court has made a pension adjustment order in respect of a retirement benefit, but the scheme member dies prior to payment of the designated benefit commencing and prior to a transfer amount being applied. In that case, an amount of money equal to the transfer amount is to be paid to the non-member spouse within three months of the death of the member. It may also be the case that the non-member spouse would also be eligible to receive a contingent benefit. In such a case, the provisions of section 17(16)(b) will apply, directing that the amount of the contingent benefit which the non-member spouse would ordinarily have received will be reduced by the amount paid out under section 17(7). Section 17(16)(a) simply provides that where a pension adjustment order is made in respect of a contingent benefit, the contingent benefit payable to the member spouse will be reduced by the amount of the order so made.

Membership of a scheme may terminate for reasons other than death, such as a transfer by a member spouse to new employment. In these circumstances and where an order has been made pursuant to section 17(2), the trustees have a discretion to take either of two approaches. Section 17(8)(i) provides that if the trustees and the spouse in whose favour the order has been made agree, the designated benefit may be valued and converted into a transfer amounts and retained by the trustees in the scheme to pay to that spouse a separate benefit of the same actuarial value as the transfer amount in question. A second option is provided for the trustees by section 17(8)(ii) to pay over the transfer amount in question to another pension scheme, with the agreement of the trustees of that scheme or they can make a payment to a life assurance company by way of a buy-out bond approved by the Revenue Commissioners. It is important to emphasise the discretion of trustees in making such a decision, although clearly the agreement of the spouse in whose favour the order is made will be required.

Section 17(9) deals with what can occur when a spouse who has the benefit of an order under section 17(2) dies before the payment of the designated benefit has begun. The trustees in such circumstances must pay over to that spouse's personal representative, within three months, an amount equal to the transfer amount in question. Where a spouse in similar circumstances dies after the payment of designated benefit has commenced, a similar timeframe applies for the payment by the trustees to the estate of the deceased spouse a sum equivalent to the part of the designated benefit which that spouse would have received were it not for their death. Thus it can be seen that the benefit of the section 17(2) order accrues to the estate of the deceased spouse and is not lost. This is in contrast with the position of a dependant family member who dies before the payment of designated benefit has commenced. In that instance, the order will lapse and no money will be paid out.

Section 17(12) provides that where a pension adjustment order is made in relation to either a contingency or retirement benefit, but the trustees have not actually implemented the pension splitting process and the member spouse ceases to be a member of the scheme, the trustees must notify both the court and the spouse in whose favour the order has been made of the cessation in membership. In these circumstances, it is possible pursuant to section 17(2) to apply to the court to have the existing retirement benefit order varied and so to attempt to limit the damage caused by the member spouse's actions in leaving the scheme. It would be possible, for example to seek an adjustment in one of the other ancillary reliefs which may have been granted to take account of the loss of the pension adjustment order.

It is not possible however to apply to vary a contingency benefit in such circumstances because section 17(3) does not permit the variation of such order. If a member spouse ceases membership of a pension scheme which was the subject of an order directing the provision of a contingency benefit for a non-member spouse or dependant family member, the contingency will be lost as the event which would have triggered the pay out of the benefit will not have occurred.

It is notable that section 17(19) provides that any order made under section 17(3) to provide a contingency benefit to a non-member spouse will cease to be of effect if the spouse dies or remarries and ceases similarly to be of effect on the death of a dependant family member.

If an order is made by the court under section 17(2), the amount of the retirement benefit which is in the scheme to be paid to the member spouse will be reduced by the amount to be paid to the non-member spouse by way of court order (section 17(15)). Similarly, section 17(16)(a) makes clear the reduction in the amount of contingency benefit payable to a member spouse if an order is made under section 17(3). Section 16(b) directs that if section 17(7) comes into operation, *i.e.* where a member spouse dies before payment of the designated benefit has commenced and monies are paid over to the spouse in whose favour the order was made, then any contingent benefit which is payable in respect of the member spouse will be diminished by the amount paid out by the trustees under section 17(7).

Section 17(7) limits the obligations placed on the trustees where they either make a payment or apply a transfer amount under section 17 subsections (5) to (10) and following any such payment they are discharged of any obligations to make further payments under the court order.

A member of a pension scheme is also defined under section 2(1) of the 1996 Act as "any person who, having been admitted to membership of the Scheme under its rules, remains entitled to any benefit under the Scheme." This includes not only active scheme members but members who are inactive and who may be enjoying deferred benefits under the scheme. Examples of "members" of a scheme include:

(i)   Current Pensioners;
(ii) Persons contributing to a personal pension plan approved under the Income Tax Act 1967;
(iii) Persons who have retained benefits under an occupational pension scheme;
(iv) Persons with paid up personal pension plans; and
(v)   Persons who are members of more than one pension scheme.

It should be noted that separate pension adjustment orders would be required for each individual pension scheme.

Section 17 contains constraints in respect of the category of person in whose favour a pension adjustment order may be made. Section 17(23)(a) provides that the court shall not make a pension adjustment order in favour of a spouse who has remarried. Section 17(19) provides that any order made pursuant to section 17(3) in respect of a contingent benefit will cease to have effect if the person in whose favour such an order was made dies or remarries.

Section 17(26) provides that any order, which may be made pursuant to section 17, may restrict or exclude the application of the provisions of section 22 of the 1996 Act to such an order. It is open therefore to the court to direct that any pension adjustment order which it might make may not be reviewed, discharged, suspended, or otherwise, and in that regard the court has the facility to vest a pension adjustment order with a certain degree of finality. However, the use of the word "may" means that unless specifically excluded or restricted the provisions of section 22 may apply to any order made under section 17, in the same way as to any other form of ancillary relief. Practitioners should consider making a specific application to the court pursuant to section 17(26) to exclude the applicability of section 22 to these orders.

In addition to the considerations which the court must apply in deciding whether to make an order pursuant to section 17, the court must also take into account all provisions of section 20 of the 1996 Act. Note also that in circumstances where a decree of judicial separation has been obtained by parties seeking a decree of divorce and where a pension adjustment order was made pursuant to section 12 of the 1995 Act, the provisions of section 26 of the 1996 Act apply insofar as the court is permitted to discharge an existing pension adjustment order from a specified date. In circumstances where such an order is not discharged, it continues in force as before. If the court can be persuaded to change the pension adjustment order already granted pursuant to section 12 of the 1995 Act, there is a possibility that an applicant spouse may obtain a new order of greater value to them in terms of the value of the pension scheme already provided for. If the court decides to discharge the first pension adjustment order, it will then have to recalculate both the period of reckonable service and the proportion of the benefit that has accrued during the period which has to be designated for the benefit of the non-member spouse. It remains to be seen what factors will influence the courts in deciding whether or not to make such orders.

The provisions of section 37 of the Divorce Act 1996 should also be noted insofar as power is granted thereunder to the court to restrain a member spouse from making any dispositions with the intention of defeating a claim for relief by the non-member spouse. This could arise in circumstances where the member spouse of a scheme moves to defeat a potential pension adjustment order by disposing of, or transferring his pension benefit to either a buy-out bond or to another scheme. This situation could also arise where the member spouse leaves the scheme and takes a refund of his member contributions.

Orders for provision for spouse out of estate of other spouse

18.—(1) Subject to the provisions of this section, where one of the spouses in respect of whom a decree of divorce has been granted dies, the court, on application to it in that behalf by the other spouse ("the applicant") not more than 6 months after representation is first granted under the Act of 1965 in respect of the estate of the deceased spouse, may by order make such provision for the applicant out of the estate of the deceased spouse as it considers appropriate having regard to the rights of any other person having an interest in the matter and specifies in the order if it is satisfied that proper provision in the circumstances was not made for the applicant during the lifetime of the deceased spouse under section 13, 14, 15, 16 or 17 for any reason (other than conduct referred to in subsection (2)(i) of section 20 of the applicant).

(2) The court shall not make an order under this section in favour of a spouse who has remarried since the granting of the decree of divorce concerned.

(3) In considering whether to make an order under this section the court shall have regard to all the circumstances of the case including—

> (a) any order under paragraph (c) of section 13(1) or a property adjustment order in favour of the applicant, and
>
> (b) any devise or bequest made by the deceased spouse to the applicant.

(4) The provision made for the applicant concerned by an order under this section together with any provision made for the applicant by an order referred to in subsection (3)(a) (the value of which for the purposes of this subsection shall be its value on the date of the order) shall not exceed in total the share (if any) of the applicant in the estate of the deceased spouse to which the applicant was entitled or (if the deceased spouse died intestate as to the whole or part of his or her estate) would have been entitled under the Act of 1965 if the marriage had not been dissolved.

(5) Notice of an application under this section shall be given by the applicant to the spouse (if any) of the deceased spouse concerned and to such (if any) other persons as the court may direct and, in deciding whether to make the order concerned and in determining the provisions of the order, the court shall have regard to any representations made by the spouse of the deceased spouse and any other such persons as aforesaid.

(6) The personal representative of a deceased spouse in respect of whom a decree of divorce has been granted shall make a reasonable attempt to ensure that notice of his or her death is brought to the attention of the other spouse concerned and, where an application is made under this section, the personal representative of the deceased spouse shall not, without the leave of the court, distribute any of the estate of that spouse until the court makes or refuses to make an order under this section.

(7) Where the personal representative of a deceased spouse in respect of whom a decree of divorce has been granted gives notice of his or her death to the other spouse concerned ("the spouse") and—

> (a) the spouse intends to apply to the court for an order under this section,
>
> (b) the spouse has applied for such an order and the application is pending, or

(c) an order has been made under this section in favour of the spouse, the spouse shall, not later than one month after the receipt of the notice, notify the personal representative of such intention, application or order, as the case may be, and, if he or she does not do so, the personal representative shall be at liberty to distribute the assets of the deceased spouse, or any part thereof, amongst the parties entitled thereto.

(8) The personal representative shall not be liable to the spouse for the assets or any part thereof so distributed unless, at the time of such distribution, he or she had notice of the intention, application or order aforesaid.

(9) Nothing in subsection (7) or (8) shall prejudice the right of the spouse to follow any such assets into the hands of any person who may have received them.

(10) On granting a decree of divorce or at any time thereafter, the court, on application to it in that behalf by either of the spouses concerned, may, during the lifetime of the other spouse or, as the case may be, the spouse concerned, if it considers it just to do so, make an order that either or both spouses shall not, on the death of either of them, be entitled to apply for an order under this section.

GENERAL NOTE

Section 18 introduced an entirely new ancillary relief, although the Family Law (Divorce) Act 1996 includes in its provisions a similar relief in the context of judicial separation by introducing section 15A of the Family Law Act 1995. This amendment was introduced by section 52(g) of the 1996 Act. During the course of the Oireachtas debates, deputies and senators commented on the new relief, which probably most strongly evidences the lack of any "clean-break" principle in Irish divorce law.

The ability to return to the court for additional relief during the lifetime of the ex-marital partners is provided for in many instances, but section 18 allows the claim for additional relief to be made after the death of the former spouse, thus indicating that even death cannot guarantee a clean break in marital obligations.

An obvious criticism of section 18 was succinctly raised by Deputy O'Dea at the Second Stage of the Bill:

> "It is extraordinary that [section 18] states that this right will only be granted "if it was not possible to make proper provision for the applicant during the lifetime of the deceased spouse." If it was not possible to do so, why was the divorce granted in the first place? Surely, [section 5(1)(c)] makes it clear that a divorce cannot be granted unless the court is satisfied that proper provision is being made." (467 *Dáil Debates* Col. 1806)

The application for relief under section 18 must be made within a period of six months after representation is first granted under the Succession Act 1965 in respect of the estate of the deceased. The personal representative must make a reasonable attempt to bring the death of the spouse to the notice of the other spouse. What constitutes a "reasonable attempt" is a matter for the discretion of the court.

Concerns were also raised in relation to the onerous duties placed upon the personal representative under section 18 and as to the possible liabilities of the personal representative in the event of a failure to comply with these duties. Legal anecdote often refers to the dire warnings of Professor Frances Moran about becoming a trustee – it would appear that this warning should now be extended to encompass personal representatives! (see Keane, *Equity and the Law of Trusts in the Republic of Ireland* (Butterworths, 1988), p. 100). A degree of protection was introduced by section 18(7), which was introduced by way of amendment at the Committee Stage of the Bill in the Seanad. Commenting upon this amendment, Minister Taylor stated that it:

"provides that, where a personal representative gives notice to a former spouse as required under subsection (6), that spouse is required within one month to notify the personal representative of any intention to make an application under section [18], any application pending or any order made. Should the former spouse fail to so notify the personal representative, he or she will be free to distribute the assets and shall not be held liable to the former spouse for any assets so distributed." (149 *Seanad Debates* Cols. 25–26)

While there was no need to include in the Act any provision similar to section 14 of the Family Law Act 1995, providing for the extinguishment of Succession Act rights as such rights would automatically cease to exist following the granting of the decree of divorce. The Minister stated:

"Where a couple divorce, the parties being no longer spouses will no longer have rights of succession" (467 *Dáil Debates* Col. 1765)

However, the Minister did appear to envisage that the range of ancillary reliefs available might be combined to compensate a spouse for such a loss. The Minister stated:

"In compensation for that loss the court will be able to make provision for a spouse by using the various financial and property adjustment provisions in . . . the Bill."(467 *Dáil Debates* Col. 1765)

This comment must be viewed in the light of section 20 of the Act which deals with matters to be taken into account in determining issues relating to ancillary financial and property reliefs consequent upon a decree of divorce. While the considerations listed in section 20 do not purport to be decisive, those particularised therein at section 20(2) include:

"(k) the value to each of the spouses of any benefit (for example, a benefit under a pension scheme) which by reason of the decree of divorce concerned, that spouse will forfeit the opportunity or possibility of acquiring . . ."

This, presumably, would include the automatic loss of spousal succession rights consequent upon a decree of divorce. The ability of the courts to provide for a *de facto* continuation of succession rights, albeit under a different heading, is supported by the remedies contained in section 18 of the 1996 Act.

It seems almost too obvious to state that when a decree of divorce is granted, the parties no longer have the status of spouses and therefore do not retain their legal rights to a share in the estate of the other. This is not explicitly stated in section 18 because the purpose of the section is to introduce an entirely new ancillary relief which enables a divorced person in specific circumstance to apply to the court for a share from the estate of their divorced spouse who has died.

This provision was not contained in the Family Law Act 1995 in the context of judicial separation, but has been inserted as section 15(A) of the 1995 Act, by section 52 (g) of the 1996 Act. The provisions of section 18 are sufficiently extensive to enable such an application to be made by a spouse whose Succession Act rights have already been extinguished by an order made pursuant to section 14 of the 1995 Act, where that person has subsequently been granted a decree of divorce. The provisions of section 18 do not extend to a spouse whose succession rights have been extinguished by an order in the course of judicial separation proceedings, other than in circumstances where such a person subsequently applies for a decree of divorce whereupon their entitlement to apply for provision out of the estate of their deceased spouse will be revived. This revival will only come into operation if no blocking order has been made on the granting of the decree of divorce pursuant to the provisions of section 18(10) of the 1996 Act.

Prior to the coming into operation of the 1996 Act, section 14 of the 1995 Act provided that when a decree of judicial separation was granted, the court could make an order extinguishing the share to which either spouse would be entitled in the estate of the other as a legal right, or on intestacy, pursuant to the Succession Act 1965. There were various conditions attached to the making of such orders which were made with a view to endeavouring to ensure "that proper provision would be made for the spouse concerned having regard to all the circumstances" and ensuring that the order was made "in the interests of justice". There is no provision in the 1996 Act equivalent to section 14 of the 1995 Act, as set out above. The loss of Succession Act rights, which automatically takes place on the granting of a decree of divorce, is one of the matters which will be taken into account by the court in deciding whether to order ancillary relief and the extent thereof.

During the course of the Oireachtas debates, much comment was made concerning the new relief, which probably most strongly evidences the lack of any "clean break" principle operating in relation to Irish divorce law. The ability to return for additional reliefs during the lifetime of the ex-marital partners is provided for in many instances, but section 18 allows the claim for additional relief to be made after the death of the former spouse, thus indicating that even death cannot guarantee an end to marital obligations.

This was finally acknowledged by McGuinness J. in *J.D. v. D.D.*, unreported, High Court, May 14, 1997. McGuinness J. stated at p. 32 that:

> "it appears to me by the subsequent enactment of the Family Law Act, 1995 and the Family Law (Divorce) Act, 1996, the Oireachtas has made it clear that a 'clean break' situation is not to be sought and that, if anything, financial finality is virtually to be prevented. Under both the 1995 Act and the 1996 Act . . . there appears to be no limit on the number of occasions on which a property adjustment order may be sought and granted. The Court, in making virtually any other order in regard to finance and property on the breakdown of a marriage, is faced with the situation where finality is not and never can be achieved."

No order may be made under section 18(2) in favour of a surviving spouse who has remarried. This is stated in mandatory terms and in this regard must be contrasted with the discretionary nature of section 18(1) and section 14 of the 1995 Act. The attitude to remarriage of an applicant spouse in this section is akin to the approach taken in the rest of the Act. The obligation to provide ceases upon remarriage. This is the only event which guarantees finality. Section 18(3) specifies that in deciding whether or not to make an order under section 18, the court, in addition to taking into account all the circumstances, has to have specific regard to whether or not a lump sum maintenance order or property adjustment order has already been made. The court may also have regard to whether or not the deceased spouse has made any devise or bequest to the applicant. There is no issue of an election between the bequest and a section 18(1) application. Rather the bequest is a factor in determining the extent, if any, to which section 18 relief ought to be given.

Section 18(4) provides that any order made under section 18, in addition to provision already made by way of lump sum maintenance order or property adjustment order, shall not exceed in total the share to which the applicant would have been entitled from the estate of the deceased spouse, either on intestacy or otherwise. In other words, the court cannot grant to the applicant spouse more than they would have got if the marriage had not been dissolved, or presumably if an order extinguishing the applicant's Succession Act rights had not been made under section 14 of the 1995 Act. This amounts to one half of the estate where there are no children and one third where there are.

If an ex-spouse wishes to make application under section 18 for this relief, they must notify any new spouse of the deceased spouse and any other person as may be directed by the court, of their intention to make such an application. Section 18(5) specifies that having been notified, any representation that these people may make shall be taken into account by the court in deciding whether or not to make an order. Section 18(6) imposes onerous new duties on the personal representative of a deceased spouse, and this caused particular concern to Deputy O'Dea:

> "This onus should not be put on a personal representative what action shall apply if it is established that the personal representative did not make a reasonable attempt to contact the spouse of somebody who has died with a view to their coming back to look for another share of the property? This represents a further onus and therefore a further disincentive for people to take on the job of being a personal representative". (467 *Dáil Debates* Col 1806)

It is hard to disagree with Deputy O'Dea's forebodings. Section 18(6) states that a personal representative must make a reasonable attempt to ensure the surviving spouse is notified of the former spouse's death. Where the surviving spouse makes an application pursuant to section 18, the personal representative must, having been so notified of that application, delay the distribution of the estate pending the outcome of such application. The personal representative cannot in fact proceed to distribute the estate until a court order permits him to do so. There is no guidance as to what would "be reasonable" for the purposes of this section, and there is not much by way of judicial interpretation in respect of same to date.

Section 18(7) specifies that once a spouse has been notified by the personal representative of the death of their former spouse, they have a period of one month within which they must notify the personal representative of their intention to make such an application, or if an order or application has already been made, they must notify them of that fact. If the former spouse does not give such notification within the one month period, the personal representative may distribute the assets of the estate without further difficulty. Unless the personal representative was given notification at the time of the distribution of the assets, he will not be liable to the former spouse for any part of those assets. However, there is protection afforded to the former spouse in this situation by section 18(9), as the former spouse can follow the assets so distributed into the hands of their recipients.

Section 18(10) opens the door to the possibility of a clean break in respect of matters of succession, in so far as any order granted pursuant to section 18(10) will have the effect of negating the provisions of section 18(1). At the time the decree of divorce is granted, or at any time thereafter, the court may block any future applications by a surviving spouse under section 18(1), thus ensuring that at least after death the surviving former spouse cannot bring a claim. It would be advisable that an application should be made in respect of the practitioner's own client's estates. This would ensure that the client would be free to dispose of all assets by way of will or settlement, without the possibility of the surviving former spouse returning to seek provision from their estate. Clearly the court could be expected to make blocking orders under section 18(10) in circumstances where the spouses had already agreed to renounce their Succession Act rights, or where a court by way of a decree of judicial separation had granted an order to do so under section 15(A)(10) of the 1995 Act.

A procedural point arises in relation to applications for blocking orders under section 18(10) of the Act. The Superior Court Rules and the Circuit Court Rules relating to divorce applications (see Appendix A and B) both require the filing of an affidavit of means where financial relief is being sought. In substantially uncontested applications, spouses are hesitant about swearing such an affidavit and in particular about disclosing the terms of the affidavit to their spouse. In many instances, the only relief being sought is the decree of divorce itself and the section 18(10) blocking order. It is submitted that the section 18(10) application constitutes financial relief and that applications made pursuant to this section require that an affidavit of means be filed. There is clearly a financial benefit to the recipient of the section 18(10) order and a financial detriment to the other party. Furthermore, this view is supported by section 20 which sets out the criteria for financial reliefs to be given and includes section 20 which sets out the criteria for financial reliefs to be given and includes section 18 in the list of applications to which the section 20 criteria are to apply.

In addition to considering the criteria set out pursuant to section 18(3), the court must also take into account the provisions of section 20, and probably, the court will also have regard to the period of time which has elapsed between the granting of the decree of divorce and the application for relief herein.

Note that the entitlement of a child to seek provision from the estate of a parent, if no provision was made for them in that parent's will, is not affected by any of the provisions outlined so far but practitioners should notice that the provisions of section 117(6) of the Succession Act 1965 are amended to shorten the time period allowed to such children for the making of applications pursuant to section 117 from 12 months to six months from the date of the grant of representation is taken out.

Orders for sale of property

19.—(1) Where the court makes a secured periodical payments order, a lump sum or a property adjustment order, thereupon, or at any time thereafter, it may make an order directing the sale of such property as may be specified in the order, being property in which, or in the proceeds of sale of which, either or both of the spouses concerned has or have a beneficial interest, either in possession or reversion.

(2) The jurisdiction conferred on the court by subsection (1) shall not be so exercised as to affect a right to occupy the family home of the spouse concerned that is enjoyed by virtue of an order under this Part.

(3) (a) An order under subsection (1) may contain such consequential or supplementary provisions as the court considers appropriate.

(b) Without prejudice to the generality of paragraph (a), an order under subsection (1) may contain—

(i) a provision specifying the manner of sale and some or all of the conditions applying to the sale of the property to which the order relates,

(ii) a provision requiring any such property to be offered for sale to a person, or a class of persons, specified in the order,

(iii) a provision directing that the order, or a specified part of it, shall not take effect until the occurrence of a specified event or the expiration of a specified period,

(iv) a provision requiring the making of a payment or payments (whether periodical payments or lump sum payments) to a specified person or persons out of the proceeds of the sale of the property to which the order relates, and

(v) a provision specifying the manner in which the proceeds of the sale of the property concerned shall be disposed of between the following persons or such of them as the court considers appropriate, that is to say, the spouses concerned and any other person having an interest therein.

(4) A provision in an order under subsection (1) providing for the making of periodical payments to one of the spouses concerned out of the proceeds of the sale of property shall, on the death or remarriage of that spouse, cease to have effect except as respects payments due on the date of the death or remarriage.

(5) Where a spouse has a beneficial interest in any property, or in the proceeds of the sale of any property, and a person (not being the other spouse) also has a beneficial interest in that property or those proceeds, then, in considering whether to make an order under this section or section 14 or 15(1)(a) in relation to that property or those proceeds, the court shall give to that person an opportunity to make representations with respect to the making of the order and the contents thereof, and any representations made by such a person shall be deemed to be included among the matters to which the court is required to have regard under section 20 in any relevant proceedings under a provision referred to in that section after the making of those representations.

(6) This section shall not apply in relation to a family home in which, fol-

lowing the grant of a decree of divorce, either of the spouses concerned, having remarried, ordinarily resides with his or her spouse.

GENERAL NOTE

Section 19 permits the court to make an order for the sale of property as a consequence of making any of the following orders:

(a) A secured periodical payments order;
(b) A lump sum payment order;
(c) A property adjustment order.

Property is understood to be very widely defined and includes property in which either of the spouses has any beneficial interest, however small, held either in possession or reversion. Property also refers to the proceeds of sale of any property owned by either of the spouses. The order for sale may be made by the court when it makes the ancillary orders referred to above, or at any time thereafter.

Section 19(2) provides that an order for sale cannot be made which would affect the right of a spouse residing in the property to occupy the property, if that spouse is enjoying that right according to the terms of an ancillary order made under Part II of the 1995 Act or Part III of the 1996 Act. Pursuant to the provisions of section 19(6) an order for sale cannot be made in respect of a family home in which either of the divorced spouses, having remarried, now resides with their new spouse. Thus, if on granting a decree of divorce, the court made a secured periodical payment order secured against a property in which the payor resides and that spouse then defaults on the payments under the secured periodical payments order, the hands of the court are tied in so far as it cannot order the sale of the family home to continue the periodical payment order made in favour of the first spouse, if the payor has remarried and resides with his new spouse in the premises in question. This is a factor which will have to be foreseen by practitioners in advising their clients as to whether or not to accept secured periodical payment orders, always assuming of course they have any choice in the matter. The options for security may be extremely limited in many cases.

Section 19(3) lists contents, which may be included by the court in making an order pursuant to section 19(1). The court may specify the manner in which the sale will take place, *i.e.* by auction or private treaty and some or all of the conditions applying to the sale, *e.g.* that a specific solicitor be appointed to have carriage of sale. The court may also require the property to be offered for sale to a particular person or number of persons and may specify that the sale will not take place until some specified event has occurred, for example, after the completion of the leaving certificate examinations being undertaken by the children. Section 19(3)(b)(iv) directs that the court may specify that monies be paid from the proceeds of sale to a person specified by the court in the order. The final provision of section 19(3) allows the court to specify the manner in which the proceeds of sale shall be distributed between all relevant parties.

Section 19(4) directs that where the court has made a secure periodical payments order and a consequential order for the sale of the secured property, the maintenance to be paid from the proceeds of sale, the periodical payments being made will cease on the event of the death or remarriage of the spouse to whom they are being paid save in respect of arrears. The provisions of section 19(5) which allow any person who has a beneficial interest in the property the subject of the sale, other than the spouses, to have an opportunity to make representations to the court in relation to the proposed order for sale and conditions attaching to same, should be noted. This subsection specifically refers to the fact that such representations are to be taken into account by the court in addition to the provisions of section 20 of the Act. Such persons are likely to be joined as notice parties in the proceedings and the situation envisaged would most usually arise in respect of property owned jointly between a spouse and a third party.

Provisions relating to certain orders under sections 12 to 18 and 22

20.—(1) In deciding whether to make an order under section 12, 13, 14, 15(1)(a), 16, 17, 18 or 22 and in determining the provisions of such an order, the court shall ensure that such provision as the court considers proper having regard to the circumstances exists or will be made for the spouses and any dependent member of the family concerned.

(2) Without prejudice to the generality of subsection (1), in deciding whether to make such an order as aforesaid and in determining the provisions of such an order, the court shall, in particular, have regard to the following matters:

    (a) the income, earning capacity, property and other financial resources which each of the spouses concerned has or is likely to have in the foreseeable future,

    (b) the financial needs, obligations and responsibilities which each of the spouses has or is likely to have in the foreseeable future (whether in the case of the remarriage of the spouse or otherwise),

    (c) the standard of living enjoyed by the family concerned before the proceedings were instituted or before the spouses commenced to live apart from one another, as the case may be,

    (d) the age of each of the spouses, the duration of their marriage and the length of time during which the spouses lived with one another,

    (e) any physical or mental disability of either of the spouses,

    (f) the contributions which each of the spouses has made or is likely in the foreseeable future to make to the welfare of the family, including any contribution made by each of them to the income, earning capacity, property and financial resources of the other spouse and any contribution made by either of them by looking after the home or caring for the family,

    (g) the effect on the earning capacity of each of the spouses of the marital responsibilities assumed by each during the period when they lived with one another and, in particular, the degree to which the future earning capacity of a spouse is impaired by reason of that spouse having relinquished or foregone the opportunity of remunerative activity in order to look after the home or care for the family,

    (h) any income or benefits to which either of the spouses is entitled by or under statute,

    (i) the conduct of each of the spouses, if that conduct is such that in the opinion of the court it would in all the circumstances of the case be unjust to disregard it,

    (j) the accommodation needs of either of the spouses,

    (k) the value to each of the spouses of any benefit (for example, a benefit under a pension scheme) which by reason of the decree of divorce concerned, that spouse will forfeit the opportunity or possibility of acquiring,

    (l) the rights of any person other than the spouses but including a person to whom either spouse is remarried.

(3) In deciding whether to make an order under a provision referred to in

subsection (1) and in determining the provisions of such an order, the court shall have regard to the terms of any separation agreement which has been entered into by the spouses and is still in force.

(4) Without prejudice to the generality of subsection (1), in deciding whether to make an order referred to in that subsection in favour of a dependent member of the family concerned and in determining the provisions of such an order, the court shall, in particular, have regard to the following matters:

    (a) the financial needs of the member,

    (b) the income, earning capacity (if any), property and other financial resources of the member,

    (c) any physical or mental disability of the member,

    (d) any income or benefits to which the member is entitled by or under statute,

    (e) the manner in which the member was being and in which the spouses concerned anticipated that the member would be educated or trained,

    (f) the matters specified in paragraphs (a), (b) and (c) of subsection (2) and in subsection (3),

    (g) the accommodation needs of the member.

(5) The court shall not make an order under a provision referred to in subsection (1) unless it would be in the interests of justice to do so.

GENERAL NOTE

This section details the criteria to which the court shall have particular regard in deciding whether to make any ancillary orders, pursuant to sections 12 to 18 and section 22, and in deciding what those orders shall contain. The criteria are to be applied in deciding financial reliefs only as section 15(1)(b) to (f) are excluded. No guidance is contained in the 1996 Act as to how the reliefs under these provisions are to be determined, but as they relate to reliefs under other family law statutes, it is to be presumed that the standards set out in the individual statutes concerned and judicial pronouncements relating thereto are applicable. Section 20 is largely the same as section 16 of the 1995 Act, although with some significant differences, the first of which emerges in section 20(1), which repeats the clearly stated provisions of section 5(1)(c) in setting out the court's duty to ensure that proper provision for the spouses and the dependant family members exists or will be made. In section 16(1) of the 1995 Act the court was charged to endeavour to ensure that adequate and reasonable provision, while having regard to all the circumstances of the case so existed. In section 20(1), the court is charged with an absolute duty to ensure the provisions of section 16(1) were adhered to, thus reflecting the terms of the constitutional amendment, and placing a more onerous duty on the court in divorce proceedings. The application of the provisions of section 16(1) of the 1995 Act were considered by McGuinness J. in *J.D. v. D.D.*, unreported, High Court, May 14, 1997, at p. 33 of the transcript.

Although practically speaking this difference in wording should have little impact as the court is charged to have regard to all relevant family circumstances and not just to those criteria specified in sections 16 and 20. The criteria set out in section 20 ultimately act as a guide to the court in ensuring that proper provision is made for the spouse and any dependant family members in the context of orders for ancillary relief. It is also a guide to practitioners when advising their clients as to how the court is likely to arrive at a decision.

The court cannot make excessive provision for one of the spouses to the detriment of either the other spouse or the dependant family members. Section 20(5) decrees that no order is to be made under the provisions of section 20(1), unless it is "in the interest of justice" to do so.

In addition to the specific factors set out in section 20(2), there are further criteria set out in section 20(4) prescribing additional criteria to which the court is to have regard in determining what orders, if any are to be made in respect of dependant family members. Similar factors are set out in section 16(4) of the Family Law Act 1995.

It is important for practitioners to ensure that evidence in respect of all matters contained in section 20(2) is before the court, in circumstances where ancillary relief is required. This places an onerous duty on practitioners who are in effect endeavouring to predict the future in assisting the court, for example to determine what financial resources either of the spouses concerned is likely to have in the future. This is where the issue of discovery becomes particularly relevant, as it is absolutely necessary that where financial or property orders are required that the court would have before it a comprehensive outline of the financial and property resources of both spouses.

The issue of discovery frequently gives rise to great difficulties in matrimonial matters. Particularly so in the context of applications for divorce where parties will have been living apart for four years, and probably want to conserve all their own resources for the future and do not wish to disclose their financial and property details. It is submitted however, that because of the possibility of the other spouse seeking a review of orders pursuant to section 22, clients should be advised that new orders can be made, if fresh information comes to light and most likely will be made if a failure to disclose assets emerges. In any event spouses are required to file an affidavit of means with the court which should contain details of all relevant matters.

Section 20(2)(a) charges the court to take into account all financial criteria applicable to each case, both present and future. Section 38(6) of the Act requires that each spouse is to furnish to the other spouse or to persons acting on behalf of dependant family members, such full particulars of their property and income, as may reasonably be required for the purposes of the proceedings. These particulars are set out in the affidavit of means, sworn and filed by each party pursuant to the Rules of the Circuit Court 1950 (S.I. No. 179 of 1950) as amended by the Circuit Court Rules (No. 1) of 1997 (S.I. No. 84 of 1997) and the Rules of the Superior Courts (No. 1) of 1990 (S.I. No. 97 of 1990), as amended by the Rules of the Superior Courts (No. 3) of 1997 (S.I. No. 343 of 1997), set out at Appendix A and B.

In circumstances where one of the parties fails to comply with the provisions of section 38(6), the court may by section 38(7) make an order directing such compliance. Any further information required to vouch or verify the details contained in the affidavit of means may be sought by way of discovery and if necessary, orders for third party discovery may be obtained. The issue arose in the Circuit Court case of *J.L. v. J.L.* [1996] 1 F.L.R. 147 and [1996] 1 F.L.J. 36 before McGuiness J., as she then was. The court confirmed that a clear and comprehensive framework of financial information should be contained in the affidavit of means sworn by each spouse. She stated that where an affidavit of means was not so filed that the Circuit Court would not grant orders for discovery "except for the most exceptional reasons", stating that it should not be the business of the trial judge to sift through large quantities of discovery documentation to try and ascertain basic information. McGuinness J. was clear that there should be a clear and systematic picture of the present financial position of each party, which was not so in the particular case.

The factors applicable to the making of orders under the Family Law (Maintenance of Spouses and Children) Act 1976 are clearly applicable to applications for ancillary reliefs under the 1996 Act with the additional element of the spouses anticipated earning capacity, property and other financial resources in the financial future. Thus the court is entitled to take into account evidence that one or other of the spouses may be about to make financial gains by way of inheritance, sale of stocks or shares, job promotion or otherwise. The court will also take into account the income generating potential of assets not heretofore used to yield cash, such as livestock, monies on deposit etc. and orders may be made where there is no actual income.

If either spouse's response is unforthcoming or economic regarding their financial position, additional evidence may be required by way of third party discovery or a bankers' books evidence order or by way simply of serving a notice to cross-examine a witness, or a witness summons or otherwise. Finally, the court must address its mind to the income and earning potential that either of the spouses might have in the foreseeable future and must assess the likelihood of the spouse's present job situation continuing into the future. For example, the court must also decide whether, an illness on the part of one of the spouses will render him or her unable to work in full-time employment in the future.

In *C.N. v. R.N.* (No. 2) 1996 I.F.L.R. 1, in the Circuit Court, McGuinness J. has held it to be "more appropriate to fix a level of maintenance in accordance with present circumstances, because of the difficulty of trying to take into account of what may happen in the future". It has also been held by the Supreme Court that where a husband is financially capable of making proper provision for the children, a wife should not be obliged to work outside the home to the detriment of the welfare of the children. This objective is clearly supported by Article 41 of the Constitution. However, this does not mean that if necessary, the court will not take into account the wife's earning capacity, if the family circumstances require it. In general, it is accepted and has been acknowledged by the courts that after the breakdown of a marriage, most families suffer a deterioration in their day-to-day financial circumstance and for this reason it is one of the most contentious and hard-fought ancillary relief applications. Section 20(2)(b) requires the court to examine the financial needs, obligations and responsibilities of each spouse.

Details as to these obligations are furnished in detail by way of the affidavits of means and welfare, which are sworn by each of the parties, where appropriate, and placed before the court. The court will take into account not only items of weekly expenditure, but also monies required to fund items of expenditure which arise on an irregular basis, for example car insurance, a holiday or new school uniforms and books. In most cases, especially where the families income is moderate or low, the issue to be determined is what periodical payment or lump sum is required to meet the basic needs of the dependant spouse and dependent family members. Clearly in cases of better financial security the court has a wider discretion based on the facts before it. As Shatter, *Family Law* (4th ed., 1997), pp. 929–951 has remarked, "this is a particularly subjective judicial exercise the outcome of which is exceedingly difficult to predict in advance of any Court hearing".

In circumstances where there is no likelihood of remarriage by either of the spouses or no evidence of such likelihood before the courts, the court must take into account items of expenditure not presently arising, but likely to do so in the future. Examples include the making of provision for university expenses or the requirement for the purchase of a new car for the dependent family members. If an applicant for ancillary relief wishes to assert that there is a likelihood of remarriage by either of the spouses, then firm evidence of that fact must be before the court. This provision first appeared in section 16 (2) of the 1995 Act.

The likelihood of remarriage must not distract the court from deciding what ancillary relief should be made available to make proper provision for the first spouse and first family, where the constitutional obligation set out in Article 41 is to ensure such proper provision "exists or will be made". If proper provision has not been previously made, it must be made by the court on granting the decree, so that a situation cannot arise whereby the decree of divorce is granted and ancillary orders made sometime in the future thus allowing a spouse against whom ancillary orders might be made to remarry in between the decree and ancillary reliefs.

Where evidence of a likely remarriage is before the court, the first spouse could ask the court for ancillary relief by way of, *e.g.* a lump sum order in addition to or instead of periodical payment orders, or a property adjustment order transferring the entire interest of the family home or other property to the first spouse. These types of order will not be affected by the remarriage. Whereas many involving an ongoing obligation will cease on the remarriage of the recipient.

As already stated, it is common place that in a significant number of cases all parties to a marital breakdown will suffer a deterioration in the standard of living enjoyed by them, before the breakdown took place. Therefore most cases coming before the courts require orders which are financially practical and which provide for the basic living needs of the parties. Frequently, clients need to be reminded of these harsh realities and it is really only in cases where there is a high income available to the parties that the courts can reasonably allow both parties and the children to retain their previous lifestyles.

The age of each of the spouses, the duration of their marriage and length of time during which they lived with one another are also significant factors to be considered. The age of the spouses informs the court of various factors, including the possible duration of any ancillary orders the court might make. Young spouses will be able to work for longer and possibly will adapt more easily to being separated than will be the case with older spouses. An older wife, for example, who has never worked outside the home might find it more difficult than her husband, who has worked throughout the marriage to obtain gainful employment and might not be in a position to take out a mortgage for a new home. The economic realities of potential employment opportunities are regularly taken into account by the court. The duration of the marriage influences the court in a similar fashion, for example, a marriage of very short duration might indicate to the courts that the parties might very quickly return to the lives they led before the marriage breakdown and clearly the length they lived together prior to and after the remarriage could also be of relevance. The longer the duration of the relationship, the more onerous the financial duties and obligations arising thereafter.

Clearly extra provision would probably be required in the case of a spouse suffering from any illness or disability requiring extra facilities, ongoing medical assistance or practical considerations, such as the provision of specially adapted accommodation or transport. The court will also take into account the vulnerability of a spouse suffering from a mental disability or illness, who might require special care. It is likely that the non-disabled spouse will probably have to bear the greater burden of the drop in living standards, usually brought about by the separation, in an effort to make proper or additional provision for the disabled spouse. In addition, if it is considered that one of the spouses is unable to take adequate care of their own affairs due to disability, it would be open to the court to impose conditions on the ancillary orders to reflect this state.

The provisions of section 20(20(f) initially appeared in section 20(2)(f) of the Judicial Separation and Family Law Reform Act 1989 and were re-enacted and incorporated into the Family Law Act 1995 and the Family Law (Divorce) Act 1996, allowing recognition of and valuations to be placed on the various types of contributions which can be made by both spouses during the marriage. It is an important provision, specifying as it does financial and non-financial contributions and allowing, most importantly, for non-financial contributions to be quantified in a manner which ultimately assists the spouse, not in a position of financial or economic strength, to have influence in the making of financial ancillary orders by the court. This position, as introduced by section 20(2)(f) of the 1989 Act, changed the fact that prior to this time, no account was taken by the court of contributions made by a spouse who cared for the family and the home, in granting to such a spouse any share in the beneficial ownership of the family home. This has been confirmed in *L. v. L.* [1996] 2 I.R. 77 where the Supreme Court held that a beneficial entitlement to matrimonial assets and in particular the family home could not be derived from Article 41 of the Constitution.

Reference is also made in section 20(2)(f) to any contribution made by a spouse to "the income, earning capacity, property and financial resources of the other spouses". An example of this would be where a spouse works to support the family while the other spouse studies to improve their career prospects. This provision allows the court to compensate a spouse for the effect their marital duties in the past and into the future have had on their earning capacity. In particular where such capacity has been diminished because they had to give up or forego the possibility of financially rewarding work to look after the home or family. This subsection would only apply to situations where the marital assets are sufficient to allow for such a compensatory measure over and above that required to make proper provision for the spouse and other dependant family members.

An amendment was proposed in the Seanad in relation to section 20(2)(f), to the effect that contributions of the respective spouses in the form of looking after any dependent parent, should be taken into account (149 *Seanad Debates* Col. 26). Rejecting this proposal, Minister Taylor indicated that he believed the provisions of section 20(2)(b), with its reference to "the financial needs, obligations and responsibilities which each of the spouses has or is likely to have in the foreseeable future" might be wide enough to extend past legal obligations, to include moral obligations. He stated:

> "In this context, though, a moral obligation and the voluntary assumption of a responsibility, provided it is reasonable, may be as relevant as a legal obligation."

While acknowledging that a court would not be obliged to accept this interpretation, the Minister continued:

"... my information and advice is that it enables it to do so in appropriate case if it is so minded." (149 *Seanad Debates* Col. 27)

While this interpretation is in some instances desirable, it is submitted that, save in exceptional circumstances, the court should only take legal obligations into consideration. To permit an interpretation of section 20(2)(b), which takes moral obligations into account, could mandate a court to take into account educational expenses of non-dependent children irrespective of age, particularly where the course of the study concerned commenced prior to dependency ceasing and also to take into account the income and expenditure of third parties with whom one of the spouses has commenced a new relationship. Arguably, a moral obligation would arise in relation to a long-term partner who does not work outside the family home, but rather is a full-time homemaker and mother.

Clearly, there is no legal obligation in relation to these categories of people, in the same way that there is no legal obligation to a dependent parent of either of the spouses. To attempt to extend the scope of relevant obligations in this manner would yield unpredictable and unwieldy results. Exceptional circumstances might include circumstances in which proper provision may be made for the family, while at the same time taking the moral obligation into account or where arguments based on estoppel, acquiescence and general equitable principles might arise.

In section 20(2), "income" refers to monies from all sources, such as employment, interest from deposits, rental income, income from the sale of any assets, gifts or inheritances from any sources, and references to benefits refers to any social welfare benefits received by either spouse, including child benefit. In cases where the sole family income consists of social welfare payments or in circumstances where it has been clearly demonstrated to the court that if a periodical payment order is made, it will not be paid, whether because of the paying party's lack of financial means or otherwise, then the court will be entitled to make either a nil periodical payment order or a very low order, thus preserving the regular social welfare payment entitlements of the receiving spouse.

Such action will have to be balanced with the legal obligations of the paying spouse to support his family and the desirability of not depriving the other spouse and dependant family members of State benefits; including medical cards, rent or mortgage allowance. A practical approach is usually adopted by the courts in these circumstances, foreseeing repeated applications for enforcement of maintenance payments and repeated applications for attachment and committal orders, which are ultimately not of any great practical assistance to the spouse awaiting monies for every day needs.

"Benefits" as referred to in section 20(2)(h), also refers to a share to which a spouse is entitled by way of legal right or intestacy on the death of the other spouse, and in making orders under section 15(A) of the 1995 Act, as inserted by section 52(g) of the 1996 Act, or under section 18 of the 1996 Act, the court will take into account the mandate of section 20(2)(h) of the 1996 Act.

Conduct plays no part in the granting a decree of divorce under section 5(1) of the 1996 Act, but it rather is one of 12 criteria which may be considered when making orders for ancillary relief. Conduct refers to all aspects of the behaviour of both spouses during the marriage both *inter se* and in relation to other members of the family unit. Typically relevant types of conduct include adultery, desertion and domestic violence. The role played by conduct in Irish matrimonial law has steadily declined.

Pursuant to section 5(3) of the Family Law (Maintenance of Spouses and Children) Act 1976, adultery was a discretionary bar to the obtaining of a maintenance order. This specific reference disappeared from the Judicial Separation and Family Law Act 1989 which included adultery by way of "referral to conduct", which is carried through to the 1996 Act, thus ensuring adultery is only one of a number of matters to be taken into account. Section 5(2) of the 1976 Act specifically provided that no maintenance order would be made by the court in circumstances where there had been desertion. This position was changed by section 38(2) of the Judicial Separation and Family Law Reform Act 1989 and section 16(3) of the Family Law Act 1995. This section rendered desertion a bar to maintenance in circumstances where:

"... the spouse had deserted the other spouse before the institution of proceedings for a Decree and had continued such desertion up to the time of the institution of such proceedings unless having regard to all the circumstances of the case (including the conduct of the other spouse) the Court is of the opinion that it would be unjust not to make the Order".

There is no specific reference to desertion in the 1996 Act, which deals with it under the umbrella heading of conduct. This distinction provoked certain Dáil deputies, during the course of the Oireachtas debates on the 1996 Act, to allege an element of discrimination between spouses applying for judicial separation and those applying for divorce. The absence of an equivalent to section 16(3)(a) was adverted to by Deputy Keogh:

"The effect of this distinction is that a deserting spouse will be treated more favourably in divorce proceedings." (467 *Dáil Debates* Col. 1793)

and by Deputy O'Donnell before the Select Committee on Legislation and Security (July 17, 1996, L6 No. 12, Col. 661). The Minister, in response, adverted to the fact that desertion is a specific ground for judicial separation under the 1989 Act and referring to section 16(3)(a) of the Family Law Act 1995 stated:

"That prohibition in separation proceedings on making financial and property orders in favour of a deserting spouse prevents a deserting spouse from benefiting from his or her desertion." (Select Committee on Legislation and Security, Col. 663)

The Minister went on to make reference to the fact that, in any event, section 16(3)(a) is not absolute in its terms.

It is arguable that the fault lies with the 1995 Act inclusion, rather than with the exclusion in the 1996 Act. The entire focus and ethos of the 1996 Act is aimed at reducing the relevance of fault. Fault is irrelevant for the granting of the decree, provided the objective criteria set out in section 5 are satisfied, the court does not have to inquire into conduct or to apportion blame. Deputy Gallagher stated:

"We are not introducing a fault based system but a system of divorce which is based on the fact that the marriage has been over, and irreconcilably so, for several years. Many people were concerned that some aspects of the behaviour of either spouse should be taken into account by the court in deciding on matters before it, in particular in relation to settlements. I am happy that those criteria have been spelt out by the Minister." (467 *Dáil Debates* Col. 1802)

While individual views may vary as to whether the attribution of fault has a role in matrimonial proceedings, the 1996 Act denies it such a central role, as did the constitutional amendment which was approved by the People. Commenting upon the no-fault basis of the divorce legislation introduced, Senator Norris stated:

". . . there is something miserable and begrudging about only allowing people to separate when at least one of the parties can be humiliated and determined to be the culprit. . . . No possibility of human healing is encouraged by trying to hang blame around the neck of one party or another". (148 *Seanad Debates* Col. 1680)

This should significantly lessen the relevance of evidence of conduct in divorce proceedings. In certain instances, it is vital in order to properly protect the spouses and/or the dependent children in terms of the required ancillary reliefs that conduct is examined. Deputy Gallagher continued:

"While the conduct of spouses is implicitly taken into account by courts in judicial separation cases, it is important that the legislation is explicit in this regard. The Minister recognised that people wanted this provision included in the legislation." (467 *Dáil Debates* Col. 1802)

Section 20(2)(i) provides that conduct may be a relevant factor, as did the equivalent provision, section 16(2)(i)) of the Family Law Act 1995. Desertion is obviously encompassed within the term "conduct" and therefore any specific reference to it would be to place an undue emphasis on a particular type of conduct, while not specifically referring to other types of conduct which are equally, or more reprehensible, *e.g.* domestic violence, which would be considered under the general "conduct" heading. Therefore, it is submitted that the provisions of section 20 of the 1996 Act deal with the issue of conduct in a more even-handed fashion.

Shatter, *Family Law* (4th ed., 1997), p. 947, echoing the views expressed by Deputy Keogh, has commented that it is anomalous that a spouse in desertion is more at risk of being deprived of ancillary relief for support purposes in judicial separation proceedings than in divorce proceedings. In addition, desertion is treated as being a more serious form of matrimonial conduct in separation proceedings than various other forms of unreasonable or disapproved behaviour, including physical assault and adultery. A great deal of court time can be saved by informing clients before the hearing of the matter, that the case will not be an opportunity for them to air all the grievances of the marriage. This is not to say however that conduct will not be taken into account by the court. The court will most likely have regard to conduct that indicates or predicts a certain type of attitude or code of behaviour is likely to be manifested in the future and the impact which such a course of action would have upon the other members of the family. Clearly, addictive problems such as gambling, alcoholism etc. may have a bearing upon future finances. Previous violent behaviour may dictate that domestic violence protection orders are required.

It is central to the duty of the court pursuant to the provisions of section 15(2), in making proper provision to ensure that where possible, proper and secure accommodation is provided for a spouse who is wholly or mainly dependant on the other spouse and for any dependant children. Section 20(2)(j) also emphasises the importance of examining the accommodation needs of all the parties. In proceedings for divorce, the spouses will not have been living for four out of the previous five years and will not be residing together in the future. Section 14 allows for the making of property adjustment orders and section 15 provides for the making of exclusion orders in respect of the family home and for orders for sale, subject to conditions. Section 20(2)(j) refers only to the accommodation needs of either spouse. The needs of dependant family members are specifically referred to at section 20(4)(g). The mechanism for the court to deal with the accommodation needs of the spouses is provided in sections 14 and 15.

Clearly, where the financial state of the parties does not allow for the purchase of two new homes, the court will endeavour to ensure that the spouse with primary care and control of the children has secure accommodation, but to the exclusion of the other spouse. The other spouse must also be accommodated in reasonable surroundings. Efforts to meet the needs of both spouses have led to court imposed arrangements, not always of a practical nature, and efforts should be made by practitioners to negotiate post-divorce living arrangements as equitably as possible before the hearing.

As the status of spouse is lost on the grant of a decree of divorce, the divorced party may also be denied certain benefits, *e.g.* a specifically stated benefit under a pension scheme, or the right to a legal right share, or a share in the other spouses estate on intestacy. Section 20(2)(k) recognises this. Despite the existence of section 18(1), applications thereunder may not be successful or indeed the other spouse may seek a blocking order, under section 18(10), which the court may grant. A similar provision first appeared at section 16(2)(k) of the 1995 Act, but it is primarily relevant to applicants for divorce. The court, pursuant to this subsection, may take into account the value to an applicant spouse of the benefit which they were to obtain in the future and adjust the value of any ancillary order accordingly.

The terms of section 20(2)(l) first appeared at section 16(2)(l) of the 1995 Act and was presumably relevant there to persons who had remarried having obtained foreign or State recognised divorces, having previously obtained judicial separation relief in Ireland. The provisions in the context of judicial separation was however somewhat prior to the incorporation of this subsection in the 1995 Act, any earnings or financial needs of new partners were not taken into account by the court (*O'K. v. O'K.*, unreported, High Court, November 16, 1982). It is to be assumed that the "rights" referred to in section 20(2)(l) are legal rights and that responsibilities towards illegitimate children would have to be taken into account under the section. The rights of creditors, judgment mortgagees or any party with a life interest or other interest in the family home would also be relevant. Section 19(5) gives to any such person the opportunity to make representations to the court when it is considering whether to make orders under sections 14, 15(1)(a) and 19. Clearly after the coming into operation of the 1996 Act there will be many more second marriages and the financial cost of sustaining such unions is a criteria to which the court shall have regard. It is possible therefore that the financial resources available to the first family will now have to sustain three separate households. However, at the time of application for a decree of divorce and ancillary orders, neither of the spouses can have remarried and therefore this subsection will have more relevance to applications for variation of ancillary orders which are made after the decree has been granted.

The factors set out in section 20(4) are the criteria to be taken into account by the courts in assessing amounts payable in respect of dependants and are largely the same as those set out in section 20(2), with a reference in section 20(4)(e) to the education and training needs of the dependant members. Specifically the issue of conduct is precluded by section 23 of the Act, from being considered by the court in assessing the needs of a dependant family member, thus continuing the principle that paramountcy of welfare of the child should be the foremost priority of the court. Practitioners should prepare detailed analyses of the financial needs of each dependant member in addition to the expenditure required for the every day running of the home, in which the dependant members reside.

Section 20(3) directs the court to have regard to the terms of any separation agreement entered into by the spouses and which is still operative. The existence of such an agreement does not preclude the court from making ancillary orders, as the court must ensure that orders for proper provision for the spouses and dependant family members are made. No reference is made to orders for judicial separation, but as with separation agreements clearly these might have an influence on the court in deciding what orders to make. If separation agreements are out of date they could be regarded as not being in force and so new ancillary orders may be required.

Section 20(4)(b) which refers to the dependant members financial resources would be particularly relevant where a child is over 18 years and in full time education and possibly working in a part-time job. Section 20(4)(e) refers the court to the educational needs of the dependant family member, which will hopefully continue as before the divorce proceedings within the confines of financial reality.

In addition, section 20(3) makes specific reference, in mandatory terms to the court having regard to the terms of any separation agreement which has been entered into between the parties which is still in force. Bringing the Family Law (Divorce) Bill 1996 to the Seanad, the Minister specifically addressed the issue of the status of separation agreements in the divorce context:

> "All existing separation deeds will stand unless they are altered by the court in the course of the divorce proceedings. One cannot provide that a separation agreement must, inevitably, stand in a divorce context which brings about a quite different legal position and result. After a separation procedure the parties are still married to each other and certain legal consequences continue to apply. After a divorce procedure the position is different. In the overwhelming majority of cases the arrangements made for a separation agreement would stand in the event of a divorce. However, there may be cases where different considerations would pertain at a later date, circumstances having changed and having regard to the fact that a new, different legal position was about to be created as a result of the divorce which would necessitate a variation in that procedure in the interests of one spouse. That possibility is provided for but this is done in a negative format in the Bill. It will stand unless the court sees a necessity for a variation." (148 *Seanad Debates* Cols. 1689–1690).

The lack of reference to separation agreement terms in a judicial separation context may be explained in the light of the granting of the decree of judicial separation being dependent upon there not having been a previous agreement to separate entered into between the parties. The Supreme Court so held in *O'D. v. O'D.*, unreported, December 12, 1997. However, in certain instances parties might have entered into agreements, not including a separation agreement, with a view to regulating their affairs in the context of difficulties in their marital relationship. It is submitted that these agreements should be considered by the court in determining ancillary reliefs and, presumably, would be taken into account in the context of the entitlement of the court to have regard to all of the circumstances and not being limited to a consideration of the listed matters in section 20 of the 1996 Act and section 16 of the 1995 Act.

Doubts remain as to the legal status of pre-nuptial agreements (O'Riordan, "Pre-Nuptial Contracts" (1997) *Bar Review* 193) and as to the extent to which the terms of such agreements should be taken into account in the context of divorce. Such agreements do not come within the specific ambit of section 20(3). The legal authorities are clear that although purporting to provide for the terms of a future separation, such agreements are not separation agreements; the latter being agreements entered into contemporaneous with and in the context of an actual separation. Arguably, such agreements would be a factor to be taken into account in the same way as the surrounding circumstances should be so taken account of. The list of considerations in section 20(2) is expressed to be "without prejudice to the generality of subsection (1)" and subsection (1) permits the court to have "regard to the circumstances", but it is submitted that the weight to be given to pre-nuptial agreements should be quite limited, partially dependent upon the length of time the marriage has lasted.

There was disagreement between Dáil deputies as to the desirability of such agreements. Deputy Keogh (467 *Dáil Debates* Col. 1790–1791) favoured such agreements as being concluded between the parties "in a much more reasonable atmosphere", with Deputy O'Dea (467 *Dáil Debates* Col. 1810) seeing such agreements as belonging to the purview of the rich, who had property to protect/divide resulting in the poor being left to have resort to litigation. While the requests made; that the legal status of such agreements be clarified, are laudable it is submitted that the real difficulties in attaching any significant weight to pre-nuptial agreements are not those referred to above, but rather that such agreements may be completely out of date by the date of separation. Furthermore, rather than being a suitable time to reach agreement as to future property distribution, the period of starry-eyed romance which normally precedes a marriage is a most inopportune time for such decision making.

Retrospective periodical payments orders

21.—(1) Where, having regard to all the circumstances of the case, the court considers it appropriate to do so, it may, in a periodical payments order, direct that—

    (a) the period in respect of which payments under the order shall be made shall begin on such date before the date of the order, not being earlier than the time of the institution of the proceedings concerned for the grant of a decree of divorce, as may be specified in the order,

    (b) any payments under the order in respect of a period before the date of the order be paid in one sum and before a specified date, and

    (c) there be deducted from any payments referred to in paragraph (b) made to the spouse concerned an amount equal to the amount of such (if any) payments made to that spouse by the other spouse as the court may determine, being payments made during the period between the making of the order for the grant of the decree aforesaid and the institution of the proceedings aforesaid.

(2) The jurisdiction conferred on the court by subsection (1)(b) is without prejudice to the generality of section 13(1)(c).

General Note

This section, identical to section 17 of the Family Law Act 1995, permits the making of backdated maintenance orders, retrospective only to the date of the institution of the proceedings. Section 21(1)(b) allows the court to direct that any arrears so arising are to be paid by way of one lump sum payment and within a specified time limit, thus awarding to an applicant spouse the possibility of an additional lump sum to that already made under section 13, but referable solely to maintenance back payments. Section 21(1)(c) permits any monies paid by a spouse by way of maintenance, and not by way of court order since the institution of proceedings, to be deducted from the payment under section 17(1)(b). Section 17(2) makes clear that such orders if made, do not encroach on the courts right to make orders under section 13(1)(c), *i.e.* lump sum orders.

The provisions of section 21 should be considered in the light of the retrospection now possible in relation to an interim maintenance pending suit under section 12. If interim retrospection is obtained, it is unlikely that further provision under section 21 will be made. The benefit of retrospection is that the payments become payable under a court order and therefore have the benefit of the enforcement mechanisms available to such orders. Defaults in agreed maintenance are usually only recoverable by specific performance proceedings. A retrospective order to cover the default period would greatly extend the range of enforcement techniques.

Variation, etc., of certain orders under this Part

22.—(1) This section applies to the following orders:
- (a) a maintenance pending suit order,
- (b) a periodical payments order,
- (c) a secured periodical payments order,
- (d) a lump sum order if and in so far as it provides for the payment of the lump sum concerned by instalments or requires the payment of any such instalments to be secured,
- (e) an order under paragraph (b), (c) or (d) of section 14(1) in so far as such application is not restricted or excluded pursuant to section 14(2),
- (f) an order under subparagraph (i) or (ii) of section 15(1)(a),
- (g) a financial compensation order,
- (h) an order under section 17(2) insofar as such application is not restricted or excluded pursuant to section 17(26),
- (i) an order under this section.

(2) Subject to the provisions of this section and section 20 and to any restriction or exclusion pursuant to section 14(2) or 17(26) and without prejudice to section 16(2)(d), the court may, on application to it in that behalf—
- (a) by either of the spouses concerned,
- (b) in the case of the death of either of the spouses, by any other person who has, in the opinion of the court, a sufficient interest in the matter or by a person on behalf of a dependent member of the family concerned, or
- (c) in the case of the remarriage of either of the spouses, by his or her spouse,

if it considers it proper to do so having regard to any change in the circumstances of the case and to any new evidence, by order vary or discharge an order to which this section applies, suspend any provision of such an order or any provision of such an order temporarily, revive the operation of such an order or provision so suspended, further vary an order previously varied under this section or further suspend or revive the operation of an order or provision previously suspended or revived under this section; and, without prejudice to the generality of the foregoing, an order under this section may require the divesting of any property vested in a person under or by virtue of an order to which this section applies.

(3) Without prejudice to the generality of section 12 or 13, that part of an order to which this section applies which provides for the making of payments for the support of a dependent member of the family shall stand discharged if the member ceases to be a dependent member of the family by reason of his or her attainment of the age of 18 years or 23 years, as may be appropriate, and shall be discharged by the court, on application to it under subsection (2), if it is satisfied that the member has for any reason ceased to be a dependent member of the family.

(4) The power of the court under subsection (2) to make an order varying, discharging or suspending an order referred to in subsection (1)(e) shall be subject to any restriction or exclusion specified in that order and shall (subject to the limitation aforesaid) be a power—

(a) to vary the settlement to which the order relates in any person's favour or to extinguish or reduce any person's interest under that settlement, and

(b) to make such supplemental provision (including a further property adjustment order or a lump sum order) as the court thinks appropriate in consequence of any variation, extinguishment or reduction made pursuant to paragraph (a), and section 19 shall apply to a case where the court makes such an order as aforesaid under subsection (2) as it applies to a case where the court makes a property adjustment order with any necessary modifications.

(5) The court shall not make an order under subsection (2) in relation to an order referred to in subsection (1)(e) unless it appears to it that the order will not prejudice the interests of any person who—

(a) has acquired any right or interest in consequence of the order referred to in subsection (1)(e), and

(b) is not a party to the marriage concerned or a dependent member of the family concerned.

(6) This section shall apply, with any necessary modifications, to instruments executed pursuant to orders to which this section applies as it applies to those orders.

(7) Where the court makes an order under subsection (2) in relation to a property adjustment order relating to land, a copy of the order under subsection (2) certified to be a true copy by the registrar or clerk of the court concerned shall, as appropriate, be lodged by him or her in the Land Registry for registration pursuant to section 69(1)(h) of the Registration of Title Act, 1964, in a register maintained under that Act or be registered in the Registry of Deeds.

GENERAL NOTE

Section 22(1) sets out all orders, which may be varied by the court on application to it. The range of variable orders is extremely wide, once again illustrating the lack of a clean break theory in Irish divorce law. It should be noted that the reference to lump sum payments which may only be varied insofar as they have been directed to be paid by way of instalment. The variation operates *de futuro* and not in relation to accrued obligations and can be made by way of discharge, suspension, revision or revival of orders previously made. Section 22 mirrors section 18 of the Family Law Act 1995, and section 22 of the Judicial Separation and Family Law Reform Act 1989. The reference in section 22(1)(i) to orders made pursuant to section 22, allows for the making of repeated applications for variation of orders previously made.

Section 26 of the 1996 Act allows the court to specify that orders already in existence and made pursuant to the Acts of 1976, 1989 and 1995 be discharged, and if not so specifically discharged, such orders remain in force. In which instance the provisions of section 22 in relation to variation of orders apply.

Section 22(2) directs that an application may be made by either of the spouses, by any person who has a sufficient interest in the matter, or by a person on behalf of a dependant family member in the event of the death of either of the spouses, and by a new spouse, in the event of either of the spouses having remarried. The fact that a new spouse can make an application pursuant to this section brings about an unsatisfactory situation whereby an application for any sort of variation may be made even though that person was not a party to the proceedings to begin with. Obviously both spouses would require an opportunity to make representations, albeit that the application has been brought by a third party. Such third party application might arise in the context of the breakdown of a second or subsequent marriage.

The provisions of section 22(2) incorporate the criteria for variation and discharge of maintenance orders previously specified in the Family Law (Maintenance of Spouses and Children) Act 1976. Any change of circumstances or any new evidence should be placed before the court in support of an application for variation. Section 22(3) specifies the automatic discharge of maintenance pending suit orders, periodical payments orders, or lump sum orders which have previously been made for the support of a dependant member of the family, who has crossed the age thresholds of 18 or 23 years, as appropriate. An application may be made to the court to have such an order discharged, in the event that a dependant member has ceased for any other reason to be so dependant, *e.g.* has ceased to be in full-time education.

Section 22(4) sets out the effect which any variation order made under section 22 shall have. Any limitations, restrictions or exclusions specified in orders previously made, now the subject of a variation order shall continue. The operative part of this section, directs that a court shall have the power to vary any settlement already made, to extinguish or reduce any persons interest under that settlement, to make additional provision by way of property adjustment order or lump sum order as may be appropriate in the light of any change of circumstances brought about by such variation, extinguishment or reduction. In circumstances therefore where a court has made such a variation, orders for sale of property may be made pursuant to section 19, in respect of the new varied order.

Section 22(5) places a restriction on the power of the court to vary property adjustment orders previously made. The court must be satisfied that in making any order to vary such a property adjustment order, that such an order will not prejudice the interest of any person who has acquired a right or interest in property, as a consequence of the property adjustment order previously made, and who is not a party to the marriage or a dependant member concerned. Section 14(2) of the 1996 Act cross-references the power to exclude the application of section 22 to such orders. Thus in seeking a variation of a property adjustment order it would have to be demonstrated to the courts that the reversal of such a property adjustment order would not effect the rights of any party not a party to the marital breakdown proceedings in the first instance. It is hard to see how this situation could be brought about other than by way of agreement between the parties.

Section 22(6) directs that the power to vary orders will apply as appropriate to instruments which have been executed pursuant to orders previously granted. Section 22(7) directs that where a variation order has been made in relation to a property adjustment order relating to land, that a copy of the variation order is to be lodged with the Land Registry for registration or in the Registry of Deeds as appropriate.

The statute provides for certain limitations on the right to apply for a variation under section 22. An order made by the court pursuant to section 14(1)(b) to (d) cannot be varied if the provisions of section 14(2) have been revoked, and accordingly practitioners should be careful where obtaining property adjustment orders and requiring them to be final, to obtain a specific order pursuant to section 14 (2), which restricts the application of section 22 to certain property transfer orders. This should ensure that a property transfer order made and properly limited will remain final.

Any orders made pursuant to section 17 for a pension adjustment order may also be restricted, under section 17(2)(b) insofar as the application of section 22 is excluded. Specific orders should be sought by the court in those terms.

Similar blocking provisions exist relating to section 18. Section 18(10) allows the court to make an order precluding an application for provision from the estate of a deceased spouse. Every other order may be the subject matter of a review by the court who will also take into account all the criteria set out in section 20 of the 1996 Act in addition to the change of circumstances.

Restriction in relation to orders for benefit of dependent members of family

23.—In deciding whether—

  (a) to include in an order under section 12 a provision requiring the making of periodical payments for the benefit of a dependent member of the family,

  (b) to make an order under paragraph (a)(ii), (b)(ii) or (c)(ii) of section 13(1),

  (c) to make an order under section 22 varying, discharging or suspending a provision referred to in paragraph (a) or an order referred to in paragraph (b),

the court shall not have regard to conduct by the spouse or spouses concerned of the kind specified in subsection (2)(i) of section 20.

GENERAL NOTE

Section 20 of the 1996 Act sets out the specific matters to which the court shall have regard in deciding whether to make or vary an order for ancillary relief, section 20(4) sets out such criteria in respect of dependent family members. Section 20(2)(i) provides that the conduct of either spouse is to be taken account by the court if it considered that to do otherwise would be "unjust." Section 20(4) does not refer to such a factor. The legislature considered however the need of a dependant family member should be assessed without the court being influenced by the behaviour of the spouse. Section 23 states that spousal conduct is to be disregarded by the court when deciding whether to make for the benefit of a dependant family member, an order for maintenance pending suit, for periodical payments, a lump sum order or an order pursuant to section 22 varying any such orders previously made. Accordingly, behaviour which might otherwise influence the court in deciding whether to make an ancillary order in favour of a spouse will not be taken into account where the order is to be made for the maintenance of a dependant family member.

Method of making payments under certain orders

24.—(1) The court may by order provide that a payment under an order to which this section applies shall be made by such method as is specified in the order and be subject to such terms and conditions as it considers appropriate and so specifies.

  (2) This section applies to an order under—

  (a) section 11(2)(b) of the Act of 1964,

  (b) section 5, 5A or 7 of the Act of 1976,

  (c) section 7, 8 or 24 of the Act of 1995, and

  (d) section 12, 13, 19 or 22.

Orders made by the court providing for maintenance under the 1996 Act, the Family Law Act 1995, the Family Law (Maintenance of Spouses and Children) Act 1976 and the Guardianship of Infants Act 1964 may have conditions attached to them by the court directing not only the method of payment, but also any other terms and conditions which have been set out in the order. For example, the court could direct that a periodical payments order under section 13(1)(a) of the 1996 Act would be effected through the local District Court clerk or by way of standing order into the recipient's bank account.

As well as terms directing the method of payment, the court may impose other conditions which must be complied with by the parties. For example, the court could direct that a periodical payment order be made specifically for the purpose of reducing a debt incurred during the course of the marriage. The court could also direct that the maintenance debtor be furnished with copy bank statements in respect of the relevant bank account. Any reasonable terms and conditions may be proposed by the parties to the court which can decide whether or not to impose same. Terms and conditions may now be imposed on orders made under the 1964 and 1976 Acts and not only in orders made on judicial separation or divorce. A similar provision is set out at section 19 of the 1995 Family Law Act.

Stay on certain orders the subject of appeal

25.—Where an appeal is brought from an order under—

  (a) section 11(2)(b) of the Act of 1964,

  (b) section 5, 5A or 7 of the Act of 1976,

  (c) section 7, paragraph (a) or (b) of section 8(1) or section 24 of the Act of 1995, or

  (d) section 12, paragraph (a) or (b) of section 13(1) or paragraph (a), (b) or (c) of section 22(1),

the operation of the order shall not be stayed unless the court that made the order or to which the appeal is brought directs otherwise.

GENERAL NOTE

Usually in family law proceedings, orders made in the District Court which are then appealed to the Circuit Court, are stayed by virtue of that appeal, provided that a recognisance where required is entered into. Section 25 specifies that in certain circumstances, orders made which are then appealed will not be stayed by virtue of the appeal, unless the court which made the original order, or the court to which the appeal is being brought, directs otherwise. The District Court has jurisdiction in respect of section 25(a) and (b).

The orders specified in section 25(a) to (d) are orders made pursuant section 11(2)(b) of the Guardiansip of Infants Act 1964 or any maintenance order made under the Family Law Act 1976 or any order for maintenance pending suit or periodical payments order made under either the 1995 Act or the 1996 Act. Orders made under these sections will not be stayed unless the court directs otherwise. They will, therefore, become immediately operative unless a successful application for a stay pending appeal is made. At High Court and Circuit Court levels, this does not represent a change in the law as stays have only been available on application and will not arise automatically. Practitioners should note that any order made under a preliminary order, made under the Domestic Violence Act 1996, will not be stayed by virtue of an appeal, nor will any order made by way of emergency care order under the Childcare Act 1991. For example, if an order is made by the court, pursuant to section 12 of the 1996 Act, granting an interim maintenance order to one spouse, and that interim order is appealed, then the order will continue to operate pending the hearing of the appeal, unless the court directs that the order shall be stayed and in such circumstances monies due may be paid to the receiving spouse by way of arrears on the determination of the appeal, if unsuccessful.

The application for a stay should be made immediately after the making of the order being appealed or as soon thereafter as possible, as the order is operative until the stay is put in place. The applicant for maintenance, even if appealing with a view to getting a high sum, will not wish to have a stay as he or she will want the payment to start as soon as possible. An application by the payor for a stay is unlikely to be successful unless the interim mode of survival is demonstrated. An interesting situation would arise in the case of an obligation to pay under an agreement where a subsequent application resulted in the maintenance payable being reduced. A stay of this order, depending on the terms of the agreement might result in the contractual obligation continuing pending the appeal.

Orders under Acts of 1976, 1989 and 1995

26.—(1) Where, while an order ("the first-mentioned order"), being—
   (a) a maintenance order, an order varying a maintenance order, or an interim order under the Act of 1976,
   (b) an order under section 14, 15, 16, 18 or 22 of the Act of 1989,
   (c) an order under section 8, 9, 10, 11, 12, 13, 14, 15 or 18 of the Act of 1995,

is in force, an application is made to the court by a spouse to whom the first-mentioned order relates for an order granting a decree of divorce or an order under this Part, the court may by order discharge the first-mentioned order as on and from such date as may be specified in the order.

(2) Where, on the grant of a decree of divorce an order specified in subsection (1) is in force, it shall, unless it is discharged by an order under subsection (1), continue in force as if it were an order made under a corresponding provision of this Act and section 22 shall apply to it accordingly.

GENERAL NOTE

Applications may come before the court in circumstances where orders have already been made by way of maintenance orders under the Family Law Act 1976, or other ancillary reliefs under the Judicial Separation and Family Law Reform Act 1989 or the Family Law Act 1995. In those circumstances, the orders may still be operative, and the court is in a position pursuant to the provisions of section 26 of the 1996 Act to direct that the orders continue in force as though they had been made under a corresponding provision in the 1996 Act. In such circumstances, it is possible to make applications to the court for variation of the orders under section 22 of the 1989 Act, notwithstanding that they were not initially made under the 1996 Act.

The court may also direct that orders made previously under a varity of matrimonial statutes, may be discharged by the court in divorce proceedings from a date specified by the court. It is unlikely however that the courts will revise arrangements previously ordered in circumstances where the financial circumstances of the family have not changed much since the order was made. The court will of course take into account the impact that the granting of a divorce might have on the financial circumstances of the family. In circumstances where ancillary reliefs are not sought under the 1996 Act, the orders made originally in previous proceedings will remain intact and in force, unless discharged under section 26(1). Matters which have been previously determined and which are *res judicata* cannot be re-opened and litigated again, *e.g.* where there was a determination as to the ownership of property under section 10(1)(b) or section 36 of the 1995 Act. In circumstances where this arises, it is always open to the applicant to seek relief under Part III of the 1996 Act and in particular a determination of property ownership under section 36 of the 1995 Act does not preclude a property adjustment order being made in relation to that property.

It should also be noted that orders made under Part II of the 1989 Act are by virtue of section 3(2)(a) of the 1995 Act treated as if made under the corresponding provisions contained in Part II of the 1995 Act. Section 26 demonstrates a consistency approach in this regard.

Section 26 deals with important transitionary arrangements which are to prevail where a decree of judicial separation and ancillary orders thereon are in being and a decree of divorce is granted. The ancillary orders in the judicial separation will continue unless discharged by the court. The Minister stated, speaking of section 26:

> "It is provided in the section that orders in relation to the separation will be continue [sic] in force unless the court orders otherwise, notwithstanding the grant of a decree of divorce." (467 *Dáil Debates* Col. 1766)

It is advisable to avoid all doubt and in particular, where the terms of the divorce are agreed between the parties, that the court would be asked to renew or confirm the orders previously made which are to continue to operate in the context of the divorce proceedings. This has the advantage of ensuring that all arrangements which are to prevail between the parties, post-divorce are incorporated in one order. Therefore it is not necessary for the parties to consider a combination of perhaps a deed of separation, ancillary orders made in the course of judicial separation proceedings and orders in divorce proceedings to establish the extent of both parties post-divorce obligations towards each other. It would appear from the section that a discharge of the previous orders should be specifically sought and obtained, if required.

Amendment of section 3 of Act of 1976

27.—Section 3(1) of the Act of 1976 is hereby amended by the insertion in the definition of "antecedent order" after paragraph (k) (inserted by the Act of 1995) of the following paragraph:

"(l) a maintenance pending suit order under the Family Law (Divorce) Act, 1996, or a periodical payments order under that Act;".

GENERAL NOTE

Section 27 amends section 3 of the Family Law (Maintenance of Spouses and Children) Act 1976. Section 3 is the interpretation clause and it is amended to include the term "antecedent order". An antecedent order is an order for maintenance made pursuant to the legislation set out in section 3(1)(a) to (i) of the 1976 Act, as amended by section 43 of the 1995 Family Law Act and section 27 of the 1996 Divorce Act.

The 1976 Act provides mechanisms to enforce payment of antecedent orders made, *e.g.* an attachment of earnings order can be made under section 10 of the 1996 Act. Section 43 of the 1995 Act added to the list of antecedent orders paragraph (j), which refers to an order for maintenance suit or a periodical payments order, under the terms of the 1989 Judicial Separation Act and paragraph (k), which refers to similar orders made under the 1995 Family Law Act. This present section extends the list to include orders under section 12 or section 13(1)(a) of the 1996 Act, so as to enable persons benefiting from such orders to avail of enforcement procedures for antecedent orders under the 1976 Act.

Transmission of periodical payments through District Court clerk

28.—Notwithstanding anything in this Act, section 9 of the Act of 1976 shall apply in relation to an order ("the relevant order"), being a maintenance pending suit order, a periodical payments order or a secured periodical payments order or any such order as aforesaid as affected by an order under section 22, with the modifications that—

(a) the reference in subsection (4) of the said section 9 to the maintenance creditor shall be construed as a reference to the person to whom payments under the relevant order concerned are required to be made,

(b) the other references in the said section 9 to the maintenance creditor shall be construed as references to the person on whose application the relevant order was made, and

(c) the reference in subsection (3) of the said section 9 to the maintenance debtor shall be construed as a reference to the person to whom payments under the relevant order are required by that order to be made,

and with any other necessary modifications.

GENERAL NOTE

Section 9 of the Family Law (Maintenance Spouses and Children) Act 1976 contains an important and widely used mechanism for providing security to a maintenance creditor by providing that maintenance payments will be received by the creditor regularly through the office of the local District Court clerk. Although section 9(1) of the 1976 Act directs that the court "shall" direct payments to be made through the District Court clerk, a practice has evolved of applicants specifying the necessity to have the order transmitted through the District Court clerk, as such method of payment is not always required.

Section 9(2) contains an important provision to assist the maintenance creditor in recovering arrears of maintenance, should they arise. The District Court clerk may, on receipt of written instructions from the maintenance creditor to do so, institute proceedings to recover those arrears, either by way of an attachment of earnings order or by seeking judgment in the amount owing to the maintenance creditor. This reduces the pressure on the maintenance creditor to institute enforcement procedures. The terms "maintenance creditor" and "maintenance debtor" employed throughout the 1976 Act are not specifically used in the 1996 Act and section 28(a) to (c) simply acknowledge that such terminology applies to persons making and receiving maintenance payments under orders made under the 1996 Act.

Application of maintenance pending suit and periodical payment orders to certain members of Defence Forces

29.—The reference in section 98(1)(h) of the Defence Act, 1954, to an order for payment of alimony shall be construed as including a reference to a maintenance pending suit order, a periodical payments order and a secured periodical payments order.

GENERAL NOTE

This section is identical to section 27 of the Judicial Separation and Family Law Reform Act 1989 and section 21 of the Family Law Act 1995. Section 98 of the Defence Act 1954 (No. 18) (the 1954 Act) provides that where an order is made pursuant to the statutes set out at section 98 (1)(a) to (h) of the Act against a serving member of the Defence Forces or a person who subsequently becomes a member of the Defence Forces, and a copy of that order is forwarded to the Minister for Defence, then a portion of that members pay shall be deducted in satisfaction of the terms of the order made. This deduction can include, if appropriate, arrears which have accrued because of the failure to discharge monies due pursuant to the order "with costs and expenses."

Section 98 (1)(h) refers to "an Order made by a Civil Court for payment of alimony." Section 29 of the 1996 Act, like section 27 of the 1989 Act and section 21 of the 1995 Act, expands the definition of "alimony" to a maintenance pending suit order, under section 12 of the 1996 Act, a periodical payments order and a secured periodical payments order under section 13 of the 1996 Act. The provisions of section 98 effectively provide for an automatic attachment of earnings order against the salary of a serving member of the Defence Forces, even if there is no evidence of default or potential default before the court.

No reference is made in section 98(1) of the 1954 Act to orders made pursuant to section 11 of the Guardianship of Infants Act 1964. However, the provisions of section 99 of the 1954 Act provide that where a member, or a person who subsequently becomes a member of the Defence Forces, deserts or leaves in "destitute circumstances," without reasonable cause, his wife or any of his legitimate children under the age of 16 years, then monies may be deducted from the pay of such member by the Minister and applied as the Minister thinks fit towards the maintenance of the wife or "legitimate children". There is a ceiling on the amount of money that can be so deducted which varies according to the rank of the member.

Amendment of Enforcement of Court Orders Act, 1940

30.—The references in subsections (1) and (7) of section 8 of the Enforcement of Court Orders Act, 1940 (as amended by section 29 of the Act of 1976 and section 22 of the Act of 1995), to an order shall be construed as including references to a maintenance pending suit order and a periodical payments order.

GENERAL NOTE

The terms of this section are identical to those of section 28 of the Judicial Separation Act 1989 and section 22 of the Family Law Act 1995, and extend the provisions of section 8 of the Enforcement of Court Orders Act 1940 (No. 23) to orders made under section 12 and parts of section 13 of the 1996 Act. Section 8 of the 1940 Act provides an enforcement mechanism in respect of certain orders for periodical maintenance payments which have been specifically ordered under the legislation set out in section 8 and subsequently by the amendment of section 8 by the Guardianship of Infants Act 1964, the Family Law (Maintenance of Spouses and Children) Act 1976, the Judicial Separation and Family Law Reform Act 1989, the 1995 Act and section 30 of the 1996 Divorce Act.

Section 8(1) of the 1940 Act provides that a "defaulter" of any maintenance payments ordered under any of these Acts may be liable to distraint or imprisonment once a period of six months has passed during which no payments have been made. An application under section 8(1) may be made to the court seeking relief by either the maintenance creditor or by the District Court clerk. A defaulting maintenance debtor may be liable to a prison sentence of up to three months, unless he or she can show that the failure to make the payments was not due to "wilful refusal" or "culpable neglect". However it is submitted that service by the maintenance debtor of any sentence imposed will not assist the maintenance creditor if the arrears due are not discharged. In practice, imprisonment is used as a remedy of last resort and is more effective as a threat to a defaulter. If the defaulter were imprisoned he would not be in a position to earn money with which to discharge the arrears and could possibly lose their job as a result of such imprisonment. Section 107 of the Defence Forces Act 1954 directs that no order may be made under section 8 of the 1940 Act against a member of the Defence Forces or a reserve member who has been called out on active service. This would not exempt members of, *e.g.* the FCA from the provisions of section 8.

PART IV

INCOME TAX, CAPITAL ACQUISITIONS TAX, CAPITAL GAINS TAX, PROBATE TAX AND STAMP DUTY

GENERAL NOTE

Part IV of the 1996 Act contains the taxation implications of a decree of divorce. During the passage of the Family Law (Divorce) Bill, 1996 through the Houses of the Oireachtas, far more wide-reaching taxation reforms were proposed by the opposition but were rejected by the Government. In particular, a proposal that VAT would not be chargable upon professional services associated with divorce and judicial separation applications was rejected. Minister for Equality and Law Reform Mervyn Taylor T.D. referred to the basis of this form of tax in European law and indicated that the amendment in the present context was inappropriate. (*Select Committee on Legislation and Security*, July 17, 1996, L6 No. 12, Col. 682; Vol. 149 *Seanad Debates* Col. 33).

A further amendment was proposed relating to stamp duty and capital tax exemptions for property transfers between previously married persons. As introduced and subsequently enacted, transfers of property between spouses consequent upon orders made by the courts in the course of a divorce application are exempt from stamp duty and capital taxes. These exemptions, contained in sections 33, 34 and 35 of the 1996 Act, are discussed further hereinafter. However, the proposal was to extend the exemptions to any transfer of property between previously married persons "in circumstances where if the, transfer had been made pursuant to a court order it would have attached the benefit of the exemptions provided for in sections [33, 34, and 35]..." (*Select Committee on Legislation and Security*, July 17, 1996, L6 No. 12, Cols. 678–679). This proposal was deemed by the Government to go too far (149 *Seanad Debates* Col. 33):

> "Under the proposed wording, it might be possible that all transfers of property between former spouses would continue to benefit from the capital taxation exemptions." (*Select Committee on Legislation and Security*, Cols. 682–683)

Payments to be made without deduction of income tax

31.—Payments of money pursuant to an order under this Act (other than under section 17) shall be made without deduction of income tax.

GENERAL NOTE

Section 26 of the Judicial Separation and Family Law Reform Act, 1989 first provided that payments of money pursuant to ancillary relief orders made under the terms of the Act would be made "without deduction of income tax." A similar provision is contained in section 37 of the Family Law Act, 1995, excluding pension adjustment orders which are likewise excluded under section 31 of the 1996 Act. This provision means, in effect that payments are to be made gross of income tax, the payments being taxable in the hands of the recipient and deductible in the hands of the payor.

Income tax treatment of divorced persons

32.—Where a payment to which section 3 of the Finance Act, 1983, applies is made in a year of assessment (within the meaning of the Income Tax Acts) by a spouse who was a party to a marriage that has been dissolved for the benefit of the other spouse and—

> (a) both spouses are resident in the State for tax purposes for that year of assessment, and
>
> (b) neither spouse has entered into another marriage,

then, the provisions of section 4 of the Finance Act, 1983, shall, with any necessary modifications, have effect in relation to the spouses for that year of assessment as if their marriage had not been dissolved.

GENERAL NOTE

Section 32 of the 1996 Act allows divorced persons who have not remarried and who have both resided in the State for tax purposes in the year of assessment to opt for joint assessment for income tax purposes; similar to the manner in which such taxation arrangements may be elected by separated couples at present. The nature and consequences of such an election were clearly stated by Minister Taylor:

> "The net effect of the section is that, through opting for joint assessment, where one

party to a dissolved marriage is paying enforceable maintenance for the benefit of the other party, the party making the maintenance payment, and not the recipient, will bear any tax referable to the maintenance payments. If the recipient has no other income, the paying party will be granted the personal allowances and tax bands appropriate to a married person. If the recipient has other income, the tax assessed on the parties will be apportioned between them but the tax referable to the maintenance payments will still be borne by the payer." (467 *Dáil Debates* Col. 1767)

If such an election is not made the parties will be singly assessed as if they were single people. Where they have children, an additional lone parent's taxation allowance can be claimed on top of the single person's allowance. Once either party remarries the option of availing of section 3 of the Finance Act 1983 ends.

Exemption of certain transfers from stamp duty

33.—(1) Subject to subsection (3), stamp duty shall not be chargeable on an instrument by which property is transferred pursuant to an order to which this subsection applies by either or both of the spouses who were parties to the marriage concerned to either or both of them.

(2) Section 74(2) of the Finance (1909–10) Act, 1910, shall not apply to a transfer to which subsection (1) applies.

(3) (a) Subsection (1) applies to an order under Part III.

(b) Subsection (1) does not apply in relation to an instrument referred to in that subsection by which any part of or beneficial interest in the property concerned is transferred to a person other than the spouses concerned.

GENERAL NOTE

The purpose of section 33 is to extend the spousal exemption for the payment of stamp duty on property transfer instruments to those instruments executed prior to a court order made under Part III of the 1996 Act. Section 114 of the Finance Act 1990 provides that property transfers made by one spouse to another will not attract a liability to stamp duty, whether such transfers were effected pursuant to a deed of separation, order of judicial separation or otherwise. Section 127 of the Finance Act 1997 is similar in its provisions to section 33 of the 1996 Act, in confirming that transfers of property made pursuant to an order under Part III of the 1996 Act do not require the payment of stamp duty.

Section 33(3) clearly states that the exemption does not apply to any instrument which transfers property from either or both of the spouses to a third party, *i.e.* not one of the spouses to the marriage which has been dissolved. It should be noted that where a marriage is dissolved by way of a foreign decree of divorce which is subsequently recognised as valid in the jurisdiction, the exemption from the payment of stamp duty will apply to property transfer instruments made on foot of an order made under Part III of the 1995 Act. Finally the provisions of section 33(2) provide that the Revenue Commissioners shall not adjudicate a transfer or conveyance between spouses as a gift or voluntary disposition.

Exemption of certain transfers from capital acquisitions tax

34.—Notwithstanding the provisions of the Capital Acquisitions Tax Act, 1976, a gift or inheritance (within the meaning, in each case, of that Act) taken by virtue or in consequence of an order under Part III by a spouse who was a party to the marriage concerned shall be exempt from any capital acquisitions tax under that Act and shall not be taken into account in computing such a tax.

Capital gains tax treatment of certain disposals by divorced persons

35.—(1) Notwithstanding the provisions of the Capital Gains Tax Acts, where, by virtue or in consequence of an order made under Part III on or following the granting of a decree of divorce either of the spouses concerned disposes of an asset to the other spouse, both spouses shall be treated for the purpose of those Acts as if the asset was acquired from the spouse making the disposal for a consideration of such amount as would secure that on the disposal neither a gain nor a loss would accrue to the spouse making the disposal:

> Provided that this subsection shall not apply if, until the disposal, the asset formed part of the trading stock of a trade carried on by the spouse making the disposal or if the asset is acquired as trading stock for the purposes of a trade carried on by the spouse acquiring the asset.

(2) Where subsection (1) applies in relation to a disposal of an asset by a spouse to the other spouse, then, in relation to a subsequent disposal of the asset (not being a disposal to which subsection (1) applies), the spouse making the disposal shall be treated for the purposes of the Capital Gains Tax Acts as if the other spouse's acquisition or provision of the asset had been his or her acquisition or provision of the asset.

GENERAL NOTE

Capital taxes on property transfers, *i.e.* capital acquisitions tax and capital gains tax will not arise due to an exemption, provided the transfer in question is covered by the divorce decree. Such an exemption does not apply to subsequent property transactions between the divorced couple who will thereafter be treated as strangers for taxation purposes.

Section 34 extends the preservation of spousal taxation relief to certain situations where capital acquisitions tax would otherwise be payable between spouses who were parties to the marriage which has been dissolved. To avail of the exemption, the gift or inheritance must have passed on foot of an ancillary order made under Part III of the 1996 Act. Any gifts or inheritance passing from either of the spouses to a third party, including a dependent member of the family will not attract the exemption. It would appear that parties who have obtained a foreign divorce and who apply for relief under Part III of the 1995 Act, subsequently obtaining orders under that Part, will also benefit from the capital acquisitions tax exemption. It must be stressed that the exemption only applies in relation to acquisitions on foot of a court order in the context of the divorce proceedings, whether such order is made contemporaneous with the decree or thereafter and not to other subsequent gifts as between the former spouses. Such a broad exemption was expressly requested by the Government during the Oireachtas debates on the Act. This gives rise to an anomaly. A post-divorce gift to a former spouse, whether by *inter vivos* disposition or upon death, will attract capital acquisitions tax. However, an order for provision under section 18 of the Act, following an application for provision out of the estate of the deceased by the former spouse, will benefit from the exemption. This anomaly is referred to in Shatter, *Family Law* (4th ed., 1997), p. 966 where the author comments that this situation does not allow for efficient tax planning in respect of the estate of the donor spouse. Furthermore, the making of further provision for a former spouse is discouraged, save where this is done in the context of litigation.

Section 35(1) provides an exemption against the payment of capital gains tax, in certain specified circumstances. Where following the grant of a decree of divorce an order has been made under Part III of the 1996 Act, whether contemporaneous with the granting of the decree or at any time thereafter, one of the spouses "disposes of" an asset to the other spouse, then such a disposal will be treated by the Revenue Commissioners as attracting neither a gain nor a loss, thus neither penalising nor benefiting the disposing spouse. An exception to this principle applies where the asset being disposed of formed, until the disposal, part of trading stock of a trade being carried on by the disposing spouse, or if the asset which is being acquired by the other spouse is acquired by them as part of trading stock for the purpose of their trade. Thus it can be seen that no exemption will apply where assets are being disposed of for commercial reasons, even where the disposal is being made pursuant to an order under Part III of the 1996 Act. Again, the exemption allowed under section 35(1) will apply only as between spouses and will apply to property disposed of pursuant to an order made under Part III of the 1995 Act where a foreign decree of divorce has been recognised in this jurisdiction. Sections 71(1) and 72(1) of the Finance Act, 1997 provide the same reliefs. Finally, section 35(2) deals with a situation where an asset is subsequently disposed of which was previously exempt from capital gains tax. The disposing spouse in that instance will be treated as if he or she had acquired the asset at the time of its acquisition by the transferring spouse and at the price paid by the transferring spouse at the time the asset was originally acquired.

Abatement and postponement of probate tax on property the subject of an order under section 18

36.—Subsection (1) of section 115A of the Finance Act, 1993 (which was inserted by the Finance Act, 1994, and provides for the abatement or postponement of probate tax payable by a surviving spouse)—

    (a) shall apply to a spouse in whose favour an order has been made under section 18 as it applies to a spouse referred to in the said section 115A, and

    (b) shall apply to property or an interest in property the subject of such an order as it applies to the share of a spouse referred to in the said section 115A in the estate of a deceased referred to in that section or the interest of such a spouse in property referred to in that section,

with any necessary modifications.

GENERAL NOTE

Probate tax is payable since 1993 in circumstances where the value of an estate exceeds the sum of £10,980 (1998 figures). As set out in section 36 of the 1996 Act, section 115A(1) of the Finance Act 1993 provided for the abatement or postponement of probate tax payable by a surviving spouse. The practical effect of this section is that the surviving spouse attracts a zero per cent rating for probate tax. However, it should be noted that in contrast with the exemption position for capital taxes, the exemption threshold of £10,980 is lost in the event of the value of the estate exceeding that amount.

The provisions of section 36 extend the zero rating for probate tax payable by a surviving spouse in circumstances where they have received a benefit pursuant to Part III of the 1996 Act, and specifically where an order has been made under section 18 providing for provision for the applicant spouse out of the estate of a deceased spouse. Probate tax is not payable on the estate of a spouse where it passes, either by will or intestacy to the other spouse. However, in circumstances where assets pass from one spouse to another after a decree of divorce has been granted, either by will or intestacy, then probate tax will be payable.

Although Part IV of the 1996 Act sets out new provisions in relation to the payment of tax by, or on behalf of divorced spouses, there is nothing novel in these provisions. The primary effect of Part IV is to extend existing spousal reliefs to parties who become former spouses consequent on a decree of divorce being granted, but only in relation to orders made under the 1996 Act. The provisions of Part IV mirror the taxation sections contained in Part IV of the Family Law Act 1995.

PART V

MISCELLANEOUS

Powers of court in relation to transactions intended to prevent or reduce relief

37.—(1) In this section—

"disposition" means any disposition of property howsoever made other than a disposition made by a will or codicil;

"relief" means the financial or other material benefits conferred by an order under section 12, 13 or 14, paragraph (a) or (b) of section 15(1) or section 16, 17, 18 or 22 (other than an order affecting an order referred to in subsection (1)(e) thereof) and references to defeating a claim for relief are references to—

> (a) preventing relief being granted to the person concerned, whether for the benefit of the person or a dependent member of the family concerned,
>
> (b) limiting the relief granted, or
>
> (c) frustrating or impeding the enforcement of an order granting relief;

"reviewable disposition", in relation to proceedings for the grant of relief brought by a spouse, means a disposition made by the other spouse concerned or any other person but does not include such a disposition made for valuable consideration (other than marriage) to a person who, at the time of the disposition, acted in good faith and without notice of an intention on the part of the respondent to defeat the claim for relief.

> (2) (a) The court, on the application of a person ("the applicant") who has instituted proceedings that have not been determined for the grant of relief, may—
>
>> (i) if it is satisfied that the other spouse concerned or any other person, with the intention of defeating the claim for relief, proposes to make any disposition of or to transfer out of the jurisdiction or otherwise deal with any property, make such order as it thinks fit for the purpose of restraining that other spouse or other person from so doing or otherwise for protecting the claim,
>>
>> (ii) if it is satisfied that that other spouse or other person has, with that intention, made a reviewable disposition and that, if the disposition were set aside, relief or different relief would be granted to the applicant, make an order setting aside the disposition.
>
> (b) Where relief has been granted by the court and the court is satisfied that the other spouse concerned or another person has, with the intention aforesaid, made a reviewable disposition, it may make an order setting aside the disposition.
>
> (c) An application under paragraph (a) shall be made in the proceedings for the grant of the relief concerned.

(3) Where the court makes an order under paragraph (a) or (b) of subsection (2), it shall include in the order such provisions (if any) as it considers

necessary for its implementation (including provisions requiring the making of any payments or the disposal of any property).

(4) Where an application is made under subsection (2) with respect to a disposition that took place less than 3 years before the date of the application or with respect to a disposition or other dealing with property that the other spouse concerned or any other person proposes to make and the court is satisfied—

    (a) in case the application is for an order under subsection (2)(a)(i), that the disposition or other dealing concerned would (apart from this section) have the consequence, or

    (b) in case the application is for an order under paragraph (a)(ii) or (b) of subsection (2), that the disposition has had the consequence,

of defeating the applicant's claim for relief, it shall be presumed, unless the contrary is shown, that that other spouse or other person disposed of or otherwise dealt with the property concerned, or, as the case may be, proposes to do so, with the intention of defeating the applicant's claim for relief.

GENERAL NOTE

Section 37 represents the continuation of the important reliefs first introduced in section 29 of the Judicial Separation and Family Law Reform Act 1989 and continued in force in the context of judicial separation, by section 35 of the Family Law Act 1995. The section has been subject to little amendment since its first introduction and provides important protective reliefs both in an interim/interlocutory context and in a permanent context. The aim of the section is to provide protection against transactions by a spouse which are calculated to reduce the remedies available to the other spouse, or which would have the effect of preventing certain reliefs being granted. Effectively, the primary purpose is to prevent the reduction of assets in a manner which would curtail the powers of the court in relation to the granting of ancillary reliefs, subsequent to the granting of a decree of divorce. It is intended to examine the provisions of the section under the following headings:

    (a) Scope and definitions;
    (b) Interim/interlocutory reliefs;
    (c) Reviewable dispositions;
    (d) Third parties;
    (e) Practice and procedure.

The section governs and can be used to attack any *inter vivos* disposition of property, although testamentary dispositions are excluded. The aim is to prevent the avoidance of financial reliefs which ought properly be granted to the non-disposing spouse and the dependent children, under the terms of Part III of the 1996 Act. The protection of the section may be invoked where property is disposed of, or attempts are made to dispose of property with a view to preventing maintenance (interim or permanent) property transfer orders, exclusive rights of occupation of the family home, orders for sale of the family home, financial compensation orders, pension adjustment orders, relief from the estate of the disposing spouse after his/her death and variations of these orders being received by a claimant spouse.

As previously stated, the aim is to prevent claims being defeated and the Act sets out three circumstances in which it is envisaged that this may occur:

    (a) Preventing reliefs being granted by the court in the first instance;
    (b) Limiting the reliefs which may be granted;
    (c) Restricting or interfering with enforcement of orders obtained.

The prohibited activities may have been completed, *i.e.* the disposition may have taken place and have been completed in which case the provisions relating to reviewable dispositions become relevant, while in some circumstances, the prohibited activities may have come to the notice of the non-disposing spouse in advance of completion and that spouse may seek protective and preventative reliefs. In this latter context, the provisions operate in a similar but not identical manner to *Mareva* type injunctions.

The equivalent provisions of section 29(2) of the 1989 Act were considered by Barron J. in *O'H v. O'H* [1990] 2 I.R. 558. In this case a wife sought to set aside a transfer of land by her husband to a child of the marriage, where the transfer had taken place prior to the coming into force of the statutory provisions in question. Relying upon the general presumption that a statute does not operate retrospectively, the relief sought was refused based on a lack of jurisdiction as there was nothing in the statutory provisions to rebut the normal presumption against retrospection.

Applications for interim/interlocutory relief in this context are made where proceedings have been instituted seeking any of the categories of relief aforementioned, but such application has not yet been determined. Section 37(2)(a) appears to limit the entitlement to apply for relief under the section to a person who has instituted proceedings. Arguably, this would preclude a respondent from seeking relief without instituting separate proceedings as applicant as even in the event of a counterclaim being made, the respondent could not be considered to be "a person, (the applicant) who has instituted proceedings".

It is submitted that in this regard the wording of section 37(2)(a) is too restrictive as a respondent may equally require the protective reliefs provided. The respondent, fearing a disposition which might interfere with his/her rights would appear to have two options. First, to institute separate proceedings or secondly, to invoke the general equitable jurisdiction of the court, as recognised in the *Mareva* case. The former option has cost implications and the latter has certain legal disadvantages which will be considered hereinafter.

The proofs required are that there is a proposed disposition or dealing with the property or transfer out of the jurisdiction and this is with the intention of defeating the claim for relief. However, the required proofs are greatly assisted by section 37(4) which provides that where the court is satisfied that the claim for relief would be defeated, the intention so to do is to be presumed. The impact of this provision is to place the burden of proving that the disposition was not for this purpose upon the prospective disposer. This statutory presumption represents a significant difference in the proofs required for section 37 relief, as compared with the required proofs for *Mareva* type relief and particularly so if application is made on an *ex parte* basis. In the context of *Mareva* injunctions the position was clarified by the Supreme Court in *O'Mahony v. Hogan* [1995] 2 I.R. 411, at 419 where Finlay C.J. stated:

> "the cases establish that there must be an intention on the part of the defendant to dispose of his assets with a view to evading his obligation to the plaintiff and to frustrate the anticipated order of the court. It is not sufficient to establish that the assets are likely to be dissipated in the ordinary course of business or in the payment of lawful debts."

The proof is assumed in the case of section 37 applications.

In an interim/interlocutory context, section 37 relief is often required as a matter of urgency. If there are fears that property will be lost, the immediate assistance of the court will be required. Therefore, in this context section 37 relief is often sought on an *ex parte* basis. Alternatively, in not so urgent cases, the application may be by motion on notice and if necessary application may be made for the abridgement of time for the service of such a motion. The notice procedure will be appropriate, if the asset or monies in question are not yet in the possession of the other spouse, but will be received in the near future. This may be the position in relation to redundancy payments, compensation from litigation and the proceeds of sale of real property, where the closing of the sale is imminent.

In circumstances where time constraints allow, the court may require that a written request be made in advance of an application to the court requesting an undertaking that the property in question will be preserved and will only grant relief where such an undertaking has not been forthcoming. However, time constraints and the lack of a desirability that notice be given of an impending application, would obviously be influential in encouraging a court to hear the matter *ex parte*. The application is usually grounded upon affidavit setting out the salient facts.

A reviewable disposition is a disposition that is open to review by the courts, having fallen foul of the provisions of section 37. Given the broad definition of "disposition", there are very specific features required for such disposition to be reviewable. In particular, a disposition to "equity's friend", *i.e.* the bona fide purchaser for value without notice, is not reviewable. It is noteworthy that the lack of notice required relates to the intention to defeat the claim for relief. However, if the criteria for reviewability are met, and this would appear to require a high degree of collusion as between the disposing spouse and the purchaser, the court is given a strong armoury to deal with the matter.

Where the disposal has taken place, it may be set aside and such setting aside may take place either prior to the determination of the proceedings or thereafter. As with interim/interlocutory relief, an intention to defeat a claim for relief or defeat orders made must be shown. However, the section 37(4) presumption of such an intention applies to dispositions made within the three years prior to the application.

The impact of a disposition being determined "reviewable" and thereafter set aside will obviously have a major impact on the third party purchaser of the property. The section does not make any specific provision for joining the third party in the application or for putting him/her on notice thereof. However, it is submitted, that prior to any order being made setting aside the disposition such third party would require to have a right to be heard. This is particularly necessary in view of the fact that the most obvious defence to the review will be that the purchaser was a bona fide purchaser for value without notice. The practice of the courts has been to join such persons as notice parties.

These would appear to be composite requirements, *i.e.* the purchaser is required to satisfy all three requirements: good faith, valuable consideration and a lack of notice. The Act does not specify the extent of such consideration and whether full market value is required, but there is no such requirement expressly stated in the section. However, proving these three elements merely provides a cast iron defence, as the definition of "reviewable disposition" is thereafter not complied with.

There are other degrees of protection afforded where perhaps only one or two of these elements exists and the remedy of setting aside the transaction is a discretionary one vested in the court. Presumably, the third party purchaser, as well as the parties to the proceedings, is entitled to make submissions to the court illustrating why he/she contends that the court should not exercise its discretion to set aside.

The provisions relating to protective reliefs and reviewable dispositions have received judicial consideration and useful guidance toward interpreting section 37 may be derived from these decisions. Perhaps the most comprehensive analysis may be found in the judgment of McGuinness J., as she then was in *J.R. v. P.R. (A.R. Notce Party)* [1996] 1 I.F.L.R. 194. The facts involved a financially modest disposition from husband, the respondent, to his brother, the notice party. In deciding whether or not the disposition was reviewable and further whether it would actually be reviewed, the court first examined the degree of knowledge of the notice party of the respondent's intention to defeat a claim for relief by the applicant and then proceeded to apply its discretion. The court noted a three-stage process:

(a) the intention of the respondent to defeat a claim for relief was to be presumed under the Act, unless rebutted by the respondent and no sufficient evidence had been advanced to achieve such a rebuttal. The court in this case was considering the 1989 Act, but there is no material difference in the wording of section 37 of the 1996 Act;

(b) the notice of the transferee of the property need not be actual notice of the intention to defeat, constructive notice is sufficient. On the facts of the case and having reviewed the English authorities the court held that this level of notice was proved, at p. 17:

> ". . . I feel that the Notice Party's awareness of the matrimonial dispute and more importantly his awareness of the District Court maintenance proceedings by the wife should have caused him to make further enquiries and therefore he is bound by constructive notice. I make this finding with some hesitation since I do not believe that the Notice Party acted with malice towards the wife. His lack of further enquiry as to his brother's intentions was careless rather than deliberate."

(c) the court was then obliged to consider its discretion and concluded in favour of using this so as not to set aside the disposition. It was stated, at p. 17:

> "... the matter must be approached with some proportionality, with a degree of ordinary common sense and in the context of the parties' present positions".

Relevant factors included that the wife was in a second relationship, the act of unravelling the transaction concerned would not necessarily realise the money at issue and would be complex and the Notice Party had not acted maliciously.

In the event that the disposition is set aside, clearly issues will arise between the disposing party and the former purchaser. The latter will in most cases have provided some consideration, even if not at full market value and consequent upon the setting aside, there will have been a total failure of consideration. In these circumstances, the purchaser is presumably entitled to recover at least the purchase price as against the disposing party. However, in circumstances in which the disposing party is not in a financial position to make such a payment, clear difficulties arise. It is difficult to see why the third party purchaser, save in circumstances of absolute and clear collusion, should be expected to subsidise the marital assets to the extent of the lost purchase monies. However, these matters are not adverted to in the section, but presumably are left to be resolved according to general legal principles.

Procedurally, much depends upon the context in which the application for relief under the section is made. As stated previously herein, interim relief may be sought on a *ex parte* basis, while interlocutory relief is sought by motion on notice. Both such applications would be grounded upon affidavit. Section 37(2)(c) indicates that where relief is sought, where the primary proceedings have not been determined, the application shall be made in the proceedings themselves. Where an application is sought to be made under section 37(3), the proceedings having been determined, presumably an application to re-enter the matter may be made and the reliefs sought by motion, whether *ex parte* or otherwise. In the context of the urgency which can sometimes prevail in relation to these applications, the 14 day notice period for High Court motions under the current Rules of the Superior Courts is likely to result in an abridgement application.

Jurisdiction of courts and venue

38.—(1) Subject to the provisions of this section, the Circuit Court shall, concurrently with the High Court, have jurisdiction to hear and determine proceedings under this Act and shall, in relation to that jurisdiction, be known as the Circuit Family Court.

(2) Where the rateable valuation of any land to which proceedings in the Circuit Family Court under this Act relate exceeds £200, that Court shall, if an application is made to it in that behalf by any person having an interest in the proceedings, transfer the proceedings to the High Court, but any order made or act done in the course of such proceedings before the transfer shall be valid unless discharged or varied by the High Court by order.

(3) The jurisdiction conferred on the Circuit Family Court by this Act may be exercised by the judge of the circuit in which any of the parties to the proceedings ordinarily resides or carries on any business, profession or occupation.

(4) The Circuit Family Court may, for the purposes of subsection (2) in relation to land that has not been given a rateable valuation or is the subject with other land of a rateable valuation, determine that its rateable valuation would exceed, or would not exceed, £200.

(5) Section 32 of the Act of 1989 shall apply to proceedings under this Act in the Circuit Family Court and sections 33 to 36 of that Act shall apply to proceedings under this Act in that Court and in the High Court.

(6) In proceedings under section 13, 14, 15(1)(a), 16, 17, 18 or 22—

    (a) each of the spouses concerned shall give to the other spouse and to, or to a person acting on behalf of, any dependent member of the family concerned, and

    (b) any dependent member of the family concerned shall give to, or to a person acting on behalf of, any other such member and to each of the spouses concerned,

such particulars of his or her property and income as may reasonably be required for the purposes of the proceedings.

(7) Where a person fails or refuses to comply with subsection (6), the court on application to it in that behalf by a person having an interest in the matter, may direct the person to comply with that subsection.

GENERAL NOTE

Section 38 sets out a number of miscellaneous details relating to procedural matters including jurisdiction, venue and the manner in which proceedings are to take place. In keeping with the provisions of the Judicial Separation and Family Law Act 1989 and the Family Law Act 1995, concurrent jurisdiction exists as between the High Court and the Circuit Court. While it remains common in Circuit Court proceedings to state that the rateable valuation of the lands the subject matter of the proceedings does not exceed £200, such a proof would not appear to be strictly necessary as the section makes it clear that there is full concurrent jurisdiction. Furthermore, it is clear from the provisions of section 38(2) that the Circuit Court is not precluded from hearing cases involving lands with a rateable valuation exceeding £200. The origins of the confusion probably derive from the Courts (Supplemental Provisions) Act 1961, as amended, which gave to the Circuit Court jurisdiction to determine property disputes relating to land with a rateable valuation not exceeding £200. However, the jurisdiction of the Circuit Court in the matrimonial context has clearly been subject to statutory extension.

The full jurisdiction of the Circuit Court is further supported by section 38(2), which indicates that if the parties are in agreement, there is nothing to prevent the Circuit Court determining disputes involving lands exceeding £200 rateable valuation. At the option of either of the parties or any party having an interest in the proceedings, the Circuit Court shall transfer the case to the High Court, if requested to do so. The pleading requirements following such a transfer to the High Court are set out at Rule 18 of the Rules of the Superior Court (No. 3), 1997 (S.I. No. 343 of 1997) (see Appendix A).

While there is not any mandatory provision in this regard, it presumably follows that where any proceedings are commenced before the High Court, where the rateable valuation of the lands concerned exceeds £200, an application to remit would be likely to be unsuccessful. The legal principles to be applied in cases of remittal are considered hereinafter. It thus follows that all cases may be brought in the Circuit Court subject to entitlement to insist upon the High Court where the rateable valuation aforementioned is exceeded.

There are certain traditional reasons why cases were pursued before the High Court, rather than the Circuit Court in the area of family law:

    (a) The waiting period for a hearing has formerly been significantly shorter in the High Court. This is certainly not the case now so far as Dublin is concerned, but might still be a factor in certain circuits around the country. The significance of this reason has substantially diminished;

    (b) The complexity of the issues, the likely duration and the value of the assets continue to be influential factors in the commencement of proceedings before the High Court;

    (c) The selected jurisdiction for judicial separation proceedings, prior to the introduction of divorce; before the High Court might be influenced by there having been previous nullity proceedings which were unsuccessful at a time when the

High Court had exclusive jurisdiction in nullity matters. This factor has diminished in significance since the granting of jurisdiction to the Circuit Court in nullity matters as contained in the Family Law Act 1995.

The traditional factors favouring the Circuit Court as a family law venue have mainly centred on costs. As the significance of legal aid in family law has continued to grow, the Civil Legal Aid Scheme and the statutory basis thereof insist that the proceedings be instituted in the first level of court having jurisdiction to determine the case concerned and in divorce cases, this is the Circuit Court.

However, the principles applicable to remittal are well established. The Rules of the Superior Courts 1986, Order 70A as amended by the Rules of the Superior Courts (No. 3) 1997 (S.I. No. 343 of 1997), states at Rule 15, that the High Court may remit proceedings at its discretion subject to the interests of justice and that such an application may be made at any time after an appearance has been entered. The original legal standard to be satisfied was set down in section 25 of the Courts of Justice Act 1924 which stated the test to be whether or not, the action was fit to be prosecuted in the High Court. If so, the action should be retained and, if not, remittal should be ordered. These provisions were modified by section 11 of the Courts of Justice Act 1936, which states that notwithstanding anything contained in section 25 of the 1924 Act, an action should not be remitted if:

> "the High Court is satisfied that, having regard to all the circumstances, and notwithstanding that such an action could have been commenced in the Circuit Court, it was reasonable that such action should have been commenced in the High Court".

This is a more onerous standard for a party seeking to remit to the Circuit Court, than was the position under the 1924 Act. In making such remittal applications, each case rests on its own facts. An analysis of the family law caselaw in this area may be found in Shatter's *Family Law* (4th ed., 1997), pp. 105–107. Perhaps most instructive in this regard is the judgment of Budd. J. in *H.K. v. P.K.*, unreported, High Court, January, 1996. The applicable test was stated to be that the case should be retained in the High Court "unless there are good reasons to the justice of the case requires" otherwise. Refusing the application, the court was influenced by the probable length of the hearing, the value of the assets concerned and the likely hearing dates, both in relation to the trial itself and associated interim motions. Of relevance was the fact that if remitted, the case would be heard on circuit outside Dublin, where family law sittings were infrequent and of one day's duration only.

The Rules of the Circuit Court (No. 1) of 1997 (S.I. No. 84 of 1997) (see Appendix B) became operative on the February 27, 1997, the same date as the Family Law (Divorce) Act 1996. These new rules dealt not only with divorce applications, but also with judicial separation applications and other matrimonial reliefs under the Family Law Act 1995. The most evident change introduced by the new procedures was the introduction of new categories of civil bill entitled "Family Law Civil Bills". These provisions replaced the previous procedures whereby matrimonial proceedings were commenced by way of application. The practical implications of these changes were that:

(a) Similar, although not identical, initiating documents are now used in the area of divorce as are used in other areas of civil law;

(b) The present rules enable motions for judgment in default of appearance or defence to be brought by an applicant where the respondent either delays in the filing of pleadings or does not intend to take any part in the proceedings at all; and

(c) In providing for the service of a notice of trial, the rules aim to have the pleadings closed and the case ready for hearing before a hearing date is allocated.

The information required for inclusion in the "Indorsement of Claim" in a family law civil bill for divorce is:

(a) The date and place of marriage of the parties;

(b) The length of time the parties have lived separately and apart and the addresses of both of the parties during that time, where known;

(c) Details of any previous matrimonial relief sought and/or obtained and details of any previous separation agreement entered into between the parties;

(d) The names and ages and dates of birth of any dependent children of the marriage;

(e) Details of the family home(s) and/or other residences of the parties including, if relevant, details of any former family home/residence to include details of the manner of occupation/ownership thereof;

(f) Whether the property concerned is registered or unregistered land;

(g) The bases of jurisdiction under the Family Law (Divorce) Act 1996, which are contained in section 38 and 39 of the 1996 Act and are considered hereinafter;

(h) The occupation of each of the parties;

(i) The grounds relied upon for the relief sought; and

(j) Each section of the 1996 Act under which relief is sought.

From the date of service of the civil bill, a 10 day period is permitted for the entry of an appearance and a further 10 day period is allowed for the filing of a defence and counterclaim, if desired. When such periods have elapsed, together with the sending of a 14 day letter warning that a default motion will issue in the event that the respondent continues to fail to act, a motion for judgment in default may be brought. In any event, the respondent is obliged to file an affidavit of means within a period of 20 days from the date of service of the civil bill. Upon issuing a family law civil bill, it must be accompanied by three separate documents:

(a) A certificate relating to alternative remedies: as required by section 6 of the 1996 Act. The provisions of section 6 and the certification procedures are considered in detail previously. In the case of the respondent, a certificate pursuant to section 7 must be filed by his/her solicitor at the same time as an appearance is entered in the proceedings. This is provided for by the Act itself in section 7;

(b) An affidavit of means: the aim of which is to give a pencil-sketch of the applicant's financial position and hopefully to reduce the need for discovery. In this objective, it has been only slightly successful and save in the most straightforward of cases, it is usual to have discovery made in the course of divorce proceedings. This can give rise to much unnecessary duplication. The fault for this probably lies with inadequate affidavits of means being sworn, a failure to demand proper vouching of the figures stated therein and with professional fears relating to advising in circumstances in which the fullest financial information is not available. In some instances, discovery will be required in addition to the affidavit of means. There are some important differences between the information to be gleaned from the affidavit of means and the information obtained on discovery. The latter gives a more historical picture, which may be particularly relevant if efforts have been made to alter the appearance of the financial position for the purposes of the proceedings; and

(c) The affidavit of welfare: is a questionnaire answered and sworn by the deponent setting out a series of practical questions concerning the dependent children. This document is only required in circumstances in which there are dependent children. As stated previously and discussed in the context of Part II of the 1996 Act herein, ensuring that the children are properly taken care of takes centre stage in the 1996 Act and the information in the affidavit of welfare will assist the court in reaching determinations on this point. It is not uncommon where disputes arise concerning children that the parents will be unable to agree on even the simplest factual matters. The affidavit of welfare highlights the areas of agreement and disagreement and aids in the identification of the areas of dispute, if any. Provision is made for a simplified affidavit of welfare to be sworn and filed by the respondent in circumstances in which he/she is in agreement with the contents of the affidavit of welfare of the applicant.

The High Court did not have specific procedures to deal with divorce applications before it until the introduction of the Rules of the Superior Courts (No. 3) 1997 (S.I. No. 343 of 1997), hereinafter "the Rules". These Rules became operative on September 1, 1997. One possible advantage of the High Court jurisdiction prior to this date, would have appeared to be the absence of an express provision for the filing of an affidavit of means, which the Circuit Court required from the outset to be filed with the civil bill or the defence; or in any event within 20 days of the service of the civil bill.

Clearly, the High Court would have been empowered by section 38(6) of the 1996 Act to require such an affidavit to be filed. This is very significant, as the disclosure of assets is perhaps one of the greatest fears in divorce proceedings, where the parties are separated along time and, in particular, where the applicant hopes that the proceedings will be uncontested and fears that disclosure of assets will only whet the appetite of the respondent! This lacuna has been closed by the Rules. Rule 6(1) states that each party is required to file and serve an affidavit of means and Rule 6(3) provides that it is to be served with the verifying affidavit "unless otherwise ordered by the Master or the Court". However, the Rules require filing with the verifying affidavit and not with the special summons.

The Rules provide that divorce proceedings before the High Court are to be commenced by special summons, a family law summons and the procedure is therefore largely unchanged from that which applied formerly in relation to judicial separation proceedings. The special endorsement of claim is required to state all necessary particulars relating to:

(a) The relief sought;

(b) Each section of the Act under which relief is sought; and

(c) The grounds upon which it is sought.

A verifying affidavit is also required. The Rules, at Rule 4, clearly specify the information required to be contained therein. The listed contents are the same for judicial separation and divorce, although arguably the pleadings in each of these instances ought to have a different emphasis. The emphasis in a judicial separation action is often more on conduct/ behaviour in relation to section 2(1)(b) and 2(1)(f) reliefs under the 1989 Act, *i.e.* unreasonable behaviour and no normal marital relationship. While in applications for divorce, conduct is of lesser significance, but rather emphasis is on the required period of living apart being satisfied and the lack of any prospect of reconciliation. However, as conduct is a factor to be taken into account by the court in relation to ancillary reliefs, details of conduct are likely to be raised and are being raised in contested divorce cases.

Section 20(2)(i) of the 1996 Act states that the conduct of the parties is a relevant consideration in determining financial reliefs if it would be unjust to disregard it. To some extent, where there has previously been a decree of judicial separation, the raising of issues of conduct pre-judicial separation at the divorce stage contains an element of *res judicata*. In relation to the verification of affidavit for divorce, special consideration should be given to the importance attached by section 20(3) of the 1996 Act, to previous separation agreements and details thereof are required to be clearly stated in the affidavit.

The contents required in a verifying affidavit in divorce proceedings are:

(a) Date and place of marriage;

(b) Duration of living apart, including the addresses at which either party resided, where known;

(c) Full particulars of children of the parties, or either of them, including whether dependent and, if so, any provision which has been made;

(d) Possibility of reconciliation;

(e) Previous matrimonial reliefs/separation agreements with a certified copy to be exhibited;

(f) Domicile at commencement date or ordinary residence for the twelve months preceding the institution of proceedings of the parties;

(g) Details of the family home and details of any other residences including manner of occupation and ownership thereof;

(h) Confirmation of whether the property is registered or unregistered and a description thereof. This facilitates compliance with section 14(4) of the 1996 Act, notification by the Registrar in relation to property adjustment orders;

(i) Rule 5 requires that the certificate pursuant to section 6 and 7 of the 1996 Act be exhibited in the verifying/replying affidavit.

As discussed previously, (see page 65) section 18 stands as a reminder that there is no "clean break" principle applicable in Irish divorce law. The substantive provisions thereof have been previously considered. However, a special procedure is provided where it is desired to institute such proceedings before the High Court and the Circuit Court. Such an application is obviously going to be made post-death and only where section 18(10) blocking orders were not made at the time of the divorce. This again raises the issue of the requirement of the affidavit of means at the divorce stage.

Both the Rules of the Superior Courts and the Circuit Court Rules and the Act itself at section 38(6), only require the filing of an affidavit of means where financial relief is sought. It must be considered whether an application for a section 18(10) blocking order is a financial relief. The term is not defined and there are conflicting opinions. It is submitted that a financial relief is any relief involving a financial benefit to the party seeking it. If this approach is correct, clearly section 18(10) is a financial relief being a valuable order with a clear financial, or at the very least potential financial benefit to the party obtaining same. The view that section 18(10) is a financial relief has caused some applicants to seek only a decree of divorce. Clearly, this may cause future difficulty as, although there is nothing to prevent a blocking order being sought at a later date, the issues would then have to be re-opened, either at the time of a later application for a blocking order or post-death in the context of relief being sought under section 18.

The contents of the verifying affidavit in these circumstances are:

(a) Date and place of marriage and date of divorce decree, exhibiting a certified copy of the decree and the marriage certificate;

(b) Details of previous matrimonial reliefs obtained by the applicant in particular lump sum and property adjustment orders;

(c) Details of other benefits received from the deceased spouse by way of agreement or otherwise, including benefits received pursuant to the will of the deceased;

(d) Date of death of deceased spouse;

(e) Date representation was first granted;

(f) Date upon which notice of the death was given to the applicant spouse;

(g) Date upon which the applicant spouse notified the personal representative of an intention to apply for relief;

(h) Marital status of deceased at date of death;

(i) Marital status of applicant at date of application and whether there has been any intervening remarriage;

(j) Details of the dependants of the deceased spouse at date of death;

(k) Details of the dependants of the applicant at the date of the application;

(l) An averment as to whether any order pursuant to section 18(10) was previously made; and

(m) Details of the value of the estate of the deceased where known.

Similar information would be required to be included in the family law civil bill indorsement of claim in which section 18 relief is sought.

As previously stated, where financial reliefs are being applied for, an affidavit of means is to be filed and served with the verifying/replying affidavit. The forms attached to the Rules indicate that this affidavit is to be in similar format to that used in the Circuit Court. No guidance is given as to the obligation of the respondent to file and serve such an affidavit where no replying affidavit is filed. Furthermore, there is no guidance as to the requirement of such filing and service where financial reliefs are not sought by the applicant, but are sought by the respondent. Rule 6(4) of the Rules would not appear to assist as it refers only to a failure to comply with the provisions in relation to the filing and serving of an affidavit of means "as hereinbefore provided for". Clearly, the statutory obligation under section 38(6) would still apply and under the terms of Rule 6(3) directions might be sought from the Master of the High Court in this regard.

The following additional points must also be considered:

(a) Vouching of the affidavit of means may be requested by the opposing side with a period of 21 days for this being allowed by the Rules;

(b) The filing/serving requirement in relation to the affidavit of means is without prejudice to the right to seek particulars, discovery or information under section 17(25), which relates to pension adjustment information;

(c) Failure to comply with these requirements can lead to an order for discovery being made or 'such order as the Court deems appropriate and necessary' including adjournments and the striking out of claims/defences.

The affidavit of welfare form, required in cases involving dependent children, is also used in High Court proceedings, which is similar to that in use in the Circuit Court with alternative forms being provided depending upon whether the respondent agrees or disagrees with the contents of the applicant's affidavit. The form is confusing as to whether it is to be sworn/affirmed or declared. It is interesting that no directions are provided in relation to the time of service/filing of the affidavit of welfare by the applicant, but the respondent is given a period of 21 days from service of same by the applicant for the service of his affidavit of welfare. The service and filing of affidavits of means and welfare, where appropriate, is expressed to be mandatory.

Defending and counterclaiming may be done by way of replying affidavit, according to Rule 17. It is submitted that this is the most unsatisfactory part of the Rules. The inclusion of a defence in a replying affidavit is difficult and cumbersome, but still more so is the inclusion of a counterclaim. There are obvious clangers and pitfalls to having pleadings contained in a sworn document particularly in response to the unsworn special indorsement of claim in the special summons.

The listed categories of interlocutory applications are:

(a) Preliminary orders made under section 11 of the 1996 Act; barring applications, family home protection applications, interim applications and orders made in relation to the welfare of children;

(b) Interim maintenance applications made pursuant to section 12 of the 1996 Act;

(c) Applications made under section 17(25) of the 1996 Act, *i.e.* information required for pension adjustment orders;

(d) *Mareva* type relief to prevent the dissipation of assets, section 37 of the 1996 Act. The requirements to be fulfilled in such applications are elaborated in Rule 20, although the Rule 20 provisions presumably apply in a broader context to simply the interlocutory situation;

(e) Applications for information relating to property or income as required by section 38(6) of the 1996 Act, which may be ordered by the court to be given under section 38(7);

(f) Social reports under section 42 of the 1996 Act; and

(g) Any other interlocutory relief; including discovery applications.

These applications are to be sought by notice of motion and require 14 days notice. This is considerably longer than is required for other High Court motions but *ex parte* applications are envisaged in cases of urgency. Applications for abridgement of time may also be made. Where appropriate, a grounding affidavit is required. This would usually be the case but may not strictly be necessary in the case of an application for discovery. Contrast an application for further and better discovery in which the grounding affidavit would be required to set out the shortcomings in discovery already made. The usual rules in relation to seeking voluntary discovery before a motion issues presumably also apply and similarly it is presumed that a request that pension information and property/income information be provided voluntarily would be a prerequisite to section 17(25) and section 38(7) applications.

The emphasis is on interlocutory applications being heard on affidavit. Where oral evidence is given, a note of this is required to be made by the applicant or the solicitor for the applicant, approved by the court and, thereafter, served upon the respondent together with a copy of the order made unless the court otherwise directs.

A useful provision in relation to motions for directions is contained in Rule 11. The scope of these motions would appear to be unduly restricted by the bringing of the motion in question being limited to the applicant or the respondent. Directions might be required by the dependent child who is *sui juris*, the third party claiming an interest in property, pension trustees, or other beneficiaries/dependants in respect of the estate of a deceased spouse.

The rules of evidence make it clear that, as a general rule, interlocutory applications should be heard on affidavit evidence only and the hearing of action should be on oral evidence, subject to the court otherwise directing. The use of affidavit evidence is, however, advocated and promoted in relation to representations by trustees regarding property adjustment orders, Rule 11(3) is expressed in mandatory terms and in relation to actuarial evidence on behalf of the parties. In this regard, the approach of the High Court is similar to the Circuit Court, presumably both being influenced by cost-reduction considerations. Notices to cross-examine may of course be served in relation to such affidavits.

Applications for subsequent ancillary reliefs or variations of previous orders, under section 22 of the 1996 Act, are to be made by way of motion, grounded upon affidavit. In the case of applications to vary, the grounding affidavit is required to fully set out the alleged changes in circumstances or new evidence to be relied upon. Rules 22 and 19 of the Rules so provide.

Section 38(5) confirms the application of previous statutory provisions aimed at preserving privacy and some degree of informality in family law proceedings. Most of these have their origins in the Judicial Separation and Family Law Reform Act 1989. The segregation of family law proceedings from other cases is preserved at Circuit Court level. The objective is a deserving one. As litigants in family law proceedings should, at least, have the comfort of knowing that when they attend court that the other litigants in attendance will be there for a similar purpose. The mixing of family law proceedings with other civil proceedings and criminal proceedings would serve to heighten the publicity and the discomfort/embarrassment.

Unfortunately, this statutory obligation is not always preserved although fortunately lapses are scarce. Informality is advocated both at High Court and Circuit Court levels, including the substantial abandonment of traditional court dress by the Judge and the barristers in attendance. There is a statutory obligation that cases be heard *in camera*. The scope of the *in camera* rule was discussed in the judgment of Laffoy J. in *M.P. v. A.P. (Dr. J.C. (applicant)* [1997] I.F.L.R. 129. The implications of this have been considered in the context of section 3 of the 1996 Act. The costs of proceedings are to be at the court's discretion. Although it should be noted that it has become more and more common in recent times for each party to bear their own costs in matrimonial proceedings, with no order for costs being made.

This development prima facie seems somewhat harsh to the financially dependent or less-well-off spouse. However, the reality that legal costs will have to be paid can be taken into account by the court in the distribution of assets and section 20 of the 1996 Act would permit this, such costs clearly being a financial obligation of the party concerned. In addition, an award of costs in litigation tends to be associated with "winning" and there is no such concept in family law litigation, rather proper provision is made for both parties which will usually involve the redistribution of assets as between the parties but not in a condemnatory manner. Awarding costs can sometimes give rise to feelings of defeat and triumphalism, which is best avoided if possible. However, in certain cases, particularly where there is considerable financial disparity between the parties, costs may be awarded.

Section 38(6) imposes a statutory obligation of financial disclosure. Failure to comply can result in an application to court to force compliance, section 38(7) and the court may direct compliance. Thereafter, the obligation gains the force of a court order and, in the case of breach, the court has a wide discretion in relation to the orders it may make including, probably as a last resort, an order for attachment and committal.

One of the greatest concerns which prospective applicants/respondents in divorce proceedings have concerns the requirement that they would have to disclose details of their financial standing in circumstances in which they have been separated from their spouse for a very considerable period of time. The concerns are primarily two fold.

First, if the financial position of the spouse has improved since the date of separation or has remained strong, it is feared that the disclosure of financial details will encourage applications for ancillary reliefs. This fear and the unfairness of any disclosure requirement is particularly felt by those who have already entered into settlements, or have previously litigated their matrimonial difficulties and have complied with the consequent court orders. The concept that a spouse might attempt to have "a second bite at the cherry" is seen as being unfair. While the entitlement to pursue such renewed claims in the divorce context is not directly related to the disclosure obligations, it is sometimes considered that seeing details of assets and income might provide an incentive for such applications.

Secondly, the intrusion in privacy following a lengthy period of separation which often means that the parties have developed unrelated and entirely independent lives causes concern. The statutory disclosure requirement is not absolute, requiring disclosure of such particulars of property and income, as may reasonably be required for the purposes of the proceedings. It is interesting that the statutory provisions refer only to a disclosure obligation of the positive aspects of one's financial affairs, no reference is made to disclosure of liabilities, debts and expenses. This is presumably based on the premise that parties will seek to hide their assets to avoid ancillary reliefs but will only be too willing to disclose their financial burdens. However, bearing in mind the intrusion to privacy mentioned above, a party may be equally anxious to keep his/her financial problems secret and undisclosed.

The Dáil Debates seem to display little sympathy for non-disclosure. At the Second Stage, Deputy O'Dea indicated that the requirements of section 38(6) did not go far enough and that all details should be disclosed not merely those reasonably required (467 *Dáil Debates* Col. 1807).

In practice, the requirements of section 38(6) are supplemented by the Rules of Court both at Circuit Court and High Court level which require that affidavits of means be filed where financial relief is being sought. In practice, this usually means that such affidavits are required in all cases as, at the very least, a section 18(10) blocking order will be being sought. This would appear to be a financial relief in so far as it provides a potential financial benefit to one party and loss to the other in precluding future claims upon the estate of the spouse obtaining the section 18(10) relief.

The form of such affidavits indicate that all financial details, negative and positive, is to be disclosed. In uncontested cases, it is common that an affidavit of means is only filed by the applicant as the decree is granted under the default of pleadings procedure with the respondent filing no documents at all or, perhaps, only an appearance and a certificate for the purposes of section 7 of the 1996 Act. However, in contested cases as well as in Circuit Court proceedings in which the "consent defence" procedure is used, the affidavit of means is required.

It should be noted that the Rules of Court at both levels, technically require the filing of an affidavit of means by the respondent, even where no defence is being filed but uncontested applications are often compromised in advance of this. It is open to the court to insist upon the filing of such affidavits by both parties before granting the decree and it is arguable that a court should insist upon this in order to properly carry out an assessment for the purposes of section 5(1)(c) of the 1996 Act, concerning "proper provision".

Exercise of jurisdiction by court in relation to divorce

39.—(1) The court may grant a decree of divorce if, but only if, one of the following requirements is satisfied—

      (a) either of the spouses concerned was domiciled in the State on the date of the institution of the proceedings concerned,

      (b) either of the spouses was ordinarily resident in the State throughout the period of one year ending on that date.

(2) Where proceedings are pending in a court in respect of an application for the grant of a decree of divorce or in respect of an appeal from the determination of such an application and the court has or had, by virtue of subsection (1), jurisdiction to determine the application, the court shall, notwithstanding section 31(4) of the Act of 1989 or section 39 of the Act of 1995, as the case may be, have jurisdiction to determine an application for the grant of a decree of judicial separation or a decree of nullity in respect of the marriage concerned.

(3) Where proceedings are pending in a court in respect of an application for the grant of a decree of nullity or in respect of an appeal from the determination of such an application and the court has or had, by virtue of section 39 of the Act of 1995, jurisdiction to determine the application, the court shall, notwithstanding subsection (1), have jurisdiction to determine an application for the grant of a decree of divorce in respect of the marriage concerned.

(4) Where proceedings are pending in a court in respect of an application for the grant of a decree of judicial separation or in respect of an appeal from the determination of such an application and the court has or had, by virtue of section 31(4) of the Act of 1989, jurisdiction to determine the application, the court shall, notwithstanding subsection (1), have jurisdiction to determine an application for the grant of a decree of divorce in respect of the marriage concerned.

GENERAL NOTE

The jurisdictional aspect of the 1996 Act exists at two levels:

(a) Is the application one which may be brought in Ireland, or in what circumstances will the Irish courts accept jurisdiction to determine an application for a decree of divorce; and

(b) If the application is being brought at Circuit Court level, which Circuit Court has jurisdiction to hear and determine the application.

In relation to the former, the provisions of the 1996 Act are clearly stated in section 39. The section indicates that if either spouse is domiciled in Ireland at the date of the institution of the proceedings or has been ordinarily resident in Ireland for a period of one year prior to the institution of proceedings the Irish courts will have jurisdiction to determine the claim. The legal concepts of "domicile" and "ordinary residence" are well known, but nevertheless the definition of such terms remains complex.

Domicile requires factual residence, but of no particular duration, together with an intention to permanently reside. Ordinary residence does not require such a high degree of intention but places greater emphasis on day-to-day residence. However, these jurisdiction rules must be considered in the light of the divorce recognition rules in the Domicile and Recognition of Foreign Divorces Act 1986. The 1986 Act continues to govern the area of divorce recognition and indicates that a foreign divorce will be recognised if and only if either of the parties to the divorce was domiciled in the jurisdiction, which granted the divorce. Therefore, section 39 of the 1996 Act provides that the Irish courts will assume jurisdiction in circumstances in which the jurisdiction of other states will not be accepted.

A lack of reciprocity in recognition rules is not unusual, but the potential problems caused are well known to lawyers specialising in the area of conflicts of laws. The potential of the "limping divorce" becomes likely, *i.e.* a circumstance in which the status of a person varies from jurisdiction to jurisdiction, being divorced in one country, but not in another. It was inevitable that such situations would arise in circumstances in which Ireland had no legal provision for the grant of domestic divorce and very restrictive recognition rules were therefore to be expected, there being no basis for reciprocity.

The existing recognition rules applicable in Ireland are based on common law principles. However, the present legislation has not dealt with recognition given the changed rules relating to domestic divorce and it is submitted that this has left the way open for problems to emerge which might well have been avoided. Over many years, the Irish courts have refused recognition notwithstanding lengthy residence on the basis of high standards of proof necessary to establish domicile. Nevertheless, the current legislation will grant a divorce based on one year's residence in Ireland.

The implications of this system are obvious. If a foreign divorce is obtained on the basis of residence where neither party was domiciled in that foreign country, the decree thus granted will not be recognised in Ireland. Therefore, either party thereto, could seek a second decree in Ireland and thus the possibility of conflicting ancillary orders and double jeopardy arises, as well as the potential for limping divorces discussed previously. It is unfortunate that the opportunity was not availed of in this legislation to widen the narrow basis upon which the Irish courts will afford recognition to foreign orders.

The Circuit Court is, under the terms of the Constitution, a court of local and limited jurisdiction. Section 38(3) specifies which circuit has jurisdiction to determine proceedings brought at the Circuit Court level. It states this to be the circuit where any of the parties ordinarily resides or carries on any trade, profession or occupation. Therefore, the circuit upon which any party lives or works is bestowed with jurisdiction, which may mean that a litigant commencing proceedings would have a choice of circuit.

In exercising such a choice, a litigant might be influenced by geographical factors, considerations of privacy, a circuit which is a distance from the place of residence may be preferred for this reason, and the waiting list for obtaining a hearing date on the particular circuits. An interesting situation arises if parties are domiciled in Ireland, but neither is ordinarily resident here. This might arise, *e.g.* where the parties are working abroad under a long-term contract. In these circumstances it would appear that the no circuit has jurisdiction and that, in consequence, proceedings must be commenced at High Court level.

Section 38(3) of the 1996 Act indicates that Circuit Court jurisdiction may be exercised by "the judge of the circuit" in question. This wording seems to indicate that there will only be one such judge. However, it should be noted that section 10 of the Courts of Justice Act 1936 provides for the temporary assignment of judges to any circuit by the President of the Circuit Court. This clearly envisages that there may be judges temporarily assigned, sitting on a particular circuit notwithstanding that there is a Circuit Judge permanently assigned thereto. Such duality regularly occurs particularly since the number of Circuit Court judicial appointments has been expanded over recent years. The wording of the 1996 Act in this regard would, however, appear restrictive. A query arises where there is a judge assigned to the circuit in question, as to whether any judge other that he who has been permanently assigned could be described as "the judge of the circuit in question". A reference to " a judge of the circuit in question" might have been less controversial and more accurate.

Notice of proceedings under Act

40.—Notice of any proceedings under this Act shall be given by the person bringing the proceedings to—

    (a) the other spouse concerned or, as the case may be, the spouses concerned, and

    (b) any other person specified by the court.

GENERAL NOTE

This section gives a wide discretion to the court as to who should be on notice of the proceedings. Normally the parties to divorce proceedings will be the marriage partners only and the only necessary notice is by the applicant to the respondent. The section provides that it is mandatory that notice be given to the other spouse or spouses concerned. The reference to giving notice to both spouses presupposes that neither spouse is the applicant for relief. This might happen in circumstances in which ancillary reliefs were being sought by or on behalf of a dependent member of the family or where a variation is sought by a new spouse following remarriage. The court is additionally empowered to require notification of any other person, which would appear to be wide enough to cover any individual or body with legal personality. While there are specific notice requirements set out in other areas of the Act, *e.g.* section 17 requires that the trustees of the pension scheme be placed on notice where an application for a pension adjustment order is being made with the trustees being given an opportunity to make representations and section 18 directs notification of the widow where the deceased had prior to his death remarried, this is a wider, more general provision.

A court is likely to direct such notice where a notice party would have an interest in the outcome of the proceedings. The likely circumstances would be where the third party claims an interest in property the subject matter of a dispute between the parties, this type of situation has previously been discussed in relation to reviewable dispositions under section 37 of the 1996 Act. Additionally, circumstances might arise where a dependent member of the family would be required to be put on notice of the proceedings, if the interests of that dependent member would be at issue and such member requires to be heard or it is in the interests of justice that such member would be heard. In this regard, it is interesting to note the provisions for the appointment of a guardian *ad litem* in respect of minor children introduced in the Children Act 1997 (No. 40).

Custody of dependent members of family after decree of divorce

41.—Where the court makes an order for the grant of a decree of divorce, it may declare either of the spouses concerned to be unfit to have custody of any dependent member of the family who is a minor and, if it does so and the spouse to whom the declaration relates is a parent of any dependent member of the family who is a minor, that spouse shall not, on the death of the other spouse, be entitled as of right to the custody of that minor.

GENERAL NOTE

Section 41 mirrors the provisions of section 41 of the Judicial Separation and Family Law Reform Act 1989 and section 46 of the Family Law Act 1995, both sections permit the court to make a declaration as to the unfitness of one of the parties to the proceedings to have custody of a minor child of the marriage, consequent on a decree of judicial separation or nullity being granted. Section 41 of the 1996 Act states that where a decree of divorce is granted, the court may declare either of the parties to the proceedings to be unfit to have custody of a minor dependent family member. This section does not permit the making of a similar order in respect of, *e.g.* a physically or mentally disabled family member who is not a minor. Section 41 goes on to provide that in the event of the death of the custodial parent of such a minor child, the other parent in respect of whom the declaration as to unfitness was made shall not be entitled as of right to custody of the minor child. In that event, an application would have to be made to the court to have the declaration of unfitness discharged or quashed. Evidence would have to be placed before the court that the conduct or behaviour of the party seeking to have the order discharged had altered in such a way that the application was now a fit and proper person to be entrusted with custody of the minor child.

If a court is contemplating making such a declaration, then it must regard the welfare of the minor child as being of the first and paramount consideration, as it is charged to do in all proceedings concerning the welfare of children, section 3 of the Guardianship of Infants Act 1964. Section 41 is silent as to the grounds on which the court might decide to make such a declaration and no guidelines or specifications appear in the legislation in that regard. Presumably, a court would feel compelled to make such a declaration if the conduct of the spouse in question has been seriously detrimental to the welfare of the minor child.

The limitations of this section should be noted. It applies to custody only and it is possible that notwithstanding an unfitness regarding custody, access might be continuing between the child and the parent concerned. Courts are reluctant to deprive children of all contact with a parent. Similarly, the provision does not relate to guardianship. Section 10(2) of the 1996 Act makes it clear that post-divorce, the joint guardianship of married or formerly married parents continues. Therefore, notwithstanding a section 41 order, guardianship rights would appear to prevail. It is unlikely that an order under section 41 would be made, save in exceptional circumstances and where serious cause for doing so is shown.

Social reports in family law proceedings

42.—Section 47 of the Act of 1995 shall apply to proceedings under this Act.

GENERAL NOTE

The role of social reports in family law proceedings is central to the efforts of parents and practitioners involved in family law disputes and the courts in resolving difficult child centered matters. These reports and the preceding assessments have played a pivotal role in recent years for various reasons. Judges faced with increasing volumes of family law matters before the courts sometimes consider that they have neither the time nor the expertise necessary to unravel bitter parenting disputes. Practitioners frequently find attempts to negotiate viable parenting arrangements fruitless in the face of the intractable positions adopted by parents. The court in an adversarial system must look beyond the views of opposing parties and have as its primary consideration the paramount welfare of the child. An assessment and report, provided usually by experts in the area are sometimes the only objective and independent means of presenting the wishes of the children to the court.

In recent years a veritable industry has grown up in the production of social reports. While in some cases such reports are a prerequisite to the resolution of a child care dispute, the cost of their production can frequently be prohibitive and the undertaking of an assessment and report can frequently extend the duration of the proceedings.

The power of the court to procure such reports was introduced in section 40 of the 1989 Judicial Separation Act, which was repealed by section 47 of the 1995 Family Law Act. The then Minister for Equality and Law Reform, Mervyn Taylor T.D., at the time of coming into operation of section 47 declared that "the reporting role of the Probation and Welfare Service and the Health Boards in a range of family law areas is now on a Statutory basis" (448 *Dáil Debates* Col. 886). However, in recent years the probation and welfare service found themselves overwhelmed by the volume of family law cases, especially in the Dublin area. Since 1992, they have been unable to provide a full service largely because of under funding from the Exchequer. The loss of the probation and welfare service in this regard has greatly hindered the ability of the courts to invoke the services of such experts without incurring great costs to both parties and the imminent restoration of an expanded service is to be welcomed.

Section 42 of the 1996 Act extends the provisions of section 47 to divorce proceedings. Section 47 permits the court, either of its own motion or on foot of an application to it by either of the parties to the proceedings, to direct that a report is to be furnished to the court addressing questions concerning the welfare of the children. Section 47(1) provided that the categories of persons who could produce such a report were:

(a) The probation and welfare service;
(b) A person nominated by the health board; and
(c) Any other person specified in the order.

Examples of those coming within category (c) are, for example a suitably qualified child psychologist, or if appropriate, a child psychiatrist.

When deciding whether or not to direct the procurement of such a report the court must, under section 47(2) of the 1995 Act have regard to submissions which may be made to it by or on behalf of either of the parties, or by "any other person to whom they relate". Section 47(3) clearly states that a copy of any such report is to be given to both parties and to any person to whom the contents of the report relate. Although it is generally assumed that the reports are not made available to the children to whom they refer. It is submitted however that this is a matter which could have been clarified in the drafting of the 1996 Act. In relation to the cost of the assessment and report, section 47(4) permits the court to determine the method of payment and the person by whom payment should be made. The author of the report may be directed, pursuant to section 47(5), to give evidence in relation to the report and consequently to be cross-examined in relation to same.

It should be noted that prior to section 11 of the Children Act 1997 (No. 40) coming into operation the provisions of section 47 did not apply to District Court proceedings. Section 11(26) of this Act has amended Part III of the Guardianship of Infants Act 1964 in this regard.

The volume and complexity of parenting disputes which arrive before the courts; together with the court's duty to regard the welfare of the infants as first and paramount, dictates that a review of family law court welfare systems would not only be timely, but is long overdue. Despite the fact that the services of the probation and welfare officer have been enshrined in legislation, this service itself has been neglected and marginalised at a cost to all who participate in the family law system.

Cost of mediation and counselling services

43.—The cost of any mediation services or counselling services provided for a spouse who is or becomes a party to proceedings under this Act, the Act of 1964 or the Act of 1989 or for a dependent member of the family of such a spouse shall be in the discretion of the court concerned.

GENERAL NOTE

Section 43 provides simply that the costs of any mediation or counselling services undertaken by either or both of the parties to proceedings under the Guardianship of Infants Act 1964, the Judicial Separation and Family Law Reform Act 1989, or the Divorce Act 1996 shall be directed to be paid by whomever and in whatever proportion the court decides. There is a similar provision in section 11(29) of the Children Act 1997 (No. 40). The court may give directions as to who shall bear the costs of such services whether they have been availed of by either of the parties concerned or by a dependent family member.

Recently, the family mediation service in Ireland has been expanded with additional Exchequer funding, which will make the service more widely available throughout the country. Until recent years this service, which is provided on a no-cost basis by the Government, was confined to the Dublin and Limerick areas. The service is now available in Cork and will shortly expand to Galway, Wexford, Athlone, Dundalk and Tralee. The services of independent mediators may also be engaged by the parties to proceedings and the court may direct that such fees be paid by either or both of the parties concerned. There is not State run and funded counselling service, although the role of marriage counselling was recognised recently by the provision of additional Department of Social, Community and Family Affairs grants to support counselling services operated by volunteers. The provision of financial support for child counselling services in relation to parental separation was included in recent funding.

Determination of questions between persons formerly engaged to each other in relation to property

44.—Where an agreement to marry is terminated, section 36 of the Act of 1995 shall apply, as if the parties to the agreement were married to each other, to any dispute between them, or claim by one of them, in relation to property in which either or both of them had a beneficial interest while the agreement was in force.

GENERAL NOTE

Section 44 of the 1996 Act effectively amends section 36 of the 1995 Family Law Act insofar as that section relates to the determination of disputes regarding property which arise between people whose agreement to marry has terminated. The purpose of section 44 is to clarify the omission in section 36(8) from the category of persons who would be treated as a spouse for the purpose of an application pursuant to section 36 of parties to an engagement which had been terminated.

The Family Law Act 1981 sets out the law applicable to the determination of such disputes and extends to the parties of a terminated engagement the right to attempt to resolve property disputes in the same manner as a married couple. In circumstances where such a dispute arises in relation to property in which during the currency of the engagement, either or both parties had a beneficial interest, either party may have recourse to the provisions of section 5(2) of the 1981 Act. This section permits such parties to institute proceedings against the other party pursuant to section 12 of the Married Women's Status Act 1957 for the determination of such dispute. A lacuna emerged however, as section 12 of the 1957 Act was repealed by the 1995 Act with the section 36 provisions of that Act replacing section 12, but only as to inter-spousal disputes. In the case of engaged couples the dispute could relate to either the home in which the parties resided or to any other property, either real or personal, in which either party had a beneficial interest as outlined above. This lacuna has been filled by extending section 36 of the 1995 Act, in accordance with section 44 of the 1996 Act.

Section 36(8) of the 1995 Act sets out the categories of persons to whom references could be made as a "spouse". Section 36(8) did not specifically refer to a reference to spouse as including parties formerly engaged to be married. Section 44 of the 1996 Act clarifies this position and states that in circumstances where an engagement is terminated, the provisions of section 36 will apply to any dispute between the parties to the broken engagement, which dispute concerns property in which either or both of them had a beneficial interest while the engagement was in force. A dispute between the parties could also refer to a claim by either of the spouses in respect of such property.

It should also be noted that the provisions of section 48 of the 1995 Act, which is clearly marked as an "avoidance of doubt" provision, clarifies the position whereby section 5(1) of the Family Law Act 1981 applies to formerly engaged couples the rules relating to the rights of spouses to the ownership of property in which either or both of them had a beneficial interest, including the presumption of advancement; albeit subject to some constitutional suspicion.

Amendment of Act of 1989

45.—The Act of 1989 is hereby amended—
(a) in section 3(2)(a), by the substitution of the following subparagraph for subparagraph (i):
"(i) is satisfied that such provision exists or has been made, or",
(b) in section 7, by the deletion of subsection (7), and
(c) by the insertion of the following section before section 8:
"Non-admissibility as evidence of certain communications relating to reconciliation or separation
7A.—An oral or written communication between either of the spouses concerned and a third party for the purpose of seeking assistance to effect a reconciliation or to reach agreement between them on some or all of the terms of a separation (whether or not made in the presence or with the knowledge of the other spouse), and any record of such a communication, made or caused to be made by either of the spouses concerned or such a third party, shall not be admissible as evidence in any court.".

GENERAL NOTE

Section 45 amends the Judicial Separation and Family Law Reform Act 1989 by directing the court not to grant a decree of judicial separation in circumstances where there are dependent children in the family, unless it is satisfied that proper provision exists or has been made for their welfare. This allows the court to decide whether existing provisions already agreed between the parties governing the welfare of the children are satisfactory. Section 3(2)(a)(ii) of the 1989 Act permits the court, on the granting of the decree, to make such provision for the welfare of the children "as is proper in the circumstances". Section 45(b) effects the deletion of section 7(7) of the 1989 Act and the replacement of same by a new section 7A which is almost identical to section 9 of the 1996 Act. The effect of both sections is to confer a privilege on communications entered into by the parties with a view to effecting a reconciliation, or with a view to concluding some or all the terms of a separation, or divorce, as per section 9 of the 1996 Act. In this regard, reference is made to the earlier discussion of section 9 (see page 24).

Amendment of Act of 1965

46.—Section 117(6) of the Act of 1965 is hereby amended by the substitution of "6 months" for "twelve months".

GENERAL NOTE

Section 46 amends section 117 of the Succession Act 1965 (the 1965 Act) by reducing the time limit allowed for such applications after representation to the deceased's estate has been taken out, from 12 to six months. Section 117 provides that in circumstances where a court is satisfied that "the Testator has failed in his moral duty to make proper provision for the child in accordance with his means, whether by Will or otherwise", the court may direct that the child receives such proper provision as it thinks just out of the estate of the testator. Section 117(2) directs the court to consider the application from the point of view of a "prudent and just" parent. The court is also obliged to consider the position of each child of the family and all other circumstances that could assist the court in reaching a fair decision for all children concerned. Section 117(3) provides that any order made pursuant to section 117(1) will not affect the legal right of the surviving spouse on intestacy, nor will it affect any devise or bequest which may have been left to that spouse, if they are the mother or father of the child in question. If however, a surviving spouse who is not the mother of the children, is bequeathed the testator's entire estate, then an application may be made by the children for relief pursuant to section 117, provided always that any orders so made will not interfere with the legal right share of the surviving spouse.

Only the provisions of section 117(6) have been altered by the 1996 Act, which now provides that any such application must be made within six months of the extraction of the grant of representation and not within 12 months, as before. The reduction of the application period places greater pressure on children who might consider making such an application to ensure that they do so within the six month period. In the context of divorce, it can be anticipated that in the future section 117 applications will be made where parents have failed to provide for all their children, whether by first or subsequent marriages.

Due to the direction contained in section 5(1)(c) of the 1996 Act, that proper provision should exist or be made for the dependant family members on the granting of a decree of divorce, it is anticipated that any section 117 application could only take into account the failure of the testator to provide for the children subsequent to a grant of divorce. In that regard, it should be noted that section 117 does not limit the definition of child to a minor or to a dependant family member under the age of 23 and accordingly applications may be made by children of any age. As with all section 117 applications, the court will have regard to provision already made for the applicant by the testator during his or her lifetime.

Amendment of Pensions Act, 1990

47.—The Pensions Act, 1990, is hereby amended as follows:

    (a) in subsection (4)(a) (inserted by the Pensions (Amendment) Act, 1996) of section 5, by the substitution of "paragraph (c) or (cc) of section 10(1)" for "section 10(1)(c),",

    (b) subsection (4) (inserted by the Pensions (Amendment) Act, 1996) of section 5 shall apply and have effect in relation to section 17 as it applies and has effect in relation to section 12 of the Act of 1995 with the modifications that—

        (i) the reference to the said section 12 shall be construed as a reference to section 17,

       (ii) the reference in paragraph (c) to the Family Law Act, 1995, shall be construed as a reference to the Family Law (Divorce) Act, 1996,

      (iii) the references to subsections (1), (2), (3), (5), (6), (7), (8), (10) and (25) of the said section 12 shall be construed as references to subsections (1), (2), (3), (5), (6), (7), (8), (10) and (25), respectively, of section 17, and

      (iv) the reference to section 2 of the Act of 1995 shall be construed as a reference to section 2,

and

  (c) in section 10(1), by the substitution for paragraph (cc) (inserted by the Pensions (Amendment) Act, 1996) of the following paragraph:
"(cc) to issue guidelines or guidance notes generally on the operation of this Act and on the provisions of the Family Law Act, 1995, and the Family Law (Divorce) Act, 1996, relating to pension schemes (within the meaning of section 2 of the Family Law Act, 1995 and section 2 of the Family Law (Divorce) Act, 1996);".

GENERAL NOTE

    Section 47 effects amendments to the law governing pensions to take account of the introduction of divorce. The legislation is primarily contained in the Pensions Act 1990 (No. 25), the Pensions (Amendment) Act 1996 (No. 18) and the Statutory Instruments and guidelines issued pursuant to this legislation. Section 5(4) of the 1990 Act was amended by the 1996 Act to deal with the availability of pension adjustment orders pursuant to section 12 of the Family Law Act 1995. Section 47 now incorporates the availability of pension adjustment orders under section 17 of the 1996 Act.

    Section 47(c) inserts a new subsection (cc) into section 10(1) of the 1990 Act, which was already amended by the Pensions (Amendment) Act 1996. The initial amendment provided for the issue of general guidelines or guidance notes on the operation of the 1990 Act and particularly on the operation of the provisions of the 1995 Act. The new section 10(1)(cc) provides for the issue of guidelines or guidance notes in relation to divorce in general.

    Section 5 of the 1990 Act provided for the making of regulations by the Minister for any purpose connected with the 1990 Act. Section 10 of the 1990 Act details the function of the Pensions Board and section 10(1)(cc) specifically directs that one of the functions of the Board will be to issue guidelines on "the duties and responsibilities of Trustees of schemes and codes of practice on specific aspects of their responsibilities."

Amendment of Criminal Damage Act, 1991

  48.—Section 1(3) of the Criminal Damage Act, 1991, is hereby amended—

    (a) in paragraph (a), by the insertion after "1976," of the following:
"or a dwelling, within the meaning of section 2(2) of the Family Home Protection Act, 1976, as amended by section 54(1)(a) of the Family Law Act, 1995, in which a person, who is a party to a marriage that has been dissolved under the Family Law (Divorce) Act, 1996, or under the law of a country or jurisdiction other than the State, being a divorce that is entitled to be recognised as valid in the State, ordinarily resided with his or her former spouse, before the dissolution",

and

(b) in paragraph (b), by the substitution of the following subparagraph for subparagraph (i):

"(i) is the spouse of a person who resides, or is entitled to reside, in the home or is a party to a marriage that has been dissolved under the Family Law (Divorce) Act, 1996, or under the law of a country or jurisdiction other than the State, being a divorce that is entitled to be recognised as valid in the State, and".

GENERAL NOTE

The Criminal Damage Act 1991 (No. 31) (the 1991 Act) sets out the law applicable to criminal damage of property, one of the basic tenets is that destruction of ones own property is not an offence, unless it can be established that an accused intended to damage or was reckless as to whether his own property was damaged and intended to "defraud" or endanger the life of another. Based on this premise, a family home intentionally damaged by an accused who did not intend to endanger life or to defraud would not come within the definition of "damaging property", as set out in sections 2 and 3 of the 1991 Act. For example, where such damage was carried out by an accused to re-assert his right of possession in respect of a property from which he has been barred.

However, the provisions of section 3(3) of the 1991 Act criminalise such an action by "a spouse of a person who resides, or is entitled to reside, in the home," being a family home within the meaning of the Family Home Protection Act 1976, where such spouse has been excluded from the family home either by a protection order, barring order or exclusion order under the Family Law Act 1995, or by any other order of a court. In such circumstances, the provisions of the 1991 Act in relation to criminal damage will apply and an accused will be liable to the same penalties as an accused found guilty of criminal damage to property not comprising the family home.

Section 48 of the 1996 Act amends section 3(3)(a) of the 1991 Act to render it an offence to cause criminal damage to a property where a person resides whose marriage has been dissolved under the 1996 Act, or who has a foreign divorce which is recognised as being valid in this jurisdiction. This provision applies where the person charged with such an offence is a spouse of a person who resides in the home, or is a spouse of a person who has been divorced pursuant either to the 1996 Act or who has obtained a validly recognised foreign divorce. Section 48 purports to amend section 1(3) of the 1991 Act, however this should read section 3(3) of the Act.

Amendment of Criminal Evidence Act, 1992

49.—Section 20 of the Criminal Evidence Act, 1992, is hereby amended in section 20—

(a) by the insertion of the following definition:

" 'decree of divorce' means a decree under section 5 of the Family Law (Divorce) Act, 1996 or any decree that was granted under the law of a country or jurisdiction other than the State and is recognised in the State;",

and

(b) by the substitution of the following definition for the definition of former spouse:

" 'former spouse' includes a person who, in respect of his or her marriage to an accused—

(a) has been granted a decree of judicial separation, or

(b) has entered into a separation agreement, or

(c) has been granted a decree of divorce;".

GENERAL NOTE

Part IV of the Criminal Evidence Act 1992 (No. 12) (the 1992 Act) deals with the competence and compellability of spouses and former spouses to give evidence in criminal proceedings involving the other spouse. The 1992 Act amended the previous position, which was that apart from a number of exceptions at common law, such as violence against the other spouse and certain statutory exceptions, a spouse of an accused was neither competent nor compellable to give evidence against the accused for the prosecution. The Criminal Justice (Evidence) Act 1924 (No. 37) provided that the spouse of an accused should be a competent defence witness, although it was unclear whether this meant that such a spouse was also compellable. The spouse of an accused was also competent to testify for a co-accused regarding certain designated offences and in any other case where the accused's spouse consented to such testimony.

Part IV of the 1992 Act makes reference to former spouses, who are defined in section 20 of the 1992 Act as including a person who:

> "in respect of his marriage to an accused; (a) has been granted a decree of Judicial Separation or (b) has entered into a Separation Agreement, where such Separation Agreement provides for the parties concerned to live separate and apart from each other."

Section 20 defines a decree of judicial separation as including a decree of divorce *a mensa et thoro*, or any decree made in another jurisdiction which has a similar effect. Section 49 of the 1996 Act amends section 20 of the 1992 Act by including in the definition of a former spouse an accused a person who has obtained a decree of divorce pursuant to the 1996 Act, or pursuant to a foreign decree of divorce which is recognised as valid in this jurisdiction.

The current position is that pursuant to section 21 of the 1992 Act, spouses or former spouses of an accused are competent to give evidence at the instance of either the prosecution or the defence in respect of the accused, or any co-accused in the same proceedings. Section 22(1) of the 1992 Act provides that the spouse of an accused shall be compellable to give evidence for the prosecution only in cases of an offence involving violence to the spouse, a child of either the spouse or the accused, or any other minor; in cases where a sexual offence is alleged to have been committed in relation to one of the above; and in cases where the offence consists of attempts or conspiracy to commit, or of aiding, abetting, counselling, procuring or inciting the commission of one of these offences. Section 22(2) provides that a former spouse of an accused is compellable to give evidence for the prosecution, unless the offence charged was alleged to have been committed at a time when the marriage was subsisting. Both sections 22(1) and (2) are subject to the provisions of section 25, which provides that where a spouse or a former spouse is charged in the same proceedings as an accused, they are neither competent to give evidence for the prosecution nor compellable to do so for a co-accused.

Amendment of Powers of Attorney Act, 1996

50.—The Powers of Attorney Act, 1996, is hereby amended—

    (a) in section 5(7), by the substitution of the following paragraph for paragraph (a):

      "(a) the marriage is annulled or dissolved either—

        (i)   under the law of the State, or

        (ii) under the law of another state and is, by reason of that annulment or divorce, not or no longer a subsisting valid marriage under the law of the State,",

    (b) in Part I of the Second Schedule, by the insertion of the following paragraph:

      "2A. The expiry of an enduring power of attorney effected in the circumstances mentioned in section 5(7) shall apply only so far as it relates to an attorney who is the spouse of the donor.".

GENERAL NOTE

The Powers of Attorney Act 1996 (No. 12) created a new legal instrument called "an enduring power of attorney." This document is intended to create an instrument which would be signed, for example, in circumstances where the onset of mental illness or mental disability, *e.g.* Alzheimers disease, would render the donor of the power of attorney unable to manage their affairs. The execution by the donor of an enduring power of attorney would allow the donee power to act on their behalf in accordance with the terms of the instrument. The enduring power of attorney comes into effect when it is registered, pursuant to section 10 of the Powers of Attorney Act 1996. Once the power of attorney is executed it cannot be revoked by the donor's subsequent mental illness or disability. This is in contrast to the previous legal position whereby a power of attorney would in such circumstances have become invalid on such mental incapacity.

Section 5 of the Powers of Attorney Act 1996 sets out the characteristics of an enduring power of attorney. Section 5(7) enumerates the circumstances in which an enduring power, granted in favour of a spouse will be rendered invalid. A power granted in favour of a spouse is invalid in the following circumstances, where:

(a) An annulment or foreign divorce has been granted (section 5(7)(a));
(b) A judicial separation has been granted either in or outside the State if the separation is recognised as valid within the State (section 5 (7)(b));
(c) A separation agreement is entered into by both parties (section 5 (7)(c));
(d) Or where relief is granted by the making of an order pursuant to the Domestic Violence Act 1996 against either the donor or the donee of the power (section 5(7((d)).

Section 50 of the Divorce Act simply amends the Powers of Attorney Act 1996 to incorporate into its terms the effect of the availability of divorce in this jurisdiction. Section 50(6) confirms that an enduring power of attorney will expire in the circumstances set ou in section 5(7) provided that the power of attorney has been made in favour of an attorney who is the spouse of the donor.

Amendment of Act of 1996

51.—The references in sections 2 and 3 of the Act of 1996 to a spouse shall be construed as including references to a person who is a party to a marriage that has been dissolved under this Act or under the law of a country or jurisdiction other than the State, being a divorce that is entitled to be recognised as valid in the State.

GENERAL NOTE

The effect of section 51 is to ensure that a former spouse who has obtained a decree of divorce either in this jurisdiction or in another jurisdiction does not lose the protection against domestic violence afforded by the Domestic Violence Act 1996 (No. 1) (the D.V. Act 1996). A person who seeks such protection, who is not a designated spouse for the purposes of the D.V. Act 1996 is required, pursuant to section 3(4) of the Act, to comply with certain conditions.

Under the terms of section 3(i)(b) of the D.V. Act 1996, a barring order cannot be granted to an applicant who is not a spouse and who has not lived with the respondent for at least six months in aggregate out of the previous nine months, prior to making the application. In addition pursuant to section 3(4), such an order cannot be granted to any applicant whose legal and beneficial interest in the family home is less than that of the respondent.

Similarly, section 2(1)(a)(ii) provides that a safety order cannot be granted to an applicant who has not co-habited with the respondent for a period of at least six months in aggregate out of the previous 12 months preceding the date of the application.

Clearly in circumstances where a divorce has been granted the parties are no longer designated spouses and would not be in a position to comply with the residency requirements. Section 51 of the 1996 Act therefore contains important relief for former spouses who continue to experience violence at the hands of their former spouse. It includes the definition of "spouse" in the Domestic Violence Act 1996 a person who is a former spouse by reason of their having obtained a divorce under the 1996 Act and thus ensure that as former spouses, they would be entitled to relief under the Domestic Violence Act 1996.

Protection, barring and safety orders in the context of an application for divorce are granted pursuant to section 15 (see page 43) and in the case of preliminary orders pursuant to section 11 of the 1996 Act.

Amendment of Act of 1995

52.—The Act of 1995 is hereby amended—
   (a) in section 8—
      (i)   in subsection (1), by the insertion of "or at any time thereafter" after "separation",
      (ii) in paragraph (c)(i) of that subsection, by the insertion of "or" after "so specified", and
      (iii) in subsection (4), by the substitution of "the spouse, or any dependent member of the family, in whose favour the order is made or the other spouse concerned" for "either of the spouses concerned",

GENERAL NOTE — SECT. 52(a)

Section 52 provides numerous and significant amendments to the Family Law Act 1995. It reflects, in the context of judicial separation, the effect of the introduction of divorce and the legal position of divorced persons. While many of the amendments are technical, section 52(g) introduces important new reliefs for a spouse by the insertion of a new section 15(A) into the 1995 Act and this section extends to judicial separation the provisions of section 18 of the 1996 Act and this enables a spouse whose Succession Act rights have been extinguished by an order under section 14 of the 1995 Act, to apply in specified circumstances to the court for an order seeking provision out of the estate of their deceased spouse.

Section 52(a) amends section 8 of the 1995 Act which provides for the making of periodical payment orders and lump sum orders on the granting of a decree of judicial separation. Section 8(1) is amended by section 52(a)(i) to provide that orders may be made either at the time of the granting of the decree of judicial separation "or at any time thereafter", thus bringing such applications in line with similar applications in the context of divorce. Section 52(a)(ii) allows the court to make an order for a lump sum payment or payments to either the other spouse, or to a dependent family member on the granting of a decree of judicial separation, or at any time thereafter. Whereas previously the 1995 Act did not seem to allow for an "either/or" situation in relation to lump sum payments, it is arguable that where section 8(1) allows the court to make "one or more of the following Orders", that that power was implicit already in the section.

   (b) in section 9(1), by the insertion of "or at any time thereafter" after "separation",

GENERAL NOTE — SECT. 52(b)

Section 52(b) empowers aan applicant for a property adjustment order applicant under section 9 of the 1995 Act to make the application either at the time of the granting of the decree of judicial separation or "at any time thereafter." This has the effect of permitting a spouse who has not remarried to make one or more applications for a property adjustment order against the other spouse. This power is not available to a spouse who has previously obtained a property adjustment order pursuant to section 15 of the Judicial Separation and Family Law Reform Act 1989 (the 1989 Act). However it would be open to such an applicant to seek a new property adjustment order pursuant to section 14 of the 1996 Act.

> (c) in section 10—
>> (i) in subsection (1), by the insertion of "or at any time thereafter" after "separation", and
>> (ii) by the insertion after subsection (2) of the following subsection:
>>> "(3) Subsection (1)(a) shall not apply in relation to a family home in which, following the grant of a decree of judicial separation, either of the spouses concerned, having remarried, ordinarily resides with his or her spouse.",

GENERAL NOTE — SECT. 52(c)

Section 52(c) amends section 10 of the 1995 Act which is now identical in its terms to section 15 of the 1996 Act. Section 52(c)(i) provides that section 10 allows the court to make miscellaneous ancillary orders either at the time of the granting of a decree of judicial separation or at any time thereafter. Section 52(c)(ii) amends section 10(3) of the 1995 Act and refers to the power of the court under section 10(1)(a)(i) and (ii) of the 1995 Act to make exclusion orders and orders for sale in respect of the family home. Before the coming into operation of the new section 10(3), parties who had obtained a validly recognised foreign divorce were obliged to rely on section 23 of the 1995 Act to prevent a sale of the family home in which they ordinarily resided having remarried with their new spouse. The insertion of the new section 10(3) provides that neither an exclusion order nor an order directing the sale of a family home in those circumstances may be made. With the availability of divorce in this jurisdiction, the necessity for relief under section 10(3) will probably arise more frequently than heretofore.

> (d) in sections 11(2)(a), 12(23)(b) and 25(1), by the substitution of "proper provision, having regard to the circumstances," for "adequate and reasonable financial provision", in each place where it occurs,

GENERAL NOTE — SECT. 52(d)

Section 52(d) amends section 11(2)(a) of the 1995 Act in relation to financial compensation orders, section 12(23)(b) in relation to pension adjustment orders, and section 25(1) in relation to orders for the provision for a spouse out of the estate of another spouse in circumstances where that marriage is the subject of a foreign divorce. The effect of the amendments is to alter the standard of "adequate and reasonable financial provision" to "proper provision having regard to the circumstances". In the context of financial compensation orders and pension adjustment orders in judicial separation, the court must decide whether by making orders pursuant to sections 8, 9 and 10 of the 1995 Act, it can ensure that the spouse and dependent family members receive proper provision.

Where an application is made under section 25 of the 1995 Act, seeking an order on behalf of an applicant who has obtained a foreign divorce for provision out of the estate of their deceased spouse, the court must address the issue of whether or not it was possible during the lifetime of that deceased spouse to properly provide for the applicant spouse, in all the circumstances, pursuant to sections 8, 9, 10, 11 and 12 of the 1995 Act. This section permits the courts to be consistent in its approach to applications for ancillary relief in the context of both judicial separation and divorce.

> (e) in section 12—
>> (i) in subsection (1), in the definition of "relevant guidelines", by the substitution of "paragraph (c) or (cc) of section 10(1)" for "section 10(1)(c)", and
>> (ii) in subsection (18), by the substitution of "40" for "41",

GENERAL NOTE — SECT. 52(e)

Section 52(e) incorporates into section 12 of the 1995 Act the amendment effected by section 47(c) of the 1996 Act which introduced section 10(i)(cc) into the Pensions Act 1990. Section 10 was inserted into the 1990 Act by the Pensions (Amendment) Act 1996 (No. 18) (the Pensions Act 1996). This section granted authority to the Minister for Social Welfare, with the consent of the now Minister for Justice, to issue detailed guidance notes on the applicability of the provisions relating to pensions adjustment orders set out in the 1995 and 1996 Acts, to pension schemes. The new section 10(1)(cc) authorised the issue of "guidelines or guidance notes generally" on the "operation of this Act and on the provisions of the Family Law Act 1995 and the Family Law Divorce Act 1996" relating to pensions schemes which could be the subject of a pensions adjustment order.

The Pensions Schemes (Family Law) Regulations 1997 (S.I. 107 of 1997) were introduced pursuant to section 10 of the 1990 Act. The regulations set out the manner in which various calculations, including the manner in which a designated benefit, a contingent benefit, or a transfer amount payable on foot of a pension adjustment order are to be calculated by the trustees of the pensions scheme. Section 52(e)(ii) corrects a mistake in section 12(18) of the 1995 Act which referred to section 41 instead of section 40 of that Act, being the section referring to notice given of proceedings under that Act.

> (f) in section 15—
>> (i) in subsection (5), by the substitution of "10(1)(a)" for "10(1)(a)(ii)", and
>> (ii) by the insertion of the following subsection after subsection (5):
>> "(6) This section shall not apply in relation to a family home in which, following the grant of a decree of judicial separation, either of the spouses concerned, having remarried, ordinarily resides with his or her spouse.",

GENERAL NOTE — SECT. 52(f)

Section 52(f) amends section 15 of the 1995 Act which allows for the making of orders for the sale of property in circumstances where a secured periodical payments order, a lump sum order, or a property adjustment order has been made. The subject property of the order must be property in which either or both spouses have an interest or would have an interest in the proceeds of sale of the property. Section 15(5) provides that where a spouse has a beneficial interest in any property or in the proceeds of sale of any property and a person who is not the other spouse also has an interest in that property, then that person must have an opportunity to make representations to the court concerning the making of a potential order pursuant to section 10(1)(a) of the 1995 Act, for either an exclusion order or an order for sale. Practitioners attention is drawn to the constraints set out in section 15 against making such orders.

Section 52(f)(ii) introduces a new subsection 6 to section 15 which provides that no order for sale property can be made in relation to a family home in which a former spouse, having remarried following the grant of a decree of judicial separation, now resides with a new spouse.

 (g) by the insertion of the following section after section 15:

  "Orders for provision for spouse out of estate of other spouse

   15A.—(1) Subject to the provisions of this section, where, following the grant of a decree of judicial separation, a court makes an order under section 14 in relation to the spouses concerned and one of the spouses dies, the court, on application to it in that behalf by the other spouse ('the applicant') not more than 6 months after representation is first granted under the Act of 1965 in respect of the estate of the deceased spouse, may by order make such provision for the applicant out of the estate of the deceased spouse as it considers appropriate having regard to the rights of any other person having an interest in the matter and specifies in the order if it is satisfied that proper provision in the circumstances was not made for the applicant during the lifetime of the deceased spouse under section 8, 9, 10(1)(a), 11 or 12 for any reason (other than conduct referred to in subsection (2)(i) of section 16 of the applicant).

   (2) The court shall not make an order under this section if the applicant concerned has remarried since the granting of the decree of judicial separation concerned.

   (3) In considering whether to make an order under this section the court shall have regard to all the circumstances of the case including—

  (a) any order under paragraph (c) of section 8(1) or a property adjustment order in favour of the applicant, and

  (b) any devise or bequest made by the deceased spouse to the applicant.

   (4) The provision made for the applicant concerned by an order under this section together with any provision made for the applicant by an order referred to in subsection (3)(a) (the value of which for the purposes of this subsection shall be its value on the date of the order) shall not exceed in total the share (if any) of the applicant in the estate of the deceased spouse to which the applicant was entitled or (if the deceased spouse died intestate as to the whole or part of his or her estate) would have been entitled under the Act of 1965 if the court had not made an order under section 14.

   (5) Notice of an application under this section shall be given by the applicant to the spouse (if any) of the deceased spouse concerned and to such (if any) other persons as the court may direct and, in deciding whether to make the order concerned and in determining the provisions of the order, the court shall have regard to any representations made by the spouse of the deceased spouse and any other such persons as aforesaid.

   (6) The personal representative of a deceased spouse in re-

spect of whom a decree of judicial separation has been granted shall make a reasonable attempt to ensure that notice of his or her death is brought to the attention of the other spouse concerned and, where an application is made under this section, the personal representative of the deceased spouse shall not, without the leave of the court, distribute any of the estate of that spouse until the court makes or refuses to make an order under this section.

(7) Where the personal representative of a deceased spouse in respect of whom a decree of judicial separation has been granted gives notice of his or her death to the other spouse concerned ("the spouse') and—

(a) the spouse intends to apply to the court for an order under this section,

(b) the spouse has applied for such an order and the application is pending, or

(c) an order has been made under this section in favour of the spouse,

the spouse shall, not later than one month after the receipt of the notice, notify the personal representative of such intention, application or order, as the case may be, and, if he or she does not do so, the personal representative shall be at liberty to distribute the assets of the deceased spouse, or any part thereof, amongst the parties entitled thereto.

(8) The personal representative shall not be liable to the spouse for the assets or any part thereof so distributed unless, at the time of such distribution, he or she had notice of the intention, application or order aforesaid.

(9) Nothing in subsection (7) or (8) shall prejudice the right of the spouse to follow any such assets into the hands of any person who may have received them.

(10) On granting a decree of judicial separation or at any time thereafter, the court, on application to it in that behalf by either of the spouses concerned, may, during the lifetime of the other spouse or, as the case may be, the spouse concerned, if it considers it just to do so, make an order that either or both spouses shall not, on the death of either of them, be entitled to apply for an order under this section.",

GENERAL NOTE — SECT. 52(g)

Section 52(g) provides for the insertion of a new section 15A into section 15 of the 1995 Act. The effect of this amendment is to provide that following the grant of a decree of judicial separation, a spouse may retain an entitlement to apply for provision out of a deceased spouse's estate at the discretion of the court. The terms of section 15A are identical to those of section 18 (1) to (10) of the 1996 Act. A spouse who renounces his or her rights in a separation agreement retains no such residual right because it is not open to them to make a subsequent application to the court for a judicial separation, see *O'D. v. O'D.* [1998] I.L.R.M. 543. However a spouse in such a position will acquire a similar right pursuant to section 18(1) of the 1996 Act on their application for a decree of divorce. Section 113 of the

Succession Act 1965 provides that the legal right of a spouse may be renounced in an ante-nuptial contract, which is entered into by both parties to a proposed marriage in writing and which renunciation must be freely given by the party to the intended marriage. Similarly a spouse may renounce a legal right in a separation agreement in respect of which they are full advised as to the legal effect of so doing.

The new section 15A provides that where a court has granted a decree of judicial separation and has made an order by way of ancillary relief, under section 14 of the 1995 Act, and one of the spouses in respect of whom the order was made dies, then the other spouse may make an application to the court within six months of the date of the grant of representation in respect of the estate of the deceased spouse for an order directing that provision be made for the applicant spouse out of the estate of the deceased spouse. Section 15A specifically refers to section 14 of the 1995 Act and accordingly it is not open to a spouse whose Succession Act rights have been extinguished by an order pursuant to section 17 of the 1989 Act to make an application for provision out of the estate of their deceased spouse. However, a person in this position who subsequently applies for a decree of divorce may make such an application pursuant to section 18(1) of the 1996 Act. The order will only be made by the court, both in the context of section 18 and section 15A, in circumstances where on the granting of a decree of judicial separation or divorce, the court has not made an order blocking the entitlement of either of the spouses to apply for an order under the section (section 15A(10) of the 1995 Act and section 18(10) of the 1996 Act).

An applicant seeking relief pursuant to section 15A(1) must make an application to the court in that regard not more than six months after the grant of representation has been taken out to the estate of the deceased spouse. The section pre-supposes knowledge on behalf of the applicant spouse of the death of the deceased spouse. Section 15A(6) directs the personal representative of a deceased spouse, in respect of whom a grant of judicial separation has been obtained to make a "reasonable attempt" to ensure that notice of that death is brought to the attention of the surviving spouse. The 1996 Act does not provide a definition of "a reasonable attempt" and thus an onerous duty can come to rest on the shoulders of a personal representative of a deceased spouse who cannot locate the former spouse. Presumably the court will decide on a definition in each individual case.

The court must have regard to the rights of any other person having an interest in the matter when directing the provisions to be made out of the estate of the deceased spouse for the former spouse. The category of persons who might have "an interest" in the matter is very wide and non-specific. It is suggested that it could have been more narrowly defined, referring perhaps to dependent family members or to a remarried spouse of the deceased's spouse. Similarly there is no definition of what comprises "an interest" in the matter. In order to make a section 15A(1) order the court must be satisfied that proper provision in the circumstances was not made for the applicant during the lifetime of the deceased spouse by way of an order for periodical payments and lump sum orders, property adjustment orders, financial compensation orders, pension adjustment orders, or any other miscellaneous ancillary orders. It is specified that the question of the applicant's conduct cannot be taken into account in arriving at this decision.

Section 15A(2) specifies that an order cannot be made by the court in favour of an applicant who has remarried since the grant of judicial separation. The court must, pursuant to section 15A(3), have regard to all circumstances of the case, including whether or not any lump sum order was made in respect of the applicant spouse or a dependent family member; whether a property adjustment order was made in favour of the applicant and whether or not any devise or bequest was made by the deceased spouse in favour of the applicant, when considering whether to make a section 15(A)(1) order. Section 15A(4) provides that if the court decides to make an order, pursuant to section 15A(1), the provision directed by the court cannot exceed, taking into account any lump sum order which may have been made in respect of the applicant spouse, the value to which the applicant would have been entitled if no order had been made pursuant to section 14 of the 1995 Act extinguishing the applicant's Succession Act rights. For example, if a testator dies following the grant of a decree of judicial separation, leaving children, the maximum entitlement of the applicant spouse is a legal right to one third of the estate of the deceased spouse. Accordingly the order directed by the court pursuant to section 15A(1), together with the value of any previous lump sum ordered cannot exceed the value of one third of the estate of the deceased spouse.

Section 15A specifies provisions relating to notice requirements of the intention to apply for an order or the fact of an application or order having been made. Such notice must be given according to section 15A(5) to any spouse of the deceased spouse and to any other persons so directed by the court. These parties are entitled to make representations to the court in connection with the provision being sought by the applicant spouse. The court in deciding whether or not to make an order, shall have regard to any such representations made. Section 15A(7) directs that where an applicant spouse has received notice of the death of a former spouse from the personal representative of the deceased, the personal representative must be notified of the surviving spouse's intention to make an application or the fact of any such application or order made, within one month of receiving such notice. If such notice is not given then the personal representative may proceed to distribute all or any part of the assets of the estate to the persons entitled. If the personal representative is not in receipt of such notice from the applicant spouse, they are not liable to the applicant spouse for any assets already distributed (section 15A(8)). The applicant spouse, in those circumstances, is entitled to follow any assets so distributed into the hands of the person who receives them (section 15A(9)). A personal representative cannot distribute any of the estate of the deceased spouse in circumstances where they have notice of the intentions of the applicant spouse without leave of the court (section 15A (6)).

An identical provision to that contained in section 18(10) is contained in section 15A(10). It provides that at the granting of a decree of judicial separation, or at any subsequent time during the lifetime of either spouse, the court may direct that either or both of the spouses will not be entitled to make an application pursuant to section 15A(1). The court may make such an order if it considers it "just to do so". Clients should be advised that if they obtain an order pursuant to section 14 of the 1995 Act, the only way to block the other spouses residual entitlement to apply for a provision out of their estate on death is to have an section 15A(10) order made simultaneously. Only when orders have been made under both sections will the client be free to dispose of assets by will, without the possibility of a surviving spouse applying for further provision out of their estate.

In summary, only the following circumstances will permit a client to be advised of any certainty in connection with disposal of their assets on judicial separation:

(a) Where both spouses have renounced Succession Act rights in a deed of separation;

(b) Where an order was made pursuant to section 17 of the 1989 Act extinguishing Succession Act rights;

(c) Where orders are made pursuant to section 14 and section 15A(10) of the 1995 Act.

An anomaly arises however in the divorce context. Despite the fact that orders may have been made pursuant to sections 14 and 15A of the 1995 Act, a surviving spouse will, under section 18 of the 1996 Act resurrect his residual entitlement to apply for provision out of the estate of a deceased spouse on their application for a divorce. This situation also applies to applicants for a divorce who have obtained orders under paragraphs (b) and (a) above. Finally it should be noted that any orders made pursuant to section 15A will not prevent the surviving spouse from receiving the benefit of any devise or bequest made in their favour by the deceased spouse.

(h) in section 16(1)—

(i) by the insertion of "15A," after "14,",

(ii) by the substitution of "exists or will be made" for "is made", and

(iii) by the substitution of "proper" for "adequate and reasonable",

GENERAL NOTE — SECT. 52(h)

Section 52(h) amends section 16 of the 1995 Act and brings it into line with the standards concerning the provision to be made in respect of an applicant spouse and dependent family members in the context of judicial separation. The standard of "proper provision" pertains and the court must ensure that proper provision "exists or will be made" for the applicant or dependent family members. (section 52 (h)(ii))

> (i) in section 18, in subsection (1)(h), by the insertion of "insofar as such application is not restricted or excluded by section 12(26)" after "section 12",

GENERAL NOTE — SECT. 52(i)

Section 52(i) amends section 18 of the 1995 Act, which governs the variability of ancillary orders in the context of judicial separation. The amendment refers to section 12(26) of the 1995 Act which permits the court to make an order restricting or excluding the applicability of section 18 to pension adjustment orders. Section 52(i) provides that an order made under section 12(2) of the 1995 Act may be varied provided the application of section 18 to such an order has not been restricted or excluded by an order made under section 12(2)(b) of the 1995 Act.

> (j) in section 25—
>> (i) in subsection (1), by the substitution, as respects applications under that section made after the commencement of the Family Law (Divorce) Act, 1996, of "6 months" for "12 months", and
>> (ii) by the substitution of the following subsections for subsection (7):
>>> "(7) The personal representative of a deceased spouse in respect of whom a decree of divorce has been granted in a country or jurisdiction other than the State shall make a reasonable attempt to ensure that notice of his or her death is brought to the attention of the other spouse concerned and, where an application is made under this section, the personal representative of the deceased spouse shall not, without the leave of the court, distribute any of the estate of that spouse until the court makes or refuses to make an order under this section.
>>> (8) Where the personal representative of a deceased spouse in respect of whom a decree of divorce has been granted in a country or jurisdiction other than the State gives notice of his or her death to the other spouse concerned ('the spouse') and—
>>> (a) the spouse intends to apply to the court for an order under this section,
>>> (b) the spouse has applied for such an order and the application is pending, or
>>> (c) an order has been made under this section in favour of the spouse,
>>> the spouse shall, not later than one month after the receipt of the notice, notify the personal representative of such intention, application or order, as the case may be, and, if he or she does not do so, the personal representative shall be at liberty to dis-

tribute the assets of the deceased spouse, or any part thereof, amongst the parties entitled thereto.

(9) The personal representative shall not be liable to the spouse for the assets or any part thereof so distributed unless, at the time of such distribution, he or she had notice of the intention, application or order aforesaid.

(10) Nothing in subsection (8) or (9) shall prejudice the right of the spouse to follow any such assets into the hands of any person who may have received them.",

GENERAL NOTE — SECT. 52(j)

Section 52(j) amends section 25 of Part III of the 1995 Act. This section refers to relief which may be granted after divorce or separation is obtained outside the State to any applicant who requires an order for provision to be made for them out of the estate of their former spouse. Section 52(j) reduces the application time limit contained in section 25(1) of the 1995 Act from 12 months to six months.

Section 25(7) of the 1995 Act is replaced by section 52(j)(ii). The new subsection 7 sets out provisions relating to the duties of personal representatives to ensure that the applicant receives notification of the death of their former spouse. These provisions are identical to those set out in section 15A(6) of the 1995 Act. Similarly, section 25(8), (9) and (10) of the 1995 Act are amended by section 52(j)(ii) which are identical to sections 15A(7), (8) and (9), but which refer to divorces granted outside the State.

(k) in section 29, by the insertion of the following subsection after subsection (10):

"(11) In this section a reference to a spouse includes a reference to a person who is a party to a marriage that has been dissolved under the Family Law (Divorce) Act, 1996.",

GENERAL NOTE — SECT. 52(k)

Section 29 of the 1995 Act facilitates an application to the court for a declaration as to the validity or otherwise of the marital status of an applicant spouse. Section 52(k) incorporates a person who has obtained a divorce pursuant to the provisions of the 1996 Act into the definition of such a spouse.

(l) in section 35(1)—

(i) by the insertion in the definition of "relief", of "15A," after "13,", and

(ii) by the insertion in that definition, after paragraph (a), of the following paragraph:

"(aa) an order under section 11(2)(b) of the Act of 1964 or section 5, 5A or 7 of the Act of 1976, or",

GENERAL NOTE — SECT. 52(l)

This subsection amends section 35 of the 1995 Act which grants to the court power to make orders setting aside transactions by one spouse which are intended to prevent or reduce relief available to the other spouse. It is similar to the terms of section 37 of the 1996 Act. The definition of "relief" set out in section 35 of the 1995 Act is hereby amended to include relief newly available under the terms of section 15A of 1995 Act. Section 35(i)(aa) includes in the definition of "relief" maintenance payable pursuant to an order made under section 11(2)(b) of the Guardianship of Infants Act 1964, maintenance payable under sections 5, 5A and 7 of the Family Law (Maintenance of Spouses and Children) Act 1976.

    (m) in section 36—

        (i) in subsection (7)(a)(i), by the insertion of "or dissolved", after "annulled", and

        (ii) in subsection (8), after paragraph (c), by the insertion of the following paragraph:

        "(cc) either of the parties to a marriage that has been dissolved under the law of the State,",

GENERAL NOTE — SECT. 52(m)

    Section 36 of the 1995 Act allows the court to determine questions which may arise between spouses after the anulment or dissolution of a marriage as to the title to, or possession of any property. Such questions would formerly have come within the ambit of section 12 of the Married Women's Status Act 1957 (No. 5) (the 1957 Act). Section 36(7)(a) permits the bringing of such an application within three years of the date of such annulment or divorce, as permitted by the insertion of the word "dissolved" in section 36(7)(a)(i) of the 1995 Act, by virtue of the amendment in section 52(m)(i) of the 1996 Act. Section 52(m)(ii) introduces a new paragraph (cc) to section 36(8) and includes references to a spouse being a party whose marriage has been dissolved under the 1996 Act.

    (n) in section 38(7), by the insertion of "15A," after "14,",

GENERAL NOTE — SECT. 52(n)

    Section 38 of the 1995 Act grants concurrent jurisdiction to the Circuit Court and the High Court to hear proceedings pursuant to the 1995 Act. Section 52(n) amends the proceedings to include proceedings pursuant to section 15A of the 1995 Act.

    (o) in section 43—

        (i) in paragraph (a), by the substitution of the following subparagraph for subparagraph (ii):

        "(ii) in the definition of 'dependent child' the substitution of '18' for 'sixteen' and '23' for 'twenty-one', and",

        and

        (ii) by the substitution of the following paragraph for paragraph (e):

        "(e) in section 23, after subsection (2), the insertion of the following subsections:

        "(3) In proceedings under this Act—

        (a) each of the spouses concerned shall give to the other spouse and to, or to a person acting on behalf of, any dependent member of the family concerned, and

        (b) any dependent member of the family concerned shall give to, or to a person acting on behalf of, any other such member and to each of the spouses concerned,

    such particulars of his or her property and income as may reasonably be required for the purpose of the proceedings.

(4) Where a person fails or refuses to comply with sub-section (3), the Court, on application to it in that behalf by a person having an interest in the matter, may direct the person to comply with that subsection.'.'',

and

GENERAL NOTE — SECT. 52(o)

Section 43 of the 1995 Act amends the Family Law (Maintenance of Spouses and Children) Act 1976 primarily by adjusting its terms to take account of changes wrought by the 1989 and the 1995 Acts. Section 43(a)(ii) is replaced by section 52(o), which amends the definition of a dependent child to one who is under the age of 18 years, or 23 years, if in full time education.

Section 43(e) refers to the obligation on both spouses in an action pursuant to the 1976 Act to exchange particulars of their income and property, failing which the court may direct them to do so. The amendment introduced by section 52(o) imposes a similar obligation on spouses to impart such information in circumstances where relief is being sought not only by the other spouse, but also by a person acting on behalf of a dependent family member. The dependent family member is also obliged to comply with such a requirement, failing which the court may direct them to do so.

(p) in section 47—
  (a) in subsection (6), by the substitution of "This section" for "Sub-section (1)", and
  (b) in subsection (7), by the substitution of "(1)(b)" for "(2)".

GENERAL NOTE — SECT. 52(p)

Section 52(p) effects technical amendments to section 47 of the 1995 Act which deals with the issue of social reports and family law proceedings. This section applies to divorce proceedings by virtue of section 42 of the 1996 Act.

Amendment of Maintenance Act, 1994

53.—The Maintenance Act, 1994 (as amended by the Act of 1995), is hereby amended—
  (a) in section 3, in subsection (1), by the insertion of the following definition:
     " 'the Act of 1996' means the Family Law (Divorce) Act, 1996;",
  (b) in section 4, by the substitution of the following paragraph for paragraph (a) of subsection (2):
     "(a) For the purposes of section 8 of the Enforcement of Court Orders Act, 1940, the Act of 1976, the Act of 1988, the Act of 1993 (as amended by this Act), the Act of 1995, the Act of 1996 and this Act, the Central Authority shall have authority to act on behalf of, as the case may be, a maintenance creditor or claimant, within the meaning of section 13(1), and references in those enactments to a maintenance creditor or such a claimant shall be construed as including references to the Central Authority.",
  (c) in section 14—
     (i) in subsection (1)(c), by the substitution of the following

subparagraph for subparagraph (i):

"(i) if the amount of the maintenance sought to be recovered exceeds the maximum amount which the District Court has jurisdiction to award under the Act of 1976 or the request is for a relief order (within the meaning of the Act of 1995) or a maintenance pending suit order, a periodical payments order, a secured periodical payments order or a lump sum order (within the meaning, in each case, of the Act of 1996), make an application to the Circuit Court,",

and

(ii) by the substitution of the following subsection for subsection (3):

"(3) An application referred to in subsection (1)(c) shall be deemed to be an application for a maintenance order under section 5 or section 5A or 21A (inserted by the Status of Children Act, 1987) of the Act of 1976, or the appropriate order referred to in subsection (1)(c)(i), as may be appropriate, and to have been made on the date on which the request of the claimant for the recovery of maintenance was received by the Central Authority of the designated jurisdiction concerned.".

GENERAL NOTE

Section 53 amends the Maintenance Act 1994 (No. 28) (the 1994 Act) to render its provisions applicable to maintenance orders made under the 1996 Act. Prior to the coming into operation of the 1994 Act, recovery procedures for foreign maintenance orders were complicated, with some orders only being enforceable through the High Court. The 1994 Act provides that foreign periodical maintenance orders and foreign lump sum maintenance orders are enforceable through the District Court, although such orders and accrued maintenance arrears may be enforced through the High Court. The Master of the High Court or the court itself must deem such enforcement appropriate "as respects the sums concerned." (section 10 of the 1994 Act) The High Court is also empowered under this legislation to enforce foreign maintenance orders where the District Court does not have jurisdiction to do so. Section 11 of the 1994 Act also provides that the District Court can enforce a foreign maintenance order where the amount payable thereunder exceeds the maximum amount payable under a domestic District Court order.

In addition, the 1994 Act enabled the State to ratify the Rome Convention between the Member States of the E.U. on the Simplification of Procedures for Recovery of Maintenance Payments 1990 and the New York Convention between Member States of the United Nations on the recovery Abroad of Maintenance 1956. Both Conventions provided for the setting up of the central authority for the recovery of maintenance payments in each signatory State. The Rome Convention, which has only been so far ratified by Ireland and Italy, allows a person who has obtained a maintenance order to apply for its enforcement to the central authority of the state in which they reside. The 1956 Convention is in force in 53 countries, although not in the United States and its terms provide that a central authority can act on instructions of a maintenance applicant to commence original maintenance proceedings where necessary in a foreign jurisdiction. Both conventions were designed to obviate the necessity of a maintenance debtor having to instruct foreign lawyers, or having to appear in person in a foreign jurisdiction to enforce a maintenance order.

Section 53 extends the remit of the central authority in this jurisdiction to enable it to act on behalf of a former spouse who has either obtained a divorce under the 1996 Act, has obtained a foreign divorce which is recognised as valid in this jurisdiction; or a spouse who, in the context of proceedings for divorce, requires the enforcement of a foreign maintenance order. Section 14 of the 1994 Act, as amended, provides that where a maintenance debtor seeks maintenance from a person for the time being resident in the State and that request is transmitted to the central authority from a central authority of a designated jurisdiction and is for maintenance pending suit order, a periodical payments order; a secured periodical payments order; or a lump sum order under the 1996 Act, then such a request may be referred to the relevant court for enforcement. Section 14(1)(c)(i), as amended by section 53 of the 1996 Act, provides that an application may be made to the Circuit Court, where the amount sought to be recovered thereunder exceeds the maximum amount awardable under the District Court jurisdiction. In the alternative, if the amount is not in excess of such limit, the application is made to the District Court. The 1994 Act also makes extensive provisions for the taking of evidence by way of affidavit, sworn deposition or live television link.

APPENDIX A

Extracts from
S.I. No. 343 of 1997

RULES OF THE SUPERIOR COURTS (No. 3) of 1997

Commencement

2. All family law proceedings other than an application under rule 27 of this Order shall be commenced by a special summons which shall be a family law summons and shall be entitled:

"The High Court
Family Law

In the matter of the..Act, 19...... (as the case may be)
Between/

A. B. the Applicant

– and –

C.B. the Respondent"

3. The endorsement of claim shall be entitled "Special Endorsement of Claim" and shall state specifically, with all necessary particulars, the relief sought and each section of the Act or Acts under which the relief is sought and the grounds upon which it is sought.

4. In any proceeding pursuant to rule 1(1) above an affidavit verifying such proceeding or in reply thereto shall contain the following, where applicable:

    (a) In the case of an application for a judicial separation or a decree of divorce:

    (1) The date and place of the marriage of the parties.
    (2) The length of time the parties have lived apart and the address of both of the parties during that time, where known.
    (3) Full particulars of any children of the applicant or respondent stating whether each or any of them is or are a dependent child of the family and stating whether and if so what provision has been made for each and any such dependent child of the applicant or respondent as the case may be.
    (4) Whether any possibility of a reconciliation between the applicant and respondent exists and if so on what basis the same might take place.

    (5) Details of any previous matrimonial relief sought and or obtained and details of any previous separation agreement entered into between the parties. (Where appropriate a certified copy of any relevant Court order and/or Deed of Separation/Separation Agreement should be exhibited with the affidavit).

    (6) Where each party is domiciled at the date of the application commencing the proceeding or where each party has been ordinarily resident for the year receding the date of such application.

    (7) Details of the family home/s and/or other residences of the parties including, if relevant, details of any former family homes/residences which should include details of the manner of occupation and ownership thereof.

    (8) Where reference is made in the summons to any immovable property whether it is registered or unregistered land and a description of the lands/premises so referred to.

4. (d) In the case of an application for the determination of property issues between spouses pursuant to section 36 of the 1995 Act or that section as applied by section 44 of the 1996 Act to engaged persons, such particulars of (a) above as are appropriate and

    (1) The description, nature and extent of the disputed property or monies.

    (2) The state of knowledge of the applicant's spouse in relation to possession or control of the disputed properties or monies at all relevant times.

    (3) The nature and extent of the interest being claimed by the applicant in the property or monies and the basis upon which such claim is made.

    (4) The nature and extent of any claim for relief being made and the basis upon which any such claim is made.

    (5) The manner in which it is claimed that the respondent has failed, neglected or refused to make to the applicant such appropriate payment or disposition in all of the circumstances and details of any payment or disposition actually made.

    (6) Sufficient particulars to show that the time limits referred to at section 36(7) of the 1995 Act have been complied with.

4. (e) In the case of an application for relief out of the estate of a deceased spouse pursuant to section 15(A) or section 25 of the 1995 Act or section 18 of the 1996 Act, such of the particulars at (a) above as are appropriate and

    (1) The date and place of the marriage and date of any decree of divorce/judicial separation. (The marriage certificate and a certified copy of the decree of divorce/separation shall be exhibited with the affidavit (with authenticated translations where appropriate)).

    (2) Details of any previous matrimonial reliefs obtained by the applicant and in particular lump sum maintenance orders and property adjustment orders, if any.

    (3) Details of any benefits received from or on behalf of the deceased spouse whether by way of agreement or otherwise and details of any benefits accruing to the applicant under the terms of the will of the deceased spouse or otherwise.

    (4) The date of death of the deceased spouse, the date upon which repre-

sentation was first granted in respect of the estate of the said spouse and, if applicable, the date upon which notice of the death of the deceased spouse was given to the applicant spouse and the date upon which the applicant spouse notified the personal representative of an intention to apply for relief pursuant to section 18(7) of the 1996 Act and section 115(A)(7) of the 1995 Act, as the case may be.

(5) The marital status of the deceased spouse at the date of death and the marital status of the applicant at the date of the application and whether the applicant has remarried since the dissolution of the marriage between the applicant and the deceased spouse.

(6) Details of the dependants of the deceased spouse at the date of death and of all the dependants of the applicant at the date of the application together with details of any other interested persons.

(7) An averment as to whether any order pursuant to section 18(10) of the 1996 Act or section 15(A)(10) of the 1995 Act has previously been made.

(8) Details of the value of the estate of the deceased spouse where known.

5. Any such affidavit filed under rule 4 shall, where appropriate, also exhibit the certificate required under section 5 or, as the case may be, section 6 of the 1989 Act or under section 6, or as the case may be, section 7 of the 1996 Act which shall be in Form Nos. 1, 2, 3 or 4 respectively as set out in the Schedule hereto.

Affidavit of Means

6. (1) Without prejudice to the right of any party to seek particulars of any matter from the other party to any proceeding or to the right of such party to make application to the Court for an order of discovery and without prejudice to the jurisdiction of the Court pursuant to section 12(25) of the 1995 Act or section 17(25) of the 1996 Act, in any case where financial relief under either of the Acts is sought each party shall file and serve an Affidavit of Means in the proceeding.

(2) The Affidavit of Means shall be in Form No. 5 as set out in the Schedule hereto.

(3) An Affidavit of Means of the applicant shall be served with the verifying affidavit grounding such proceeding and the Affidavit of Means of any respondent or any other party shall be served with the replying affidavit in the proceeding unless otherwise ordered by the Master or the Court. Subsequent to the service of an Affidavit of Means either party may request the other party to vouch all or any of the items referred to therein within 21 days of the said request.

(4) In the event of a party failing properly to comply with the provisions in relation to the filing and serving of an Affidavit of Means as hereinbefore provided for or failing properly to vouch the matters set out therein, the Court may, on application by notice of motion, grant an order for discovery and/or make any such order as the Court deems appropriate and necessary, including an order that such party shall not be entitled to pursue or defend as appropriate such claim for any ancillary relief under the Act save as permitted by the Court and upon such terms as the Court may determine are appropriate or the Court may adjourn the proceeding for a specified period of time to enable compliance with any such previous request or order of the Court.

Affidavit of Welfare

7. In any case in which there is a dependant child or children of the spouses or either of them an Affidavit of Welfare shall be filed and served on behalf of the applicant and shall be in Form No. 6 as set out in the Schedule hereto. In a case in which the respondent agrees with the facts as averred to in the Affidavit of Welfare filed and served by the applicant, the respondent may file and serve an Affidavit of Welfare in the alternative form provided in Form No. 3 of the Schedule hereto. In a case in which the respondent disagrees with all or any of the Affidavit of Welfare served and filed by an applicant, a separate Affidavit of Welfare in the said Form No. 6 herein shall be sworn, filed and served by the respondent within 21 days from the date of service of the applicant's Affidavit of Welfare.

Ex parte application to seek relief under section 23 of the 1995 Act

8. (1) An applicant for relief under section 23 of the 1995 Act may issue but not serve a special summons and shall as soon as may be after the issue of such summons apply ex parte to the Court for leave to make the application for the relief claimed in the summons.

    (2) The applicant shall by affidavit verify the requirements specified in section 27 of the 1995 Act and shall set forth the substantial grounds relied upon for seeking relief.

    (3) The Court may upon such application, if appropriate, grant or refuse such application or may, in circumstances which seem appropriate, adjourn the application to allow the applicant to put further evidence before the Court on any relevant matter.

    (4) If upon application made to it the Court shall grant leave to make the application for the relief claimed in the summons, the applicant may thereupon proceed to serve the summons in the manner provided for by these rules and the matter shall thereupon proceed in accordance with the provisions of this Order.

Interim and Interlocutory Relief

9. (1) An application for:

    (a) a preliminary order pursuant to section 6 of the 1995 Act; or
    (b) a preliminary order pursuant to section 11 of the 1996 Act; or
    (c) maintenance pending suit pursuant to section 7 of the 1995 Act; or
    (d) maintenance pending relief pursuant to section 24 of the 1995 Act; or
    (e) maintenance pending suit pursuant to section 12 of the 1996 Act; or
    (f) calculations pursuant to section 12(25) of the 1995 Act; or
    (g) calculations pursuant to section 17(25) of the 1996 Act; or
    (h) relief pursuant to section 35 of the 1995 Act; or
    (i) relief pursuant to section 37 of the 1996 Act; or
    (j) relief pursuant to section 38(8) of the 1995 Act; or
    (k) relief pursuant to section 38(7) of the 1996 Act; or
    (l) a report pursuant to section 47 of the 1995 Act; or
    (m) a report pursuant to section 42 of the 1996 Act; or
    for any other interlocutory relief, shall be by notice of motion to the Court.

Such notice shall be served upon the other party or parties to the proceeding 14 clear days before the return date and shall, where appropriate, be grounded upon the affidavit or affidavits of the parties concerned.

(2) An application may be made ex parte to the Court in any case in which interim relief of an urgent and immediate nature is required by the applicant and the Court may in any case, where it is satisfied that it is appropriate, grant such relief or make such order as appears proper in the circumstances.

(3) Any interim or interlocutory application shall be heard on affidavit unless the Court otherwise directs. Where any oral evidence is heard by the Court in the course of any such application ex parte, a note of such evidence shall be prepared by the applicant or the applicant's solicitor and approved by the Court and shall be served upon the respondent forthwith together with a copy of the order made, if any, unless otherwise directed by the Court.

Notice to Trustees

10. An applicant who seeks an order under Part II of the 1995 Act or under Part III of the 1996 Act affecting a pension in any way shall give notice to the trustees thereof in the Form No. 7 as set out in the Schedule hereto informing them of the application and of the right to make representations in relation thereto to the Court.

Motion for Directions

11. (1) An applicant or respondent may, at any stage, bring a motion for directions to the Court:

    (a) Where there are any dependant children who are sui juris and whose welfare or position is or is likely to be affected by the determination of the proceeding or of any issue in the proceeding;

    (b) Where an order is sought concerning the sale of any property in respect of which any other party has or may have an interest;

    (c) Where an order of any type is sought which will affect the rules of a pension scheme or require non-compliance therewith; or

    (d) Where an application is brought seeking provision out of the estate of a deceased spouse,

or in any other case in which it is appropriate. Such notice of motion shall be grounded upon the affidavit of the applicant which shall, in particular, identify the party or parties whose interests are or are likely to be affected by the determination of the proceeding or any issue in the proceeding and who ought to be put on notice of the said proceeding and given an opportunity of being heard.

(2) The Court may, upon such motion or of its own motion, make such order or give such direction pursuant to section 40 of the 1995 Act or section 40 of the 1996 Act as appears appropriate and may, where any order affecting the rules of a pension scheme is sought, direct that further notice be given to the trustees of such pension scheme in accordance with the Form No. 7 set out in the Schedule hereto or in such variation thereof as the Court may direct, as appropriate.

(3) Save where the Court shall otherwise direct, a notice party who wishes to make representations to the Court shall make such representations by affidavit which shall be filed and served on all parties to the proceeding within 28 days of service upon them of the notice of application for relief or within such further time as the Court may direct.

12. The Court may, at any stage, direct that the parties to any proceeding exchange pleadings in relation to all or any of the issues arising in the proceeding between the parties or between the parties or any of them and any third party on such terms as appear appropriate and may give such directions in relation to the matter as appear necessary.

Hearing

13. (1) Save where the Court otherwise directs, the hearing of any interim or interlocutory application brought under the Acts shall be on the affidavits of the parties subject to the right of the parties to seek to cross examine the opposing party on their affidavit. Any party may serve a notice to cross examine in relation to the deponent of any affidavit served on him.

   (2) Save where the Court otherwise directs the hearing of any application under the Acts shall be on the oral evidence of the parties.

   (3) Where relief is sought by the applicant or the respondent pursuant to section 12 of the 1995 Act or section 17 of the 1996 Act, evidence of the actuarial value of the benefit under the scheme shall be by affidavit filed on behalf of the applicant or respondent as the case may be. Such affidavit on behalf of an applicant shall be sworn and served on all parties to the proceeding and filed at least 28 days in advance of the hearing and subject to the right to serve notice of cross examination in relation to the affidavit. When one of the parties has adduced evidence of the actuarial value of the benefit by such affidavit as provided herein which the other party intends to dispute, he shall do so by affidavit which shall be filed at least 14 days in advance of the hearing, subject to the right to serve notice of cross examination in relation to same.

14. Where any relief is sought which has not been specifically claimed, the Court may adjourn the proceeding to allow such amendments to the Family Law Summons as may be necessary and upon such terms and conditions as it seems fit.

15. (1) Where any action or proceeding is pending in the High Court which might have been commenced in the Circuit Court or the District Court any party to such action or proceeding may apply to the High Court that the action be remitted or transferred to the Circuit Court or the District Court (as the case may be) and if the High Court should, in the exercise of its discretion, consider such an order to be in the interests of justice it shall remit or transfer such action or proceeding to the Circuit Court or the District Court (as the case may be) to be prosecuted before the Judge assigned to such Circuit or (as the case may require) the Judge assigned to such District as may appear to the Court suitable and convenient, upon such terms and subject to such conditions as to costs or otherwise as may appear just.

   (2) An application under this rule to remit or transfer an action or proceeding may be made at any time after an appearance has been entered.

16. The provisions of Order 49, rules 1, 2, 3 and 6 shall apply to any proceeding commenced under rule 2 above.

17. Any respondent in family law proceedings may counterclaim by way of a replying affidavit and such affidavit shall clearly set out the relief claimed and the grounds upon which it is claimed in like manner as if he were an applicant and subject to the provisions of this order.

18. In any proceeding which has been transferred to the High Court pursuant to section 31(3) of the 1989 Act, the applicant and the respondent shall each within fourteen days from the making of the order or such further time as the Master may allow, file in the Central Office an affidavit or supplemental affidavits as shall appear necessary to conform to the requirements of this order as if the proceeding had commenced in the High Court, together with a certified copy of the order transferring the same and the proceeding shall thereupon be listed for hearing.

19. An application by either spouse or on behalf of a dependent member pursuant to section 18 of the 1995 Act or section 22 of the 1996 Act shall be made to the Court by motion in the proceeding on notice to the party concerned and shall be supported by an affidavit verifying the same and shall set out fully how, when and in what respect circumstances have changed or what new evidence exists as a result of which the Court should vary or discharge or otherwise modify in any respect an order to which the section applies.

20. An application pursuant to section 35 of the 1995 Act or pursuant to section 37 of the 1996 Act may, at any time, be made to the Court by motion on notice in the proceeding to the party concerned and shall be supported by an affidavit verifying the facts alleged in relation to the disposition complained of and shall specify the relief claimed and the way in which the disposition is said to be intended to defeat the relief claimed or to affect it in any way and the Court may make such order upon such motion as appears proper in the circumstances and may, if necessary, adjourn the motion in order to give notice of the application to any party affected by the disposition complained of or the disposal of the property concerned.

21. An application pursuant to section 8 the 1989 Act, for the rescission of a grant of a decree of judicial separation shall be preceded by a notice of re-entry which shall have been given at least one month before the date of the application and shall be grounded on an affidavit sworn by each of the spouses seeking such rescission which shall specify the nature and extent of the reconciliation including whether they have resumed cohabiting as husband and wife and shall also specify such necessary ancillary orders (if any) as they require the Court to make or to consider making in the circumstances.

Subsequent Ancillary Relief

22. Subsequent to the grant of a decree of judicial separation or of a decree of divorce any party who seeks any or any further ancillary relief under Part II of the 1995 Act or under Part III of the 1996 Act shall do so by notice of motion in the proceeding. Such notice shall be served on any party concerned and shall be grounded on the affidavit of the moving party.

Service of Orders

23. In all cases in which the Registrar of the Court is required to serve or lodge a copy of an order upon any person or persons or body such service or lodgement may be effected by the service of a certified copy of the said order by registered post to the said person or persons or body.

28. The provisions of Order 119 rules 2 and 3 shall not apply to any cause, action or proceeding under Order 70 or Order 70A.

SCHEDULE OF FORMS

FORM NO. I

THE HIGH COURT

FAMILY LAW

IN THE MATTER OF THE JUDICIAL SEPARATION AND FAMILY LAW
REFORM ACT, 1989
AND IN THE MATTER OF THE FAMILY LAW ACT, 1995

BETWEEN/

A.B.

Applicant

– and –

C.D.

Respondent

CERTIFICATE PURSUANT TO SECTION 5 OF THE JUDICIAL
SEPARATION AND FAMILY LAW REFORM ACT, 1989

I,   , the Solicitor acting for the above Applicant do hereby certify as
follows:

1. I have discussed with the Applicant the possibility of reconciliation with
   the Respondent and I have given the Applicant the names and addresses of
   persons qualified to help effect a reconciliation between spouses who have
   become estranged.
2. I have discussed with the Applicant the possibility of engaging in mediation to help effect a separation on an agreed basis with the Respondent and
   I have given the Applicant the names and addresses of persons and organisations qualified to provide a mediation service.
3. I have discussed with the Applicant the possibility of effecting a separation by the negotiation and conclusion of a Separation Deed or written
   Separation Agreement with the Respondent.

Dated the   day of   19   .

Signed: ....

Solicitor

Address:

FORM NO. 2

THE HIGH COURT

FAMILY LAW

IN THE MATTER OF THE JUDICIAL SEPARATION AND FAMILY LAW REFORM ACT, 1989 AND IN THE MATTER OF THE FAMILY LAW ACT, 1995

BETWEEN/

A.B.

Applicant

– and –

C.D.

Respondent

CERTIFICATE PURSUANT TO SECTION 6 OF THE JUDICIAL SEPARATION AND FAMILY LAW REFORM ACT, 1989

I,   , the Solicitor acting for the above Respondent do hereby certify as follows:

1. I have discussed with the Respondent the possibility of reconciliation with the Applicant and I have given the Respondent the names and addresses of persons qualified to help effect a reconciliation between spouses who have become estranged.
2. I have discussed with the Respondent the possibility of engaging in mediation to help effect a separation on an agreed basis with the Applicant and I have given the Respondent the names and addresses of persons and organisations qualified to provide a mediation service.
3. I have discussed with the Respondent the possibility of effecting a separation by the negotiation and conclusion of a Separation Deed or written Separation Agreement with the Applicant.

Dated the   day of   19   .

Signed: ....

Solicitor

Address:

Family Law (Divorce) Act 1996

FORM NO. 3

THE HIGH COURT

FAMILY LAW

IN THE MATTER OF THE FAMILY LAW (DIVORCE) ACT, 1996

BETWEEN/

A.B.

Applicant

– and –

C.D.

Respondent

CERTIFICATE PURSUANT TO SECTION 6 OF THE FAMILY LAW (DIVORCE) ACT, 1996

I,   , the Solicitor acting for the above Applicant do hereby certify as follows:

1. I have discussed with the Applicant the possibility of reconciliation with the Respondent and I have given the Applicant the names and addresses of persons qualified to help effect a reconciliation between spouses who have become estranged.
    (The following paragraphs to be inserted where appropriate].

2. I have discussed with the Applicant the possibility of engaging in mediation to help effect a separation on an agreed basis (the spouses the parties hereto not being separated) or a divorce on the basis agreed between the Applicant with the Respondent and I have given the Applicant the names and addresses of persons and organisations qualified to provide a mediation service for spouses who have become estranged.

3. I have discussed with the Applicant the possibility of effecting a separation by the negotiation and conclusion of a Separation Deed or written Separation Agreement with the Respondent.

4. I have ensured that the Applicant is aware of judicial separation as an alternative to divorce, no decree of judicial separation in relation to the Applicant and the Respondent being in force.

Dated the   day of   19   .

Signed: ....

       Solicitor

Address:

FORM NO. 4

THE HIGH COURT

FAMILY LAW

IN THE MATTER OF THE FAMILY LAW (DIVORCE) ACT, 1996

BETWEEN/

A.B.

Applicant

– and –

C.D.

Respondent

CERTIFICATE PURSUANT TO SECTION 7 OF THE
FAMILY LAW (DIVORCE) ACT, 1996

I,   , the solicitor acting for the above Respondent do hereby certify as follows:-

1. I have discussed with the Respondent the possibility of reconciliation with the Applicant and 1 have given the Respondent the names and addresses of persons qualified to help effect a reconciliation between spouses who have become estranged.

[The following paragraphs to be inserted where appropriate].

2. I have discussed with the Respondent the possibility of engaging in mediation to help effect a separation on an agreed basis (the spouses the parties hereto not being separated) or a divorce on the basis agreed between the Respondent with the Applicant and 1 have given the Respondent the names and addresses of persons and organisations qualified to provide a mediation service for spouses who have become estranged.

3. I have discussed with the Respondent the possibility of effecting a separation by the negotiation and conclusion of a Separation Deed or written Separation Agreement with the Applicant.

4. I have ensured that the Respondent is aware of judicial separation as an alternative to divorce, no decree of judicial separation in relation to the Respondent and the Applicant being in force.

Dated the   day of   , 19   .

Signed: ....

Solicitor

Address:

FORM NO. 5

THE HIGH COURT

FAMILY LAW
[insert as appropriate]

IN THE MATTER OF THE JUDICIAL SEPARATION AND FAMILY LAW REFORM ACT, 1989
IN THE MATTER OF THE FAMILY LAW ACT, 1995
IN THE MATTER OF THE FAMILY LAW (DIVORCE) ACT, 1996

BETWEEN/

A.B.

Applicant

– and –

C.D.

Respondent

AFFIDAVIT OF MEANS

I,   , [insert occupation],
of   , aged 18 years and upwards MAKE OATH and say as
follows:-

1. I say that I am the Applicant/Respondent [DELETE AS APPROPRIATE] in the above entitled proceedings and I make this Affidavit from facts within my own knowledge save where otherwise appears and where so appearing I believe the same to be true.

2. I say that I have set out in the First Schedule hereto all the assets to which I am legally or beneficially entitled and the manner in which such property is held.

3. I say that I have set out in the Second Schedule hereto all income which I receive and the source(s) of such income.

4. I say that I have set out in the Third Schedule hereto all my debts and/or liabilities and the persons to whom such debts and liabilities are due.

5. I say that my weekly outgoings amount to the sum of £   and I say that the details of such outgoings have been set out in the Fourth Schedule hereto.

6. I say that to the best of my knowledge, information and belief, all pension information known to me relevant to the within proceedings is set out in the Fifth Schedule hereto. [Where information has been obtained from the trustees of the pension scheme concerned under the Pensions Act, 1990, such information should be exhibited and where such information has not

been obtained, the Deponent should depose to the reason(s) why such information has not been obtained].

First Schedule

[Here set out in numbered paragraphs all assets whether held in the Applicant/ Respondent's sole name or jointly with another, whether held legally or beneficially, the manner in which the assets are held, whether they are subject to a mortgage or other charge or lien and such further and other details as are appropriate].

Second Schedule

[Here set out in numbered paragraphs all income from whatever source(s)].

Third Schedule

[Here set out in numbered paragraphs all debts and/or liabilities and the persons/ institutions to which such debts and/or liabilities are due].

Fourth Schedule

[Here set out full details of weekly personal outgoings].

Fifth Schedule

[Here full details of nature of pension scheme, benefits payable thereunder, normal pensionable age and period of reckonable service should be listed to the best of the Deponent's knowledge, information and belief].

SWORN etc.

FORM NO. 6

THE HIGH COURT

FAMILY LAW

[insert as appropriate]

IN THE MATTER OF THE JUDICIAL SEPARATION AND FAMILY LAW REFORM ACT, 1989
IN THE MATTER OF THE FAMILY LAW ACT, 1995
IN THE MATTER OF THE FAMILY LAW (DIVORCE) ACT, 1996

BETWEEN/

A.B.

Applicant

– and –

C.D.

Respondent

AFFIDAVIT OF WELFARE

I,   [insert occupation],
of   , aged 18 years and upwards MAKE OATH and say
as follows;

1. I say that I am the Applicant/Respondent [DELETE AS APPROPRIATE] in the above entitled proceedings and 1 make this Affidavit from facts within my own knowledge save where otherwise appears and where so appearing I believe the same to be true.

2. I say and believe that the facts set out in the Schedule hereto are true.

[In circumstances in which the Respondent does not dispute the facts deposed to by the Applicant in his/her Affidavit of Welfare, the following averment shall be included, replacing paragraph 2 hereof, and in such circumstances, the Schedule shall not be completed by the Respondent:

2. I say that I am fully in agreement with the facts as averred to by the Applicant in his/her Affidavit of Welfare sworn herein on the day of 19   and I say and believe that the facts set out in the Schedule hereto are true].

SCHEDULE

Part I – details of the children

1. Details of children born to the Applicant and the Respondent or adopted by both the Applicant and the Respondent.

Forenames   Surname   Date of Birth

2. Details of other children of the family or to which the parents or either of them are in loco parentis

   Forenames   Surname   Date of Birth Relationship to Applicant/Respondent

Part II – Arrangements for the children of the family

3. Home details

   (a) The address or addresses at which the children now live.

   (b) Give details of the number of living rooms, bedrooms, etc., at the addresses in (a) above.

   (c) Is the house rented or owned and, if so, name the tenant(s) or owner(s).

   (d) Is the rent or mortgage being regularly paid and, if so, by whom?

   (e) Give the name of all other persons living with the children either on a full-time or part-time basis and state their relationship to the children, if any.

   (f) Will there be any change in these arrangements and, if so, give details.

Part III – Education and Training Details

   (a) Give the names of the school, college or place of training attended by each child.

   (b) Do the children have any special educational needs. If so, please specify.

   (c) Is the school, college or place of training fee-paying. If so, give details of how much the fees are per term/year. Are fees regularly paid and, if so, by whom?

   (d) Will there by any change in these circumstances? If so, give details.

Part IV – Childcare Details

   (a) Which parent looks after the children from day to day? If responsibility is shared, please give details.

   (b) Give details of work commitments of both parents.

   (c) Does someone look after the children when the parent is not there? If yes, give details.

   (d) Who looks after the children during school holidays?

   (e) Will there be any change in these arrangements? If yes, give details.

Part V – Maintenance

   (a) Does the Applicant/Respondent pay towards the upkeep of the children? If yes, give details. Please specify any other source of maintenance.

(b) Is the maintenance referred to at (a) above paid under court order? If yes, give details.

(c) Has maintenance for the children been agreed? If yes, give details.

(d) If not, will you be applying for a maintenance order from the Court?

Part VI – Details of Contact with the Children

(a) Do the children see the Applicant/Respondent? Please give details.

(b) Do the children stay overnight and/or have holiday visits with the Applicant/Respondent? Please give details.

(c) Will there be any change to these arrangements? Please give details.

Part VII – Details of Health

(a) Are the children generally in good health? Please give details of any serious disability or chronic illness suffered by any of the children.

(b) Do the children or any of them have any special health needs? Please give details of the care needed and how it is to be provided.

(c) Are the Applicant or Respondent generally in good health? If not, please give details.

Part VIII – Details of Care and Other Court Proceedings

(a) Are the children or any of them in the care of a health board or under the supervision of a social worker or probation officer? If so, please specify.

(b) Are there or have there been any proceeding in any Court involving the children or any of them? If so, please specify. (All relevant court orders relating to the children or any of them should be annexed hereto).

Part IX - Declaration

I   , Applicant/Respondent [delete as appropriate], declare that the information I have given herein is correct and complete to the best of my knowledge.

Signed: ....

                Applicant/Respondent

Witnessed:

Date:

Part X – Agreement of Respondent (where applicable)

I   , Respondent, declare that the information given by the Applicant herein is correct and complete to the best of my knowledge and I agree with the arrangements and proposals contained herein. . ,

Signed: ....

          Respondent

Witnessed:

Date:

FORM NO. 7

THE HIGH COURT

FAMILY LAW

[insert as appropriate]

IN THE MATTER OF THE JUDICIAL SEPARATION AND FAMILY LAW REFORM ACT, 1989
IN THE MATTER OF THE FAMILY LAW ACT, 1995
IN THE MATTER OF THE FAMILY LAW (DIVORCE) ACT, 1996

BETWEEN/

          A.B.

                            Applicant

          – and –

          C.D.

                          Respondent

NOTICE TO TRUSTEES

TAKE NOTICE that relief has been claimed by the Applicant/Respondent in the above entitled proceedings pursuant to section(s) 12 and/or 13 of the Family Law Act, 1995 or section 17 of the Family Law (Divorce) Act, 1996 or section 8B of the Family Law (Maintenance of Spouses) Act, 1976 and in particular in relation to [here insert details of pension in respect of which relief is claimed].

AND FURTHER TAKE NOTICE that any representations to be made to the Court pursuant to section 12(18) or section 13(2) of the 1995 Act or section 17(18) of the 1996 Act may be made by way of Affidavit of Representation to be filed and served on all parties herein within 28 days of the date of service of this Notice upon you.

Dated the   day of   19   .

Signed: ....

Solicitors for the Applicant/Respondent

To: The County Registrar

and

To: The Trustees of the pension scheme concerned

and

To: Applicant/Respondent [or solicitors where appropriate]"

APPENDIX B

Extracts from
S.I. No. 84 of 1997

CIRCUIT COURT RULES (No.1) 1997

ORDER 78

JUDICIAL SEPARATION AND FAMILY LAW REFORM ACT, 1989 AND FAMILY LAW ACT, 1995 AND FAMILY LAW (DIVORCE) ACT, 1996

Introduction, Substitution, and Revocation

1.　In this Order "the 1996 Act" means the Family Law (Divorce) Act, 1996 (No.33 of 1996) and "the 1995 Act" means the Family Law Act, 1995 (No. 26 of 1995) and "the 1989 Act" means the Judicial Separation and Family Law Reform Act, 1989 (No. 6 of 1989). These Rules shall be substituted for the Rules contained in Circuit Court Rules (No. 1) of 1989 (S.I. No. 289 of 1989) and Circuit Court Rules (No. 1) of 1994 (S.I. No. 225 of 1994) which are hereby revoked, subject only to the provisions contained in Rule 2 hereof.

Transitional

2.　All applications made or proceedings taken before these Rules shall have come into operation but which are in accordance with the then existing Rules and practice of the Court shall have the same validity as applications made or proceedings taken in accordance with these Rules.

Venue

3.　Any proceedings under this Order shall be brought in the County where any party to the proceedings ordinarily resides or carries on any profession, business or occupation.

Commencement

4.　(a)　All proceedings for divorce, judicial separation, relief after foreign divorce or separation outside the State, nullity, declarations of marital status, the determination of property issues between spouses pursuant to section 36 of the 1995 Act/ formerly engaged couples pursuant to section 44 of the 1996 Act and relief pursuant to section 25 of the 1995 Act, section 18 of the 1996 Act or section 15A of the 1995 Act under this Order, shall be instituted by the issuing out of the Office of the County Registrar for the appropriate County (hereinafter referred to as "the appropriate Office") of the appropriate Family Law Civil Bill in the format and manner hereinafter provided save that no Family Law Civil Bill for relief after foreign divorce or separation outside the State shall be issued until requirements set down in Rule 4(b) of these Rules have been complied with. Upon issue, the Family Law Civil Bill shall be served in a manner provided for hereunder.

(b) No proceedings for a relief order after foreign divorce or separation out-side the State shall issue without the leave of the appropriate Court in accordance with section 23(3) of the 1995 Act. Such application for leave to issue proceedings shall be made ex parte by way of ex parte docket grounded upon the Affidavit of the Applicant or another appropriate person. The aforementioned Affidavit shall exhibit a draft of the Family Law Civil Bill for relief after divorce or separation outside the State which the Applicant seeks leave to issue as well as the foreign divorce or separation decree, shall set forth fully the reasons why relief is being sought and shall make specific averment to the fact that, to the knowledge, information and belief of the Applicant, the jurisdictional requirements of section 27 of the 1995 Act are complied with in the particular case, specifying the particular basis of jurisdiction being relied upon.

Form of Proceedings

5. Every Family Law Civil Bill shall be in numbered paragraphs setting out the relief sought and the grounds relied upon in support of the application. The Civil Bill shall be in accordance with the form set out in Form 1 herein or such modification thereof as may be appropriate, subject to the requirements hereinafter set out.

(a) A Family Law Civil Bill for a Decree of Divorce shall, in all cases, include the following details:

(i) the date and place of marriage of the parties;

(ii) the length of time the parties have lived apart, including the date upon which the parties commenced living apart, and the addresses of both of the parties during that time, where known;

(iii) details of any previous matrimonial relief sought and/or obtained and details of any previous separation agreement entered into between the parties (where appropriate a certified copy of any relevant court order and/or deed of separation/separation agreement should be annexed to the Civil Bill);

(iv) the names and ages and dates of birth of any dependent children of the marriage;

(v) details of the family home(s) and/or other residences, of the parties including, if relevant, details of any former family home/residence to include details of the manner of occupation/ownership thereof;

(vi) where reference is made in the Civil Bill to any immovable property, whether it is registered or unregistered land and a description of the land/premises so referred to;

(vii) the basis of jurisdiction under the 1996 Act;

(viii) the occupation(s) of each party;

(ix) the grounds relied upon for the relief sought;

(x) each section of the 1996 Act under which relief is sought.

5. (f) A Family Law Civil Bill for the determination of property issues between spouses, pursuant to section 36 of the 1995 Act/ formerly engaged couples, pursuant to section 44 of the 1996 Act, shall, in all cases, include the following details:

(i)   the description, nature and extent of the disputed property or monies;

(ii)   the state of knowledge of the Applicant spouse in relation to possession and control of the disputed property or monies at all relevant times;

(iii) the nature and extent of the interest being claimed by the Applicant in the property or monies and the basis upon which such a claim is made;

(iv) the nature and extent of any claim for relief being made and the basis upon which any such claim for relief is being made;

(v)   where reference is made in the Civil Bill to any immovable property, whether it is registered or unregistered land and a description of the land/premises so referred to;

(vi) the manner in which it is claimed that the Respondent spouse has failed, neglected or refused to make to the Applicant spouse such appropriate payment or disposition in all of the circumstances and details of any payment or disposition made;

(vii) that the time limits referred to at section 36(7) of the 1995 Act have been complied with;

(viii) any other relevant matters.

(g) A Family Law Civil Bill for relief pursuant to section 18 of the Family Law (Divorce) Act, 1996 or section 15A or section 25 of the Family Law Act, 1995 shall, in all cases include the following details:

(i)   the date and place of marriage and the date of any decree of divorce/judicial separation and the marriage certificate and a certified copy of the decree of divorce/separation shall be annexed to the Civil Bill (with authenticated translations, where appropriate);

(ii)   details of previous matrimonial relief obtained by the Applicant and in particular lump sum maintenance orders and property adjustment orders, if any;

(iii) details of any benefits previously received from or on behalf of the deceased spouse whether by way of agreement or otherwise and details of any benefits accruing to the Applicant under the terms of the Will of the deceased spouse or otherwise;

(iv) the date of death of the deceased spouse, the date on which representation was first granted in respect of the estate of the said spouse and, if applicable, the date upon which notice of the death of the deceased spouse was given to the Applicant spouse and the date upon which the Applicant spouse notified the personal representative of his/her intention to apply for relief pursuant to section 18(7) of the 1996 Act and section 15A(7) of the 1995 Act;

(v)   the nature and extent of any claim for relief being made and the basis upon which any such claim for relief is being made;

(vi) the marital status of the deceased spouse at the date of death and the marital status of the Applicant at the date of the application and whether the Applicant has remarried since the dissolution of the marriage between the Applicant and the deceased spouse;

(vii) details of all dependents of the deceased spouse at the date of death and of all dependents of the Applicant at the date of the application together with details of any other interested persons;

(viii) that no Order pursuant to section 18(10) of the 1996 Act or section

15A(10) of the 1995 Act has previously been made;

(ix) details of the value of the estate of the deceased spouse, where known;

(x) any other relevant facts.

Applications pursuant to section 15A(6) or section 25(7) of the 995 Act or section 18(6) of the 1996 Act by the personal representative in relation to the distribution of the estate shall be by motion, grounded on Affidavit, on notice to the Applicant spouse and such other persons as the Court shall direct.

6. All Family Law Civil Bills shall be dated and shall bear the name, address and description of the Applicant and an address for service of proceedings, and shall be signed by the party's solicitor, if any, or, where the Applicant does not have a solicitor, by that party personally. The address to which a Respondent should apply in order to receive information in relation to legal aid shall also be included in such Civil Bills.

Issuing and Entry

7. On the issuing of a Family Law Civil Bill the original thereof shall be filed, together with the appropriate certificate (pursuant to section 5 of the 1989 Act or section 6 of the 1996 Act), an Affidavit of Means in the intended action sworn by the Applicant in compliance with Rules 18 and 19 hereof and, in all circumstances where there are dependent children, an Affidavit of Welfare in the intended action in compliance with Rule 20 hereof, and the County Registrar shall thereupon enter same.

Service

8. (a) All Family Law Civil Bills shall be served by registered post on the Respondent at his/her last-known address or alternatively shall be served personally on the Respondent by any person over the age of eighteen years together with the appropriate certificate in the form set out in Forms 7 and 9 herein (pursuant to section 5 of the 1989 Act or section 6 of the 1996 Act), an Affidavit of Means in compliance with Rules 18 and 19 hereof in the form set out in Form 2 herein or such modification thereof as may be appropriate and in all cases where there are dependent children, an Affidavit of Welfare in compliance with Rule 20 hereof in the form set out in Form 3 herein. Where relief pursuant to section 12 and/or section 13 of the 1995 Act or section 17 of the 1996 Act is sought, notice thereof in accordance with Form 4 herein shall also be served on the trustees of the pension scheme in, question by registered post at their registered office or other appropriate address and an Affidavit of such service shall be sworn and filed within fourteen days of service of the Civil Bill. Service shall be endorsed upon all Family Law Civil Bills in accordance with the provisions of Order 10, Rule 22 of the Circuit Court Rules, 1950, as amended. All other pleadings may be served by ordinary pre-paid post.

(b) In all cases in which a declaration of marital status under section 29 of the 1995 Act is sought, the Family Law Civil Bill shall, in addition to the provisions of Rule 8(a) hereof, be served upon the parties to the marriage or, where no longer living, their personal representatives (all of whom shall be parties to the proceedings) and to such other persons as the Court may direct, including the Attorney General, in accordance with the provisions as to service of Family Law Civil Bills hereinbefore set out in respect of the Respondent to proceedings which said persons (excepting the Attorney General) may be made parties to the application in accordance with section 29(6) of the 1995 Act. The Attorney General shall, however, be entitled to interplead in such proceedings.

(c) Where relief is sought pursuant to sections 15A or 25 of the 1995 Act or section 18 of the 1996 Act, the Family Law Civil Bill shall be served in accordance with these Rules on the personal representative of the deceased and on the spouse (if any) of the deceased and on such other person or persons as the Court shall direct.

Appearance

9. If a Respondent intends to contest the application, or participate in proceedings, or any part thereof, he/she shall enter an Appearance in the Office within 10 days of the service upon him/her of the Family Law Civil Bill and shall serve a copy of the Appearance on the Applicant's solicitors or, where appropriate, on the Applicant. The Appearance shall bear an address for service of any interlocutory applications and shall be signed by the Respondent's solicitor or, if the Respondent does not have a solicitor, by the Respondent personally.

Defence

10. (a) A Respondent shall at the same time as entering an Appearance, or within 10 clear days from the date of service of the Appearance, or such further time as may be agreed between the parties or allowed by the Court, file and serve a Defence, together with the appropriate certificate in the form set out in Forms 8 and 10 herein (pursuant to section 6 of the 1989 Act and section 7 of the 1996 Act), an Affidavit of Means in compliance with Rules 18 and 19 hereof and, in all cases where there are dependent children, an Affidavit of Welfare in compliance with Rule 20 hereof in the form set out in Form 3 herein, on the Applicant, or the Applicant's solicitor, if any, and on the County Registrar in the form set out in Form 2 herein or such modification thereof as may be appropriate. Where relief pursuant to section 12 and/or section 13 of the 1995 Act or section 17 of the 1996 Act is sought by way of Counterclaim, notice thereof in accordance with Form 4 herein shall also be served on the trustees of the pension scheme in question by registered post at their registered office and a Affidavit of such service shall be sworn and filed within 7 days of service of the Defence and Counterclaim.

(b) No Appearance or Defence shall be entered after the time specified in these Rules without the leave of the Court or of the County Registrar or the agreement of the parties, and no Defence shall be entered unless the Respondent has previously entered an Appearance as required by these Rules.

(c) Whether or not a Defence is filed and served in any proceedings, the Respondent shall, where appropriate, in any event be obliged to file and serve an Affidavit of Means and a Welfare Statement in accordance with these Rules of Court within 20 days after the service of the Family Law Civil Bill upon him/her subject to Rule 36 hereof.

(d) Without prejudice to the entitlement of the Court to permit representations in relation to the making or refusal of an attachment of earnings order at the hearing of the action, such representations for the purposes of section 8(6)(b) of the 1995 Act or section 13(6)(b) of the 1996 Act may be included in the Defence and for the purposes of section 10(3)(a) of the Family Law (Maintenance of Spouses and Children) Act, 1976 may be included in the Answer provided for by Rule 15 of the Circuit Court Rules (No. 6) of 1982 (S.I. No. 158 of 1982) and Form 9 scheduled thereto.

Motions for Judgment

11. (a) In any case in which a Respondent has made default in entering an Appearance or filing a Defence, as the case may be, the Applicant may, subject to the provisions of the following sub-rules of this Rule, at any time after such default, on notice to be served on the Respondent and, where relief pursuant to section 12 and/or 13 of the 1995 Act and section 17 of the 1996 Act is sought, on the trustees of the pension scheme concerned, not less than fourteen clear days before the hearing, apply to the Court for judgment in default of appearance/defence.

(b) No notice-of motion for Judgment in default of defence shall be served unless the Applicant has, at least fourteen days prior to the service of such notice, written to the Respondent giving him/her notice of his/her intention to serve a notice of motion for Judgment in default of appearance/defence and at the same time consenting to the late filing of a Defence within fourteen days from the date of the letter.

(c) If no defence is delivered within the said period the Applicant shall be at liberty to serve a notice of motion for Judgment in default of defence which shall be returnable to a date not less than fourteen clear days from the date of the service of the notice, such notice of motion to be filed not later than six days before the return date.

(d) If, not later than seven days after the service of such notice of motion for Judgment in default of appearance/defence, the defendant delivers a Defence to the Applicant and not less than six days before the return date lodges a copy thereof in the appropriate Office with a certified copy of the said notice of motion attached thereto, the said motion for Judgment shall not be put in the Judge's List but shall stand struck out and the Respondent shall pay to the Applicant the appropriate sum for his/her costs of the said motion for Judgment.

(e) If in any case the Applicant can establish special reasons for making it necessary to serve a notice of motion for Judgment in default of appearance/defence in the cases provided for by this Rule with greater urgency than in accordance with the provisions hereinbefore contained, he/she may apply ex parte to the Court or the County Registrar for an Order giving him/her liberty to serve a notice of motion for Judgment in default of appearance/defence giving not less than four clear days' notice to the Respondent, or in the alternative the Judge or the County Registrar may deem good the service of a Notice of Motion giving not less than four clear days' notice to the Respondent.

(f) Upon the hearing of such application the Court may, on proof of such default as aforesaid, and upon hearing such evidence, oral or otherwise, as may be adduced, give judgment upon the Applicant's claim endorsed upon the Family Law Civil Bill, or may give leave to the Respondent to defend the whole or part of the claim upon such terms as he or she may consider just.

(g) Upon the hearing of an application for judgment under this Order the Court may make such order as to costs as the Court considers just.

(h) In any case in which the parties are agreed in respect of all of the reliefs being sought and a Defence in accordance with Rule 10 hereof has been filed and served by the Respondent which reflects this agreement, the Applicant or the Respondent may, subject to the provisions of the following sub-rules of this Rule, at any time after such Defence has been filed and served, on notice to be served on the other party and, where relief pursuant to section 12 and/or 13 of the 1995 Act and section 17 of the 1996 Act is sought, on the trustees of the pension scheme concerned, not less than fourteen clear days before the hearing, apply to the Court for judgment, the application to be by way of motion on notice.

(i) Upon the hearing of such application the Court may, upon hearing such evidence, oral or otherwise, as may be adduced
    (i) give judgment in the terms agreed between the parties or,
    (ii) give such directions in relation to the service of a Notice of Trial/Notice to fix a date for Trial as to the Court appears just.

(j) Upon the hearing of an application for judgment under this Order the Court may make such order as to costs as the Court considers just.

Notice of trial/ Notice to fix a date for trial

12. Subject to Rule 11(h), (i) and (j) herein, when a Defence has been duly entered and served, the Applicant may serve a notice of trial or a notice to fix a date for trial, as appropriate..

Notice of trial (Circuits other than Dublin Circuit)

13. Not less than ten days' notice of trial shall be served upon the Respondent and all other necessary parties and, where relief is sought under sections 12 and/or 13 of the 11.195 Act or section 17 of the 1996 Act, upon the trustees of the pension scheme in question, and shall be for the Sittings next ensuing after the expiration of the time mentioned in the said notice, and same shall be filed at the appropriate Office not later than seven days before the opening of such Sittings. Such notice of trial and filing thereof shall operate to set down the action or matter (including Counterclaim if any) for hearing at the next ensuing Sittings. This Rule shall not apply to the Dublin Circuit.

Notice to fix a date for trial (Dublin Circuit)

14. This Rule shall apply only to the Dublin Circuit. Ten days notice to fix a date for trial shall be necessary and sufficient and shall be served upon the Respondent and all other necessary parties and, where relief is, sought under sections 12 and/or 13 of the 1995 Act or section 17 of the 1996 Act, upon the trustees of the pension scheme in question, and filed at the appropriate Office. Such notice to fix a date for a trial shall set out the date upon which a date for hearing shall be fixed by the County Registrar and shall operate to set down the action or matter (including a Counterclaim if any) for hearing upon such date as may be fixed by the County Registrar. A notice to fix a date for trial shall be in accordance with Form 5 herein.

Service by Respondent

15. Where the Applicant has failed to serve a notice of trial or notice to fix a date for trial, as appropriate, within ten days after the service and entry of the Defence, the Respondent may do so and may file the same in accordance with these Rules.

Joinder

16. The Court, if it considers it desirable, may order that two or more actions be tried together, and on such terms as to costs as the Court shall deem just.

Affidavits of Representation

17. (a) Save where the Court shall otherwise direct, any notice of party, including the trustees of a pension scheme, who wishes to make representations to the Court pursuant to section 12(18) and/or section 13(2) of the 1995 Act or section 17(18) of the 1996 Act shall make such representations by Affidavit of Representation to be filed and served on all parties to the proceedings within 28 days of service upon them of notice of the application for relief under section 12 and/or 13 of the 1995 Act or section 17 of the 1996 Act in accordance with Rules 8 and 10 hereof or within such time or in such manner as the Court may direct.

(b) Without prejudice to the entitlement of the Court to permit representations by persons having a beneficial interest in property (not being the other spouse) pursuant to section 15(5) of the 1995 Act and section 19(5) of the 1996 Act or by interested persons pursuant to section 15A(5) or section 25(6) of the 1995 Act and section 18(5) of the 1996 Act at the hearing of the action, such representations may be made by way of Affidavit of Representation to be filed and served on all parties to the proceedings as directed by the Court.

Affidavit of Means

18. Without prejudice to the right of each party to make application to the Court for an Order of Discovery pursuant to the Rules of this Honourable Court and without prejudice to the jurisdiction of the Court pursuant to section 12(25) of the 1995 Act and section 17(25) of the 1996 Act, in any case where financial relief under the Acts is sought, the parties shall file Affidavits of Means in accordance with Rules 7 and 10 hereof in respect of which the following Rules shall be applicable –

(a) either party may request the other party to vouch any or all items referred to therein within 14 days of the request;

(b) in the event of a party failing to properly comply with the provisions in relation to the filing and serving of Affidavits of Means as set down in these Rules or failing to properly vouch the matters set out therein the Court may on application grant an Order for Discovery and/or may make such Orders as the Court deems appropriate and necessary (including an Order that such party shall not be entitled to pursue or defend as appropriate such claim for any ancillary reliefs under the Acts save as permitted by the Court upon such terms as the Court may determine are appropriate and/or adjourning the proceedings for a specified period of time to enable compliance) and furthermore and/or in the alternative relief pursuant to section 38(8) of the 1995 Act or section 38(7) of he 1996 Act may be sought in accordance with Rule 24 hereof.

19. The Affidavit of Means shall set out in schedule form details of the party's income, assets, debts, expenditure and other liabilities wherever situated and from whatever source and, to the best of the deponent's knowledge, information and belief the income, assets, debts, expenditure and other liabilities wherever situated and from whatever source of any dependent member of the family and shall be in accordance with the form set out in Form 2 herein or such modification thereof as may be appropriate. Where relief pursuant to section 12 of the 1995 Act is sought, the Affidavit of Means shall also state to the best of the deponent's knowledge, information and belief, the nature of the scheme, the benefits payable thereunder, the normal pensionable age and the period of reckonable service of the member spouse and where information relating to the pension scheme has been obtained from the trustees of the scheme under the Pensions Acts 1990–1996, such information should be exhibited in the Affidavit of Means and where such information has not been obtained a specific averment shall be included in the Affidavit of Means as to why such information has not been obtained.

Affidavit of Welfare

20. An Affidavit of Welfare shall be in the form set out in Form 3 herein. In circumstances in which the Respondent agrees with the facts as averred to in the Affidavit of Welfare filed and served by the Applicant, the Respondent may file and serve an Affidavit of Welfare in the alternative form provided for in Form 3 herein. In circumstances in which the Respondent disagrees with the Affidavit of Welfare filed and served by the Applicant, a separate Affidavit of Welfare, including the schedule provided for in the form set out in Form 3 herein shall be sworn, filed and served by the Respondent in accordance with Rule 10 hereof.

Counterclaims

21. Save where otherwise directed by the Court, a Counterclaim, if any, brought by a Respondent shall be included in and served with the Defence, in accordance with the provisions of these Rules relating thereto, and shall, in particular, set out in numbered paragraphs

    (a) in the case of an application for a decree of divorce
        (i)   the facts specified at Rule 5(a) hereof in like manner as in the Family Law Civil Bill;
        (ii) outline the ground(s) for a decree of divorce, if sought;
        (iii) specify any ground upon which the Respondent intends to rely in support of any ancillary relief claimed; and
        (iv) the relief sought pursuant to the 1996 Act;

21. (f) in the case of an application for the determination of property issues be-

tween spouses, pursuant to section 36 of the 1995 Act/ formerly engaged couples pursuant to section 44 of the 1996 Act

(i)   the facts specified at Rule 5(f) hereof in like manner as in the Family Law Civil Bill;

(ii)   specify any additional ground upon which the Respondent intends to rely in support of any relief claimed; and

(iii)   the relief sought pursuant to the 1995 Act;

and shall be in the form set out in Form 6 herein or such modification thereof as may be appropriate.

Evidence

22. Save where the Court otherwise directs and subject to Rules 17, 23 or 26 hereof, every Application under this Order shall be heard on oral evidence, such hearings to be held in camera.

23. Notwithstanding the provisions of Rule 22 hereof, where relief pursuant to section 12 of the 1995 Act or section 17 of the 1996 Act is sought by the Applicant or the Respondent, evidence of the actuarial value of a benefit under the scheme (as defined in section 12(1) of the 1995 Act and section 17(1) of the 1996 Act) may be by Affidavit filed on behalf of the Applicant/Respondent, such Affidavit to be sworn by an appropriate person and served on all parties to the proceedings and filed at least 14 days in advance of the hearing and subject to the right of the Respondent/Applicant to serve Notice of cross-examination in relation to same. Where one of the parties has adduced evidence of the actuarial value of a benefit by Affidavit as provided for herein and the other party intends to adduce similar or contra oral evidence, notice of such intention shall be served by the disputing party upon all other parties at least 10 days in advance of the hearing.

Interim and Interlocutory Applications

24. (a) An application for Preliminary Orders pursuant to section 6 of the 1995 Act or section 11 of the 1996 Act or for maintenance pending suit/relief pursuant to section 7 or section 24 of the 1995 Act or section 12 of the 1996 Act or for information pursuant to section 12(25) of the 1995 Act of section 17(25) of the 1996 Act or for relief pursuant to section 35 of the 1995 Act or section 37 of the 1996 Act or for relief pursuant to section 38(8) of the 1995 Act or section 38(7) of the 1996 Act or for a report pursuant to section 47 of the 1995 Act or section 42 of the 1995 Act or for any other interlocutory relief shall be by Notice of Motion to be served upon the parties to the proceedings and, in the case of applications pursuant to section 12(25) of the 1995 Act or section 17(25) of the 1996 Act, upon the trustees of the pension scheme concerned.

(b) Prior to any interlocutory application for discovery or for information pursuant to section 12(25) of the 1995 Act or section 17(25) of the 1996 Act being made, the information being sought shall be requested in writing voluntarily at least 14 days prior to the issuing of the motion for the relief concerned and upon failure to make such a request, the judge may adjourn the motion or strike out the motion or make such other order, including an order as to costs, as to the Court may appear appropriate.

(e) In any case where the Court is satisfied that the delay caused by proceeding by Motion on Notice under this Order would or might entail serious harm or mischief, the Court may make an Order ex parte as it shall consider just. Urgent applications under this Rule may be made to a Judge at any time or place approved by him, by arrangement with the County Registrar for the County in question.

(f) Interim and interlocutory applications shall where appropriate be made to the County Registrar in accordance with the Second Schedule to the Courts and Court Officers Act, 1995 and Orders 15 and 16 of the Circuit Court Rules, 1950, as amended.

25. If on the date for hearing of any application under this Order the matter is not dealt with by the Court for any reason, and, in particular, on foot of an adjournment sought by either party, the other party, whether consenting to the adjournment or not, may apply for, and the Court may grant, such interim or interlocutory relief as to it shall seem appropriate without the necessity of service of a Notice of Motion.

26. Any interim or interlocutory application shall be heard on Affidavit, unless the Court otherwise directs, save that the Deponent of any Affidavit must be available to the Court to give oral evidence or to be cross-examined as to the Court shall seem appropriate, save that a Motion for Discovery and a Motion in the course of nullity proceedings for the appointment of medical/psychiatric inspectors shall be heard on a Notice of Motion only. Where any oral evidence is heard by the Court in the course of such applications ex parte, a note of such evidence shall be prepared by the Applicant or the Applicant's solicitor and approved by the Judge and shall be served upon the Respondent forthwith together with a copy of the Order made (if any), unless otherwise directed by the Court.

Further relief and applications on behalf of dependent persons

27. (a) Where either party or a person on behalf of a dependent member of the family wishes at any time after the hearing of the of application to seek further relief as provided for in the 1995 Act or the 1996 Act or to vary or discharge an Order previously made by the Court, that party shall issue a Notice of Motion to re-enter or to vary or discharge as the case may be grounded upon an Affidavit seeking such relief. Such Motions shall be subject to the provisions of Rules 8, 17, 18, 19, 22 and 23 hereof, as appropriate.

(b) Where a person on behalf of a dependent member of the family wishes to make application for ancillary reliefs at the hearing of the action, such application shall be by way of Notice of Motion to be served on all other parties to the proceedings setting out the reliefs sought grounded on Affidavit which said Motion shall be listed for hearing on the same date as the hearing of the action contemporaneously therewith. Such Motions shall be subject to the provisions of Rules 8, 17, 18, 19, 22 and 23 hereof, as appropriate.

Costs

35. (a) The costs as between party and party may be measured by the Judge, and

if not so measured shall be taxed, in default of agreement by the parties, by the County Registrar according to such scale of costs as may be prescribed. Any party aggrieved by such taxation may appeal to the Court and have the costs reviewed by it.

(b) Where necessary, the Court may make an order determining who shall bear any costs incurred by trustees of a pension scheme pursuant to section 12(22) of the 1995 Act or section 17(22) of the 1996 Act and in making such determination the Court shall have regard, inter alia, to the representations made by the trustees pursuant to Rule 17 hereof, if any.

General

36. The Court may, upon such terms (if any) as it may think reasonable, enlarge or abridge any of the times fixed by these Rules for taking any step or doing any act in any proceeding, and may also, upon such terms as to costs or otherwise as it shall think fit, declare any step taken or act done to be sufficient, even though not taken or done within the time or in the manner prescribed by these Rules.

Certificates

37. (a) The Certificate required by section 5 of the 1989 Act shall be in accordance with Form No. 7 in the Schedule attached hereto.

(b) The Certificate required by section 6 of the 1989 Act shall be in accordance with Form No. 8 in the Schedule attached hereto.

(c) The Certificate required by section 6 of the 1996 Act shall be in accordance with Form No. 9 in the Schedule attached hereto.

(d) The Certificate required by section 7 of the 1996 Act shall be in accordance with Form No. 10 in the Schedule attached hereto.

Service of orders by the Registrar of the Court

38. In all circumstances in which the Registrar of the Court and/or the County Registrar is required to serve or lodge a copy of an order upon any person(s) or body such service of lodgment shall be satisfied by the service of a certified copy of the said order by registered post to the said person(s) or body.

SCHEDULE

FORM NO. 1

AN CHUIRT TEAGHLAIGH CHUARDA

(THE CIRCUIT FAMILY COURT)

CIRCUIT   COUNTY OF

[insert as appropriate]

IN THE MATTER OF THE JUDICIAL SEPARATION AND
FAMILY LAW REFORM ACT, 1989
IN THE MATTER OF THE FAMILY LAW ACT, 1995
IN THE MATTER OF THE FAMILY LAW (DIVORCE) ACT, 1996

BETWEEN

A.B.

Applicant

– and –

C.D.

Respondent

FAMILY LAW CIVIL BILL

INDORSEMENT OF CLAIM

YOU ARE HEREBY REQUIRED within ten days after the service of this Civil Bill upon you, to enter, or cause to be entered with the County Registrar, at his or her Office at   an Appearance to answer the Claim of   of   in the County of   the Applicant herein as indorsed hereon.

AND TAKE NOTICE THAT unless you do enter an Appearance, you will be held to have admitted the said claim and the Applicant may proceed therein and judgment may be given against you in your absence without further notice.

AND FURTHER TAKE NOTICE THAT if you intend to defend the proceedings on any grounds, you must not only enter an Appearance as aforesaid, but also within ten days after the Appearance deliver a statement in writing showing the nature and grounds of your Defence.
The Appearance and Defence may be entered by posting same to the said Office and by giving copies to the Applicant and his/her Solicitor by post.

Dated the   day of   19   .

To: The Respondent

Signed:..

Applicant/Solicitor for the Applicant

[Here set out in numbered paragraphs details of the relief(s) being claimed by the Applicant specifying the matters required by Rule 5 of these Rules]

AND THE APPLICANT CLAIMS:

[Here set out in numbered paragraphs the reliefs (including decrees and declarations) being claimed pursuant to the 1989 Act, the 1995 Act or the 1996 Act specifying, where appropriate, the statutory basis upon which each such relief is sought].

AND FURTHER TAKE NOTICE that, in any cases where financial relief is sought by either party you must file with the Defence herein or in any event within 20 days after the service of this Civil Bill upon you at the aforementioned Circuit Court Office an Affidavit of Means and, where appropriate, an Affidavit of Welfare in the Manner prescribed by the Rules of this Court and serve a copy of same as provided by the Rules of this Court on the Applicant or his/her Solicitor at the address provided below.

Dated the   day of   19 .

The address for service of proceedings upon the Applicant is as follows:

(here insert address of Applicant or his/her solicitor)

Signed:..

Applicant/Solicitor for the Applicant

To: The Registrar Circuit Family Court

Address

and

To: Respondent or Solicitor for Respondent

Address

TAKE NOTICE that it is in your interest to have legal advice in regard to these proceedings. If you cannot afford a private solicitor, you may be entitled to legal aid provided by the State at a minimum cost to you. Details of this legal aid service are available at the following address:

Legal Aid Board,
St. Stephens Green House
Dublin 2.
Telephone No. (01) 6615811

where you can obtain the addresses and telephone numbers of the Legal Aid Centres in your area.

FORM NO. 2

AN CHUIRT TEAGHLAIGH CHUARDA

(THE CIRCUIT FAMILY COURT)

CIRCUIT   COUNTY OF

[Insert as appropriate]

IN THE MATTER OF THE JUDICIAL SEPARATION AND
FAMILY LAW REFORM ACT, 1989
IN THE MATTER OF THE FAMILY LAW ACT, 1995
IN THE MATTER OF THE FAMILY LAW (DIVORCE) ACT, 1996

BETWEEN

A.B.

Applicant

– and –

C.D.

Respondent

AFFIDAVIT OF MEANS

I,   , [insert occupation]   , of   aged 18 years
and upwards MAKE OATH and say as follows:

1. I say that I am the Applicant/Respondent [delete as appropriate] in the
    above entitled proceedings and 1 make this Affidavit from facts within my
    own knowledge save where otherwise appears and where so appearing I
    believe the same to be true.

2. I say that I have set out in the First Schedule hereto all the assets to which
    I am legally or beneficially entitled and the manner in which such property
    is held.

3. I say that I have set out in the Second Schedule hereto all income which I
    receive and the source(s) of such income.

4. I say that I have set out in the Third Schedule hereto all my debts and/or
    liabilities and the persons to whom such debts and liabilities are due.

5. I say that my weekly outgoings amount to the sum of £   and I say that
    the details of such outgoings have been set out in the Fourth Schedule
    hereto.

6. I say that to the best of my knowledge, information and belief, all pension
    information known to me relevant to the within proceedings is set out in
    the Fifth Schedule hereto. [Where information has been obtained from the
    trustees of the pension scheme concerned under the Pensions Act, 1990,
    such information should be exhibited and where such information has not
    been obtained, the Deponent should depose to the reason(s) why such in-
    formation has not been obtained].

First Schedule

[Here set out, in numbered paragraphs all assets whether held in the Appiicaints/ Respondent's sole name or jointly with another, whether held legally or benefi- cially, the manner in which the assets are held, whether they are subject to a mort- gage or other charge or lien and such further and other details as are appropriate.]

Second Schedule

[Here set out in numbered paragraphs all income from whatever source(s)

Third Schedule

[Here set out in numbered paragraphs all debts and/or liabilities and the persons/ institutions to which such debts and/or liabilities are due.]

Fourth Schedule

[Here set out full details of weekly personal outgoings.]

Fifth Schedule

[Here full details of nature of pension scheme, benefits payable thereunder, normal pensionable age and period of reckonable service should be listed to the best of the Deponent's knowledge, information and belief.]

SWORN etc.

FORM NO. 3

AN CHUIRT TEAGHLAIGH CHUARDA

(THE CIRCUIT FAMILY COURT)

CIRCUIT   COUNTY OF

[Insert as appropriate]

IN THE MATTER OF THE JUDICIAL SEPARATION AND
FAMILY LAW REFORM ACT, 1989
IN THE MATTER OF THE FAMILY LAW ACT 1995
IN THE MATTER OF THE FAMILY LAW (DIVORCE) ACT, 1996

BETWEEN

A.B.

Applicant

– and –

C.D.

Respondent

AFFIDAVIT OF WELFARE

I,   , [insert occupation]   , of   aged 18 years
and upwards MAKE OATH and say as follows:

1. I say that I am the Applicant/Respondent [delete as appropriate] in the
    above entitled proceedings and 1 make this Affidavit from facts within my
    own knowledge save where otherwise appears and where so appearing I
    believe the same to be true.

2. I say and believe that the facts set out in the Schedule hereto are true.
    [In circumstances in which the Respondent does not dispute the facts as
    deposed to by the Applicant in his/her Affidavit of Welfare, the following
    averment shall be included, replacing Paragraph 2 hereof, and in such
    circumstances, the Schedule shall not be completed by the Respondent:

3. I say that I am fully in agreement with the facts as averred to by the Appli-
    cant in his/her Affidavit of Welfare sworn herein on the day of 19 and I say
    and believe that the facts set out in the Schedule thereto are true.]

SCHEDULE

Part I – Details of the children

1. Details of children born to the Applicant and the Respondent or adopted by
    both the Applicant and the Respondent

Forenames	Surname	Date of Birth

2. Details of other children of the family or to which the parties or either of them are in loco parentis

Forenames	Surname	Date of Birth	Relationship to Applicant/Respondent

Part II – Arrangements for the children of the family

3. Home Details
    (a) The address or addresses at which the children now live.
    (b) Give details of the number of living rooms, bedrooms, etc. at the addresses in (a) above.
    (c) Is the house rented or owned and, if so, name the tenant(s) or owner(s)?
    (d) Is the rent or mortgage being regularly paid and, if so, by whom?
    (e) Give the names of all other persons living with the children either on a full-time or part-time basis and state their relationship to the children, if any.
    (f) Will there be any change in these arrangements and, if so, give details.

Part III – Education and training details

(a) Give the names of the school, college or place of training attended by each child.
(b) Do the children have any special educational needs? If so, please specify.
(c) Is the school, college or place of training fee-paying? If so, give details of how much the fees are per term/year. Are fees being regularly paid and, if so, by whom?
(d) Will there be any change in these circumstances? If so, give details.

Part IV – Childcare details

(a) Which parent looks after the children from day to day? If responsibility is shared, please give details.
(b) Give details of work commitments of both parents.
(c) Does someone look after the children when the parent is not there? If yes, give details.
(d) Who looks after the children during school holidays?
(e) Will there be any change in these arrangements? If yes, give details.

Part V – Maintenance

(a) Does the Applicant/Respondent pay towards the upkeep of the children? If yes, give details. Please specify any other source of maintenance.
(b) Is the maintenance referred to at (a) above paid under court order? If yes, give details.
(c) Has maintenance for the children been agreed? If yes, give details.
(d) If not, will you be applying for a maintenance order from the Court?

Part VI – Details of contact with the children

(a) Do the children see the Applicant/Respondent? Please give details.
(b) Do the children stay overnight and/or have holiday visits with the Applicant/Respondent? Please give details.
(c) Will there be any change to these arrangements? Please give details.

Part VII – Details of health

(a) Are the children generally in good health? Please give details of any serious disability or chronic illness suffered by any of the children.
(b) Do the children or any of them have any special health needs? Please give details of the care needed and how it is to be provided.
(c) Are the Applicant or Respondent generally in good health? If not, please give details.

Part VIII – Details of care and other court proceedings

(a) Are the children or any of them in the care of a health board or under the supervision of a social worker or probation officer? If so, please specify.
(b) Are there of have there been any proceedings in any Court involving the children or any of them? If so, please specify. (All relevant Court orders relating to the children or any of them should be annexed hereto.)

SWORN etc.

FORM NO. 4

AN CHUIRT TEAGHLAIGH CHUARDA

(THE CIRCUIT FAMILY COURT)

CIRCUIT   COUNTY OF

[Insert as appropriate]

IN THE MATTER OF THE JUDICIAL SEPARATION AND FAMILY LAW
REFORM ACT, 1989
IN THE MATTER OF THE FAMILY LAW ACT, 1995
IN THE MATTER OF THE FAMILY LAW (DIVORCE) ACT, 1996

BETWEEN

A.B.

Applicant

– and –

C.D.

Respondent

NOTICE TO TRUSTEES

TAKE NOTICE that relief has been claimed by the Applicant/Respondent in the above entitled proceedings pursuant to section(s) 12 and/or 13 of the Family Law Act, 1995 or section 17 of the Family Law (Divorce) Act, 1996 or section 813 of the Family Law (Maintenance of Spouses and Children) Act, 1976 and in particular in relation to ....[here insert details of pension in respect of which relief is claimed].

AND FURTHER TAKE NOTICE that a Notice of Trial or a Notice to fix a date for Trial will be served upon you in due course in accordance with the Rules of the Circuit Court.

Dated the .... day of 19   .

Signed:..
            Solicitors for the Applicant/Respondent

To: The County Registrar

and

To: The trustees of the pension scheme concerned

and

To: Applicant/Respondent [or Solicitors where appropriate]

FORM NO. 5

AN CHUIRT TEAGHLAIGH CHUARDA

(THE CIRCUIT FAMILY COURT)

CIRCUIT   COUNTY OF:

[insert as appropriate]

IN THE MATTER OF THE JUDICIAL SEPARATION AND FAMILY LAW
REFORM ACT, 1989
IN THE MATTER OF THE FAMILY LAW ACT, 1995
IN THE MATTER OF THE FAMILY LAW (DIVORCE) ACT, 1996

BETWEEN

A.B.

Applicant

– and –

C.D.

Respondent

NOTICE TO FIX DATE FOR TRIAL

TAKE NOTICE that the above matter will be listed before this Honourable Court/
the County Registrar sitting at   on the day of   19   at
o'clock in the forenoon for the purpose of fixing a date for the trial hereof.

Dated this   day of   19   .

Signed:..

Solicitor for the Applicant/Respondent (delete as appropriate)

To: The County Registrar

and

To: The Respondent/Applicant (delete as appropriate) or the solicitors for the Re-
spondent/Applicant, if appropriate.

To: The trustees of the pension scheme concerned if relief is sought under sections
12 and/or 13 of the 1995 Act or section 17 of the 1996 Act.

Family Law (Divorce) Act 1996

FORM NO. 6

AN CHUIRT TEAGHLAIGH CHUARDA

(THE CIRCUIT FAMILY COURT)

CIRCUIT   COUNTY OF:

[insert as appropriate]

IN THE MATTER OF THE JUDICIAL SEPARATION AND FAMILY LAW
REFORM ACT, 1989
IN THE MATTER OF THE FAMILY LAW ACT, 1995
IN THE MATTER OF THE FAMILY LAW (DIVORCE) ACT, 1996

BETWEEN

A.B.

Applicant

– and –

C.D.

Respondent

DEFENCE AND COUNTERCLAIM

TAKE NOTICE that the Respondent   of
in the County of   disputes the claims made In the
Applicant's Family Law Civil Bill pursuant to sections   of the above entitled Acts, which Civil Bill was served on the Respondent on the   day of
19

AND TAKE NOTICE that the Respondent will rely upon the following matters in
disputing the Applicant's claim:

[Here set out in numbered paragraphs the matters disputed or denied by the Respondent. Indicate clearly the extent (if any) to which the Applicant's claim or claims
are admitted.]

COUNTERCLAIM

AND TAKE NOTICE that the Respondent will rely on the following matters in
support of his/her Counterclaim:

[Here set out in numbered paragraphs details of the relief(s) being claimed by the
Respondent specifying the matters required by Rule 21 of these Rules.]

AND THE RESPONDENT CLAIMS:

[Here set out in numbered paragraphs the reliefs (including decrees and declarations) being claimed pursuant to the 1989 Act, the 1995 Act or the 1996 Act speci-

fying, where appropriate, the statutory basis upon which each such relief is sought.]

Dated the   day of   19   .

The address for the service of proceedings on the Respondent is as follows:

[Here insert address of Respondent/Solicitor for the Respondent]

Signed:..

　　　　　Respondent/Solicitor for the Respondent

To: The County Registrar

        Address

and

To: The Applicant/Solicitors for the Applicant

        Address

FORM NO. 7

AN CHUIRT TEAGHLAIGH CHUARDA

(THE CIRCUIT FAMILY COURT)

CIRCUIT   COUNTY OF

IN THE MATTER OF THE JUDICIAL SEPARATION AND FAMILY LAW REFORM ACT, 1989 AND IN THE MATTER OF THE FAMILY LAW ACT, 1996

BETWEEN

A.B.

Applicant

– and –

C.D.

Respondent

CERTIFICATE PURSUANT TO SECTION 6 OF THE JUDICIAL

SEPARATION AND FAMILY LAW REFORM ACT, 1989

I,   , the Solicitor acting for the above Applicant do hereby certify as follows:

1. I have discussed with the Applicant the possibility of reconciliation with the Respondent and I have given the Applicant the names and addresses of persons qualified to help effect a reconciliation between spouses who have become estranged.
2. I have discussed with the Applicant the possibility of engaging in mediation to help effect a separation on an agreed basis with the Respondent and I have given the Applicant the names and addresses of persons and organisations qualified to provide a mediation service.
3. I have discussed with the Applicant the possibility of effecting a separation by the negotiation and conclusion of a Separation Deed or written Separation Agreement with the Respondent.

Dated the   day of   , 19   .

Signed:...

Solicitor

Address:

FORM NO. 8

AN CHUIRT TEAGHLAIGH CHUARDA

(THE CIRCUIT FAMILY COURT)

CIRCUIT   COUNTY OF

IN THE MATTER OF THE JUDICIAL SEPARATION AND FAMILY LAW
REFORM ACT, 1989 AND IN THE MATTER OF THE FAMILY LAW ACT,
1995

BETWEEN

A.B.

Applicant

– and –

C.D.

Respondent

CERTIFICATE PURSUANT TO SECTION 6 OF THE JUDICIAL

SEPARATION AND FAMILY LAW REFORM ACT, 1989

I ,   , the Solicitor acting for the above Respondent do hereby certify as
follows:

1. I have discussed with the Respondent the possibility of reconciliation with
   the Applicant and I have given the Respondent the names and addresses of
   persons qualified to help effect a reconciliation between spouses who have
   become estranged.
2. I have discussed with the Respondent the possibility of engaging in mediation to help effect a separation on an agreed basis with the Applicant
   and I have given the Respondent the names and addresses of persons and
   organisations qualified to provide a mediation service.
3. I have discussed with the Respondent the possibility of effecting a separation by the negotiation and conclusion of a Separation Deed or written
   Separation Agreement with the Applicant.

Dated the   day of   , 19   .

Signed:..

       Solicitor

Address:

173

FORM NO. 9

AN CHUIRT TEAGHLAIGH CHUARDA

(THE CIRCUIT FAMILY COURT)

CIRCUIT   COUNTY OF

IN THE MATTER OF THE FAMILY LAW (DIVORCE) ACT, 1996

BETWEEN

A.B.

Applicant

-and-

C.D.

Respondent

CERTIFICATE PURSUANT TO SECTION 6 OF THE FAMILY LAW
(DIVORCE) ACT, 1996

I,   , the Solicitor acting for the above Applicant do hereby certify as
follows:

1. I have discussed with the Applicant the possibility of reconciliation with
    the Respondent and I have given the Applicant the names and addresses of
    persons qualified to help effect a reconciliation between spouses who have
    become estranged.
    [The following paragraphs to be inserted where appropriate.]
2. I have discussed with the Applicant the possibility of engaging in media-
    tion to help effect a separation on an agreed basis (the spouses the parties
    hereto not being separated) or a divorce on a basis agreed between the
    Applicant with the Respondent and I have given the Applicant the names
    and addresses of persons and organisations qualified to provide a media-
    tion service for spouses who have become estranged.
3. I have discussed with the Applicant the possibility of effecting a separa-
    tion by the negotiation and conclusion of a Separation Deed or written
    Separation Agreement with the Respondent.
4. I have ensured that the Applicant is aware of judicial separation as an
    alternative to divorce, no decree of judicial separation in relation to the
    Applicant and the Respondent being in force.

Dated the   day of   , 19   .

Signed:...

Solicitor

Address:

FORM NO. 10

AN CHUIRT TEAGHLAIGH CHUARDA

(THE CIRCUIT FAMILY COURT)

CIRCUIT   COUNTY OF

IN THE MATTER OF THE FAMILY LAW (DIVORCE) ACT, 1996

BETWEEN

A.B.

Applicant

– and –

C.D.

Respondent

CERTIFICATE PURSUANT TO SECTION 7 OF THE FAMILY LAW (DIVORCE) ACT, 1996

I,   , the Solicitor acting for the above Respondent do hereby certify as follows:-

1. I have discussed with the Respondent the possibility of reconciliation with the Applicant and I have given the Respondent the names and addresses of persons qualified to help effect a reconciliation between spouses who have become estranged.
   [The following paragraphs to be inserted where appropriate.]
2. I have discussed with the Respondent the possibility of engaging in mediation to help effect a separation on an agreed basis (the spouses the parties hereto not being separated) or a divorce on a basis agreed between the Respondent with the Applicant and 1 have given the Respondent the names and addresses of persons and organisations qualified to provide a mediation service for spouses who have become estranged.
3. I have discussed with the Respondent the possibility of effecting a separation by the negotiation and conclusion of a Separation Deed or written Separation Agreement with the Applicant.
4. I have ensured that the Respondent is aware of judicial separation as an alternative to divorce, no decree of judicial separation in relation to the Respondent and the Applicant being in force.

Dated the   day of, 19

Signed:...

                   Solicitor

Address:

APPENDIX C

Extracts from
THE PENSIONS BOARD*
PENSION PROVISIONS OF FAMILY LAW ACT, 1995
& FAMILY LAW (DIVORCE) ACT, 1996
GUIDANCE NOTES

PART 2

INTRODUCTION

This Part of the notes sets out the various items of information which must be provided in order to satisfy the requirements of the legislation.

General – [s. 38(7) 1995; s. 12(25) 1995; s. 12(13) 1995; s. 38(6) 1996; s. 17((25) 1996; s. 17(13) 1996]

50. In deciding whether or not to make an *order, the legislation* enables the *Court* to obtain various items of information in respect of the *member spouse's scheme* benefits. Furthermore, after an *order* is made, the *trustees* of the *scheme* in question are obliged, under certain circumstances, to provide information to the person named in the *order* and to the *Court. The trustees* may also require information from the person concerned to enable them to give effect to the *order.* This Part of the notes sets out the various items of information which must be provided in order to satisfy the requirements of the *legislation.* Where appropriate, the notes also specify the information which may be provided, and the procedures which may be applied, by the *trustees* (although not required by *the legislation)* in order to satisfy best practice and facilitate the efficient operation of a pension adjustment order.

Assessment of Value and Amount of Scheme Benefits – [s. 38(7) 1995; s. 38(6) 1996]

51. If proceedings have been instituted for any of the orders specified in the *legislation, each spouse* is required to give particulars of his/her property and income to the other *spouse* (or to a person for the benefit of a *dependent member of the family).* In this context, property would be deemed to include rights under a *scheme.*

[s. 12(24); 1995; s. 17(24) 1996]

52. Under section 54 of the Pensions Act of 1990 (Disclosure of Information), *the spouse* of a *member* of an *occupational pension scheme* is entitled on request to receive basic information in relation to that *scheme* (including: *scheme* documentation; annual reports; and copies of audited accounts and actuarial valuation reports, where these are produced). The provisions of the disclosure of information *legislation* will apply if proceedings for the granting of a *decree* have been instituted and will continue to apply following the granting of a *decree.*

---

*Reproduced by kind permission of the Pensions Board.

Sections and articles in **bold** refer to provisions of the Family Law Act 1995, the Family Law (Divorce) Act 1996 or the Pension Schemes (Family Law) Regulations 1997 (S.I. No. 107 of 1997).

[s. 12(25) 1995; s. 17(25) 1996; Art. 47 1997]

53. The *Court* may direct the *trustees* to provide more specific information (as set out in paragraphs 54 to 61) in respect of the *member spouse's scheme* benefits. The *Court* may issue such a direction on its own initiative but must do so following a request by either of the *spouses* (or any other person concerned). Such information must be provided by the *trustees* within the period specified by the *Court.*

General Membership Information

54. In order to satisfy the requirements of the *legislation,* the following general membership information must be provided:-

   (1) Name of the *scheme* (or other appropriate identification).

   (2) Name of *member spouse.*

   (3) Date on which *member spouse* first began to accrue *retirement benefit* and/or was first provided with *contingent benefit* under the *scheme.*

   (4) Current pensionable salary and the method of its calculation (if relevant).

   (5) Details of the amount of any *additional voluntary contributions (AVCs),* the period during which these were paid, and the additional *retirement benefit or contingent benefit* which will be provided in respect of the *AVCs.*

   (6) Details of the benefits provided following a transfer of accrued rights from another *scheme* (if any) and the period of service in that *scheme to* which this relates.

55. Paragraphs 56 to 60 set out the information which must be provided in relation to *retirement benefit* that is payable (or which, but for the granting of the *decree,* would have been payable) under the *scheme.* The information must relate to a date specified by the *trustees,* not being earlier than 12 months before the date on which the *trustees* were directed to provide the information. When provided, the information must be accompanied by the name and address of the person to be contacted if there is any further enquiry. With the consent of the *member spouse, the trustees* should, if possible, provide the information voluntarily to avoid putting the parties to the expense of obtaining a *Court* order.

Retirement Benefit – Defined Benefit – [Art. 48 1997]

56. If part, or all, of the *member spouse's retirement benefit* under the *scheme is* calculated on a *defined benefit basis,* in order to satisfy the requirements of the *legislation* the following information must be provided:-

   (1) Calculation of the amount of each element of accrued *retirement benefit* payable under the *rules* of the *scheme* at the time of the date of the *decree* assuming termination of the *member spouse's reckonable service* on the date specified by the *trustees* (see paragraph 55).

   (2) The method by which the amounts in (1) have been calculated. *(Where additional retirement benefit has been secured or granted by way of*

> *AVCs or a transfer of accrued rights from a previous scheme, the amount of such benefits should be either included in the main calculation - with a statement to this effect - or shown separately).*

(3) The date or dates on which such benefit becomes payable.

(4) The provision for increases in such benefits. If there is no provision for increases this must be stated.

(5) *The actuarial value* of such benefits, as at the date specified by the *trustees*.

Where the *scheme* concerned is an *occupational pension scheme* which is a funded *scheme* within the meaning of that term under Section 2(1) of the Pensions Act 1990, the *trustees* should include a general statement to the effect that the ability to make any payment from the *scheme* is subject to the availability of sufficient resources. In particular, the *legislation* provides that, where, in the opinion of the *actuary, the scheme* is not adequately funded, the magnitude of any *transfer amount* (or other amount payable following the death of the *member spouse* or the *non-member spouse*) made in lieu of the *designated benefit* may be adjusted to take account of the inadequacy of the funding of the *scheme*. If, at the time the information is being provided, the *actuary* to the *scheme* is of the opinion that such adjustment would be necessary, were a *transfer amount* payable in lieu of *designated benefit* arising under an *order,* this opinion should be conveyed by the *trustees* when providing information in respect of the *member spouse's retirement benefits*.

[s. 12(1) 1995; s. 17(1) 1996; Art. 3 1997]

57. *Actuarial value* means the equivalent cash value of a benefit (including, where appropriate, provision for any revaluation of such benefit) under a *scheme* calculated by reference to appropriate financial assumptions and making due allowance for the probability of survival to normal pensionable age and thereafter in accordance with normal life expectancy on the assumption that the *member spouse* is in a normal state of health having regard to his/her age.

58. *The actuarial value* should be calculated on a basis which an *actuary* has approved as being consistent with the appropriate guidelines issued by the Society of Actuaries in Ireland.

Retirement Benefit – Defined Contribution – [Art. 49 1997]

59. If part, or all, of the *member spouse's retirement benefit* under the *scheme is* calculated on a *defined contribution basis,* the following information must be provided:–

(1) *The accumulated value* at a specified date (see paragraph 55) of the contributions paid by, or in respect of, the *member spouse* for the purpose of *retirement benefit* to the date of the *decree* assuming termination of the *member spouse's reckonable service* on the specified date.

(2) The date or dates on which *retirement benefit* falls due together with a brief explanation as to how the *accumulated value* would be applied to provide *retirement benefit*.

Information Required Prior to the Decree – [Art. 47 1997]

60. Where the *Court* directs the *trustees* to provide information prior to the granting of the *decree,* the information in paragraphs 56 and 59 should be provided upon the assumption that the *decree* is granted at the specified date (see paragraph 55).

Contingent Benefit – [Art. 50 1997]

61. The following information must be provided in relation to *contingent benefit* that is payable (or which, but for the granting of the *decree,* would have been payable) under the *scheme:–*

(1) Calculation of the amount of each element *of contingent benefit payable* under the *rules* of the *scheme* assuming the *member spouse* died on the specified date, together with a reference to the specific rule or policy number under which each such element is provided.

(2) The method by which the amounts in (1) have been calculated.

Making of a Pension Adjustment Order – [s. 12(18) 1995; s. 12(20) 1995; s. 17(18) 1996; s. 17(20) 1996]

62. A person who applies for an *order* under the *legislation* must give notice thereof to the *trustees* of the *scheme* in question. In deciding whether or not to make an *order,* and in determining the provisions of the *order,* the *Court* shall have regard to any representations made by the *trustees.* Where the *order* will involve non-compliance with the *rules* of the *scheme* or with the Pensions Act 1990, the *trustees* should request that the *order* would include a direction to the *trustees* so that they will have the protection of Section 12 (20) of the Family Law Act, 1995 or Section 17(20) of the Family Law (Divorce) Act, 1996 (which provides that *trustees* are not liable for any loss or damage caused by non-compliance with the *rules* of the *scheme* or with the Pensions Act of 1990 if the non-compliance is occasioned by compliance with a direction of the *Court* under *the legislation).*

[s. 12(21) 1995; s. 17(2I) 1996]

63. If *an order* is made, the registrar or clerk of the *Court* concerned will serve a copy of the *order* on the *trustees* of each *scheme* in question.

Following the Making of an Order

64. Following the making of an *order(s) the trustees* should notify the person specified in the *order* of the amount and nature of the *designated benefit* and/or the amount of *contingent benefit* that is payable under the *order(s).* (The methodology for calculating the designated benefit and/or the contingent benefit that may be payable under an *order* is set out in Part 4 and Part 8 of these guidance notes, respectively.) They should also notify the specified person of the options available regarding any *transfer amount* that may be payable in lieu of *the designated benefit. (Transfer amounts* are covered in Part 7 of these guidance notes.) The *trustees* should request the specified person to maintain contact with *the scheme* (e.g. by suggesting that the person notifies the *trustees* of any changes in his/her address) and to ensure that arrangements are made for his/her personal representatives to notify the *trustees* in the event of his/her death. The *trustees* will not be liable for any loss where the specified person has not maintained contact with the *scheme* or made the necessary arrangements in relation to the notification of his/her death.

Transfer Amount at Request of Non-Member Spouse – [s. 12(4) 1995; s. 12(5) 1995; s. 17(4) 1996; s. 17(5) 1996; Art. 30]

65. If an *order in* relation to the *member spouse's retirement benefit* has been made in favour of the *non-member spouse,* he/she may apply to the *trustees* for a *transfer amount* in lieu of receiving the *designated benefit* (see paragraph 262). Such an application should be made in writing and should be accompanied by the following information:-

(1) evidence of date of birth of *non-member spouse* (if relevant);

(2) the name of the *occupational pension scheme* to which *the transfer amount* should be applied (if relevant) and the written agreement of the *trustees* thereof to accept such payment;

(3) the name of the life assurance company to which the *transfer amount* should be applied (if relevant)

Transfer Amount Initiated by Trustees – [s. 12(6) 1995; s. 12(8) 1995; s. 12(13) 1995; s. 17(6) 1996; s. 17(8) 1996 s. 17(13) 1996; Art. 34]

66. If *the order* relates to the *member spouse's retirement benefit, the trustees* may, in certain circumstances, give effect to the *order* by applying a *transfer amount* without obtaining the consent of the person in whose favour it has been made. Paragraphs 277 and 278 set out the criteria governing the application of *transfer amounts* without consent. Following such a transfer, the *trustees* must notify both the person named in the *order* and the registrar or clerk of the *Court* concerned. They must also provide details of the *transfer amount* and particulars of the *scheme* or life assurance company to which it has been applied.

Member Spouse Ceases to be Active Member – [s. 12(12) 1995; s. 17(12) 1996]

67. If, following the making of an *order* in relation to an *occupational pension scheme* (and prior to the payment of a *transfer amount), the member spouse* ceases to be an *active member* of the *scheme, the trustees* must notify both the registrar or clerk of the *Court* concerned and the *non-member spouse* of such cessation.

Death of Non-Member Spouse – [s. 12(9) 1995; s. 12(10) 1995; s. 17(9) 1996; s. 17(10) 1996; Art. 38; Art. 41]

68. If the *non-member spouse* predeceases the *member spouse,* either before or after commencement of the *designated benefit* (and prior to the payment of a *transfer amount)* a benefit becomes payable to the personal representatives of the deceased *spouse* as outlined in paragraphs 215 and 241. The *trustees* should require evidence of death prior to making any payment to the personal representatives.

Commencement of Designated Benefit

69. When, following the making of an *order* in relation to the *member spouse's retirement benefit* in favour of the *non-member spouse* (and prior to the payment of a transfer amount), the member spouse's retirement benefit is about to commence, the *trustees* should notify the *non-member spouse* of the amount and nature of the *designated benefit. The trustees* may also choose (but are not obliged) to notify the *non-member spouse:*–

(1) whether they would be prepared to provide an alternative benefit to, or in respect of, the *non-member spouse* under the *scheme* and, if so, the amount of such alternative benefit;

(2) the amount of the *transfer amount* which could be provided in lieu of *the designated benefit.*

Payments Under an Order Remain Valid

70. Prior to making any payment in connection with an *order(s) the trustees* should satisfy themselves that the person in whose favour the *order(s)* is made remains eligible to receive such payment (e.g. that the person in whose favour the *order* is made is alive and has not remarried or ceased to be a *dependent member of the family,* if relevant). The *trustees* may, in the absence of evidence to the contrary, rely on the statement of such person.

PART 3

PENSION ADJUSTMENT ORDERS

This Part of the notes sets out the sequence of events leading to the making of a pension adjustment order and the details that will be contained in the order.

Application – [s. 12(2) 1995; s. 12(3) 1995; s. 12(23) 1995; s. 17(2) 1996; s. 17(3) 1996; s. 17(23) 1996]

75. Either *spouse (or* a person on behalf of a *dependent member of the family)* may apply for an *order* in relation to *retirement benefit* and/or *contingent benefit* under a *scheme* of which one of the *spouses* is a *member.* The *Court* will not make *an order* if the *spouse* who applies for it has remarried.

[s. 12(2) 1995; s. 17(2) 1996]

76. *An order* in relation to either *spouse's retirement benefit* may be made at the time of the granting of the *decree* or at any time thereafter during the *member spouse's* lifetime (including following commencement of his/her *retirement benefit).*

[s. 12(3) 1995; s. 17(3) 1996]

77. An *order* in relation to either *spouse's contingent benefit* under a *scheme* must be made within 12 months following the granting of the *decree.*

Considerations – [s. 12(18) 1995; s. 12(23) 1995; s. 17(18) 1996; s. 17(23) 1996]

78. The person applying for the *order* must give notice to the *trustees* of the *scheme* concerned. In deciding whether or not to make an *order,* and in determining the provisions of the *order,* the *Court* must have regard to any representations made by the *trustees. The trustees* should, where reasonably possible, co-operate with the parties in endeavouring to facilitate the making of *an order* on a consensual basis, in order to minimise the necessity of *Court* appearances on behalf of the *trustees,* with the resultant costs to the parties. The *Court* must also consider whether adequate and reasonable financial provision already exists for the *non-member spouse* and any other *dependent member of the family* (or can be made by any of the other *order(s)* that are available under Part II of the Family Law Act, 1995 or Part III of the Family Law (Divorce) Act, 1996.

Information Contained in Pension Adjustment Order(s) – [s. 12(2) 1995; s. 12(20) 1995; s. 12(21) 1995; s. 17(2) 1996; s. 17(20) 1996; s. 17(21) 1996]

79. The *Court* may make an *order* in relation to either *spouse's retirement benefit*. Such an *order* will provide for the payment of a benefit to either the *non-member spouse* (and his/her personal representatives on death) or a specified person for the benefit of a person who is (and for so long only as he/she remains) a *dependent member of the family. The order* will be served on the *trustees* of each *scheme* of which the *member spouse* was a *member* during the *relevant period* and will contain the following information:–

   (i)   the name of the *scheme* (or other appropriate identification);

   (ii) the name of the *member spouse;*

   (iii) the name and address of the person in whose favour the *order* is made;

   (iv) the name of the *dependent member of the family* (if relevant);

   (v) type of *order* (i.e. pension adjustment order in relation to *retirement benefit* made under section 12(2) of the Family Law Act, 1995 or section 17(2) of the Family Law (Divorce) Act, 1996);

   (vi) date of commencement of period of *reckonable service of member spouse* to be taken into account;

   (vii) date of ending of period of *reckonable service of member spouse* to be taken into account (but not later than date of granting of *decree);*

   (viii) percentage of the *retirement benefit* accrued during the period between (vi) and (vii) above, to be paid to the person specified in (iii) above;

   (ix) such directions (if any) to the *trustees* of the *scheme* as the *Court* considers appropriate for the purposes of the *order* including directions compliance with which occasions non-compliance with the *rules* of the *scheme* or the Pensions Act of 1990.

[s. 12(3) 1995; s. 12(20) 1995; s. 12(21) 1995; s. 17(3) 1996; s. 17(20) 1996; s. 17(21) 1996]

80. The *Court* may make an *order* in relation to the *contingent benefit* that is payable (or which, but for the making of the *decree,* would have been payable) under the *scheme* of which either *spouse* is a *member.* Such an *order* will provide for the payment of a benefit on the death of the *member spouse* to the *non-member spouse* and/or a specified person for the benefit of a person who is (and for so long only as he/she remains) a *dependent member of the family.* This means that a single *order* (in relation to *contingent benefit)* may be made for the benefit of more than one person. The *order* will be served on the *trustees* of the *scheme* and will contain the following information:–

   (i)   the name of *the scheme* (or other appropriate identification);

   (ii) the name of the *member spouse;*

   (iii) the name and address of the person(s) in whose favour the *order is* made;

   (iv) the name of the *dependent member(s) of the family* (if relevant);

   (v) type of *order* (i.e. pension adjustment order in relation to *contingent benefit* made under section 12(3) of the Family Law Act, 1995 or section 17(3) of the Family Law (Divorce) Act, 1996);

   (vi) identification of the *contingent benefit* to which the *order* applies (i.e. identified by reference to appropriate *scheme rules* or policy or contract number);

   (vii) percentage of *contingent benefit* in (vi) to be paid to each of the person(s) specified under (iii), above;

   (viii)such directions (if any) to the *trustees* of the *scheme* as the *Court* considers appropriate for the purposes of the *order* including directions compliance with which occasions noncompliance with the *rules* of the *scheme* or the Pensions Act of 1990.

Calculations – [s. 12(1) 1995; s. 17(1) 1996; Art. 5 1997]

81.   *An order* will not specify the amount of the *designated benefit* or the amount of *contingent benefit* to be paid under the *order(s). The trustees* will give effectto the *order(s)* by calculating the amounts using the procedures laid down in the *legislation* and in these notes.

Variation of Orders – [s. 18(1) 1995; s. 18(2) 1995; s. 22(1) 1996; s. 22(2) 1996]

82.   Subject to paragraph 83, the *Court* may vary or discharge an *order* made in relation to either *spouse's retirement benefit.* The variation may be made on application to the *Court* by either of the *spouses* or, in the case of the death of either of the *spouses,* by any other person who, in the opinion of the *Court,* has a sufficient interest in the matter, or by a person for the benefit of a *dependent member of the family.*

[s. 12(26) 1995; s. 17(26) 1996]

83.   When making an *order* in relation to either *spouse's retirement benefit,* the *Court* may restrict the circumstances under which the *order* may be varied or it may remove the power to vary the *order.*

[s. 18(1) 1995; s. 22(1) 1996]

84.   There is no power to vary an *order* made in relation to *contingent benefit.*

PART 4

CALCULATION OF DESIGNATED BENEFIT

This Part of the notes sets out the procedure to be used by the trustees of each scheme in calculating the designated benefit payable from the scheme following a pension adjustment order in relation to the member spouse's retirement benefit tinder that scheme.

General – [s. 12(1) 1995; s. 17(1) 1996; Art. 4 1997]

90. *The legislation* defines the element of the *member spouse's retirement benefit* which is paid to the *nonmember spouse* (or to a specified person for the benefit of *a dependent member of the family*) from each *scheme* under an *order* as the *"designated benefit"*. This Part of the notes sets out the procedure to be used by *the trustees* of each *scheme* in calculating the *designated benefit* payable from that *scheme*.

Retirement Benefit Service – [Art. 3 1997]

91. *Retirement benefit service* in relation to a *scheme* means the period of *reckonable service* within that *scheme* but excluding any period of *reckonable service* where:

(1) the only benefit in respect of such service is in respect of death before *normal pensionable age;* or

(2) the *member* has been notified in writing by the *trustees,* or the rules of *the scheme* so provide, that a period of service does not entitle him/her *to retirement benefit; or*

(3) in the case of *AVCs, a scheme* year (as defined in the Regulations to Part V of the Pensions Act of 1990) in which no *AVC* was made; or

(4) in the case of a *Section 235 retirement annuity contract* or a *trust scheme, a* year beginning on 6th April in which no contribution was made.

Rules in Force – [Art. 3 1997]

92. The calculation of the *designated benefit* will depend on the *rules* of the *scheme* in force at the date of the *decree* as they apply to the *member spouse's retirement benefit.* *"Rules in force"* where used in these notes should be taken to mean the *rules* of the *scheme* in force at the date of the *decree* (subject to any overriding provisions of the Pensions Act of 1990).

Information in Pension Adjustment Order – [s. 12(1) 1995; s 12(2) 1995; s. 17(1) 1996; s. 17(2) 1996; Art. 3 1997; Art. 5 1997]

93. In calculating the *designated benefit, the trustees* of each *scheme* must give effect to the provisions of the *order.* This will contain specified information (see paragraph 79) including the following:–

(1) the period of *reckonable service* of the *member spouse* prior to the

granting of the *decree* which is to be taken into account (the *"relevant period"*);

(2) the percentage of the *retirement benefit* accrued during the *relevant period* to be paid to the person specified in the *order (the "relevant percentage").*

[s. 12(2) 1995; s. 17(2) 1996]

94. The *Court* is not empowered to specify a *relevant period* which ends after the date of the granting of the *decree* but it may specify a *relevant period* which ends at an earlier date.

Determination of Type of Scheme – [Art. 6 1997]

95. The procedure for calculating the *designated benefit* payable from a *scheme* will depend on whether the *retirement benefit* in question arises from *a defined benefit* or a *defined contribution scheme.* Where under the *rules in force the retirement benefit* is calculated partly on a *defined benefit basis* and partly on *a defined contribution basis, the defined benefit* element of the *designated benefit* is calculated using the procedures set out for *defined benefit schemes* and the remaining part is calculated using the procedures set out for *defined contribution schemes.*

96. Any part of the *member spouse's retirement benefit* which is not directly determined by the amount of the contributions paid by, or in respect of, the *member spouse* is deemed to be calculated on a *defined benefit basis.*

97. Any part of the *member spouse's retirement benefit* which is directly determined by the amount of the contributions paid by, or in respect of, the *member spouse* is deemed to be calculated on a *defined contribution basis.*

98. Where certain specified benefits are being targeted but, under the *rules of the scheme, the member spouse's retirement benefit* will ultimately be determined by the amount of contributions paid, such a *scheme* is a *defined contribution scheme* and not a *defined benefit scheme.*

99. A *Section 235 retirement annuity contract* or a *trust scheme is a defined contribution scheme* and the *designated benefit* should be calculated accordingly.

100. A *buy-out bond* is a *defined contribution scheme* and the *designated benefit* should be calcuiated as for a transfer of accrued rights from another *scheme.*

Defined Benefit Schemes

101. If retirement benefit is calculated on a *defined benefit basis* the calculation of *the designated benefit* will depend on the status of the *member spouse* at the date of the making of the *order* (i.e. whether the *member spouse* is then an *active member, a deferred pensioner* or a *current pensioner* of the *scheme* in question). Furthermore, if *the member spouse* is an *active member* of the *scheme,* the calculation of the *designated benefit* depends on whether the *member spouse:-*

(1) commences to receive *retirement benefit* from the *scheme* on retirement at *normal pensionable age;*

(2) commences to receive *retirement benefit* from the *scheme* on retirement earlier or later than *normal pensionable age;* or

(3) withdraws from *reckonable service* and, on a later date, commences to receive *retirement benefit* from the *scheme.*

Active Member – Designated Benefit on Retirement at NPA – [Art. 7 1997]

104. If the *member spouse* is an *active member* of the *scheme* in question at the date of the *order, the designated benefit* on his/her subsequent retirement at *normal pensionable age* will be calculated using the principle of uniform accrual (i.e. *retirement benefit* will be assumed to have accrued uniformly over the *member spouse's* entire period of *retirement benefit service). The designated benefit* will be calculated using the formula:

$$A \times \frac{B}{C} \times p$$

A = the amount of *retirement benefit at normal pensionable age,* payable in accordance with the *rules in force* (excluding benefits secured by *AVCs* or a transfer of accrued rights from *another scheme).*

B = the period of *retirement benefit service* which the *member spouse has* completed within the *relevant period.*

C = the period of *retirement retirement benefit service* which the *member spouse has* completed at *normal pensionable age* as defined under the *rules in force.*

p = *the relevant percentage.*

105. In determining B and C above, *retirement benefit service* is calculated disregarding any rule of the *scheme* under which the number of years taken into account in calculating *retirement benefit* is subject to an upper limit (e.g. if the *member spouse* has completed 45 years' *retirement benefit service,* C equals 45 years, even if a maximum of 40 *years' scheme* service is taken into account in calculating *retirement benefit).*

Example

A scheme provides a retirement pension of 1/60th of final pensionable salary for each year of pensionable service at *normal pensionable age* of 65. Final pensionable salary is defined as the average salary earned in the three years preceding *normal pensionable age.* Pensionable service is defined as complete years of service with the company after attaining age 25. *Members* qualify for contingent benefit on joining the company but must be over age 25 to be eligible for *retirement benefit.*

An employee, whose date of birth is 1st January, 1961, joined the company on 1st January, 1981 (i.e. at age 20).

The employee married on 1st January, 1983 and was subsequently granted a decree on 1st January, 2001.

At the time of the granting of the decree the *Court* made an order which specified:

Relevant period: 1st January, 1983 to 1st January, 2001
Relevant percentage: 50%

At *normal pensionable age* the member spouse retires and final pensionable salary is calculated as follows:

Calendar Year	Earned Salary
2023	£87,500
2024	£90,000
2025	£92,500

The *designated benefit* to be paid to the person specified in the order is specified as folows:–

$$A = (87,500 + 90,000 + 92,500) \div 3 \times \frac{40}{60} \qquad = \quad £60,000$$

B =   1st January, 1986 to 1st January, 2001   =   15 years*
C =   1st January, 1986 to 1st January, 2026   =   40 years*
p =   50%

$$\text{Designated Benefit} = £60,000 \times \frac{15}{40} \times 50\% \qquad = \quad £11,250$$

*B and C count from the commencement of service for retirement benefit purposes within the relevant period (1986) rather than the commencement of reckonable service within the relevant period (1983).

108. The procedure described in paragraph 107 applies equally to the calculation of any lump sum payable on retirement at normal pensionable age (whether in commutation of part of the *member spouse's* pension or as a separate gratuity) and to any other element *of retirement benefit.* Where, under the *rules in force, the scheme* from which the *retirement benefit* is payable provides an independent lump sum or gratuity or has a rule allowing the *member spouse,* as of right, or subject to the consent of the employer/*trustees,* to receive part of his/her retirement pension as a lump sum, the *non-member spouse* (or other beneficiary) must be given an equivalent right/option in relation to the *designated benefit.* The *member spouse* and the *non-member spouse* (or other beneficiary) may exercise their rights/options independently of one another.

Calculation of a Contingent Benefit

The court will determine whether a pension adjustment order should be made and the provisions of the order. Specifically the order will detail the person or persons in whose favour it is made; this may be the dependant spouse and/or person representing the children and each element of the contingent benefit that is to be payable to such person or persons.

On the death of the member's spouse during the period of employment or self-employment to which the pension scheme relates, the percentage of contingent benefits as specified in the order must be paid to the appropriate person or persons. The contingent benefits in question are those applying based on the rules of the scheme at the date of the judicial separation or divorce, *i.e.* subsequent improvements or reductions in contingent benefits are ignored and if relevant, the member spouse's salary, or pensionable salary at the date of death.

Example

The rules of a pension scheme provide for a lump sum death benefit of four times the salary at the date of death to be paid in the event of the death of the scheme member during employment.

A pension order is made in relation to the member spouse's contingent benefits, in favour of the dependent spouse, which specifies:

Contingent Benefit: lump sum of four times salary at date of death

*Percentage of contingent benefit
to be paid to dependant spouse*: 50%

The member spouse dies while in employment. The spouse's salary at date of death is £50,000.

The amount of benefit paid in accordance with the order is calculated as:

$$4 \times £50,000 \times 50\% = £100,000$$

Thus, an amount of £100,000 is paid to the dependant spouse.

PART 5

PAYMENT OF DESIGNATED BENEFIT

This Part of the notes sets out the conditions governing the payment of the designated benefit and the circumstances under which the value of the designated benefit may crystallise and become payable as a transfer amount.

General – [s. 12(2) 1995; s. 17(2) 1996]

200. The *legislation* empowers the *Court* to make an *order*, in relation to *retirement benefit* under a *scheme* of which either *spouse* is a *member*, providing for the payment of part, or all, of the *member spouse's retirement benefit* which had accrued to the date of the *decree*, to the *non-member spouse*, or to a specified person for the benefit of a *dependent member of the family*. The amount of the *retirement benefit* to be paid is called the *designated benefit*.

201. The methodology for calculating the *designated benefit* is described in Part 4 of these notes.

202. The circumstances under which a *transfer amount* may, or must, be paid from the *scheme* as an alternative to paying the *designated benefit* are set out in Part 7 of these notes.

203. This Part sets out the conditions under which the *designated benefit is* payable. Paragraphs 204 to 232 deal with *designated benefit* which is calculated on *a defined benefit basis*. Paragraphs 233 to 243 deal with *designated benefit* which is calculated on a *defined contribution basis*.

Defined Benefit Schemes – [s. 12(14) 1995; s. 17(14) 1996; Art. 35 1997]

204. Other than in the circumstances described in Part 7 of these notes (i.e. where a transfer of *designated benefit* is either requested by the *non-member spouse,* or is initiated by the *trustees) the designated benefit* arising from the *member spouse's* membership of a *defined benefit scheme* will generally be paid from the *scheme* at the same time, and in the same format, as the residual *retirement benefit* payable to the *member spouse.* In other words, any *retirement benefit* payable to, or in respect of, the *member spouse* under the *rules in force* will result in a corresponding payment of *designated benefit to* the person specified in the *order.* The various types of payment are discussed in the following paragraphs.

Retirement of Member Spouse

205. The procedures set out in Part 4 of these notes will be applied to the *retirement benefit* payable to the *member spouse* in order to calculate the amount of the corresponding *designated benefit.* In some circumstances in order to calculate *the designated benefit* it may be necessary to make separate calculations in respect of the various elements of *retirement benefit* payable from the *scheme* (e.g. if part is calculated on a *defined benefit basis* and part is calculated on a *defined contribution basis).*

[s. 12(14) 1995; s. 17(14) 1996; Art. 35 1997]

206. The *designated benefit* is payable in accordance with the *rules in force* governing the payment of *retirement benefit.*

[s. 12(14) 1995; s. 17(14) 1996; Art. 35 1997]

207. Where the *order* is made in favour of the *non-member spouse, the designated benefit* which is in the form of a pension payable during the lifetime of the *member spouse* will commence on his/her retirement and will be paid for as long as both the *member spouse* and the *non-member spouse* are alive. Where the *order* is made in favour of a person, for the benefit of a *dependent member of the family,* it will be paid for as long as both (i) the *member spouse* is alive and (ii) the *dependent member of the family* is alive and remains a *dependent member of the family.* If, however, the *rules in force* provide for the guaranteed payment of the *member spouse's* pension in respect of a period after his/her death, the *designated benefit* would continue to be paid during this period to the *non-member spouse* (if living) or for the benefit of the *dependent member of the family* (if living, and still a *dependent member of the family).*

Dependent Member of the family – [s. 2(1) 1995; s. 2(1) 1996; Art. 3 1997]

208. The *legislation* defines a *dependent member of the family* and it is this definition, rather than any definition contained in the *rules* of the *scheme, that* applies. The *legislation* defines a *dependent member of the family* as any child of both *spouses,* or of either *spouse,* who is under the age of 18 years, or is under the age of 23 years and receiving full-time education, or has a mental or physical disability regardless of age.

Benefits on Death of Member Spouse following Commencement of Designated Benefit – [s. 12(14) 1995; s. 17(14) 1996; Art. 35 1997]

209. Where an *order* is made in relation to *retirement benefit* and the *rules in force* provide for the payment of a spouse's/dependant's pension, a similar benefit must be paid to the person in receipt of the *designated benefit* for his/her lifetime or *dependency,* as appropriate. Where on the *member spouse's* death, the person in whose favour the *order* is made has already died, or the *dependent member of the family* ceased to be dependent as the case may be, the *order* ceases to have any effect. (See Part 6 of these notes in relation to the calculation of *member spouse's retirement benefit* under the *scheme*).

Options

210. The *rules in force* may permit certain options. These may relate exclusively to the *member spouse's retirement benefit* (e.g. exchange of part of the *member spouse's* pension into a lump sum) or may involve the provision of benefits to a third party (e.g. allocation of part of *member spouse's* pension to provide for a dependant's pension).

[s. 12(14) 1995; s. 17(14) 1996; Art. 37 1997]

211. Where the *rules in force* allow the member spouse the option of exchanging part of his/her pension for a lump sum and the *member spouse* has not retired at the date of the *order*, an equivalent option must be provided to the person in whose favour the *order* is made in respect of the part of the *designated benefit* which relates to the *member spouse's* pension (i.e. the *non-member spouse* must be given an equivalent option, but he/she may exercise that option independently). Where the *non-member spouse* chooses to exercise the option, the rate of exchange of *designated benefit* for lump sum will be the same as the rate of exchange applying to the *member spouse's benefit.*

Example

A *member* joined a *scheme* on. lst January, 1980 and retires (at *normal pensionable age*) on 1st January, 2020. Her *retirement benefits* are calculated *as follows:*

Option A
    Scheme pension of   £60,000 p.a.

Option B
    Lump sum of   £135,000 p.a.
      plus
    Reduced pension of   £46,224 p.a.

An *order* was made in favour of the non-member spouse shortly before the *member spouse* retired which specified:–

    Relevant period: 1st January, 1983 to 1st January, 2001
    Relevant percentage: 50%

Option A
    Pension of   £15,000 (i.e. £60,000 x $\frac{20}{40}$ x 50%)

Option B

Lump sum of £33,750 (i.e. £135,000 x $\frac{20}{40}$ x 50%)

plus

Reduced pension of £11,556 (i.e. £46,224 x $\frac{20}{40}$ x 50%)

Option B is available to the *non-member spouse* regardless of whether the *member spouse* opts for a lump sum and reduced pension under the *scheme*.

212. If the *member spouse* elects to exchange part of his/her pension to provide benefits on his/her death after retirement to a third party, this option must not affect the calculation or payment of the *designated benefit*. In these circumstances, *the designated benefit* must be calculated and paid ignoring any such option exercised by the *member spouse*.

Pension Increases – [s. 12(14) 1995; s. 17(14) 1996]

213. If:–

(1) the *rules in force* provide for guaranteed increases in the *retirement benefit* payable in pension form, or

(2) the *rules in force* permit, and the appropriate person or persons exercise, a discretion to grant a cost of living increase in the *retirement benefit* payable to all, or a certain category of, pensioners,

and the *member spouse's retirement be?iefit* is increased as a result, the same increase must be applied to the *designated benefit*.

[Art. l4 1997]

214. The principle in paragraph 213 does not, however, extend to rule changes or benefit augmentations awarded to *current pensioners*. As described in paragraph 120, such rule changes or augmentations will only be taken into account for the purposes of calculating the *designated benefit* where the augmentation took place prior to the date of the *decree*.

Benefits on Death of Person Specified in the Order following Commencement of Designated Benefit – [s. 12(10) 1995; s. 17(10) 1996; Art. 38 1997]

215. If *the order* is made in favour of the *non-member spouse,* and he/she predeceases the *member spouse* following commencement of the *designated benefit, the legislation* requires the *trustees* to provide for the payment of an amount to the personal representatives of the deceased *spouse* within 3 months of the death of *the spouse*. The amount is calculated as the *actuarial value*, at the date of death, of *the designated benefit* which would otherwise have been payable to the *non-member spouse* during the lifetime of the *member spouse*. It will exclude the value of benefits which would have been payable to the *non-member spouse* following the *member spouse's* death.

216. Such an actuarial value should be calculated on a basis which an actuary has approved as being consistent with the appropriate guidelines issued by the Society of Actuaries in Ireland. Where the *scheme* is an *occupational pension scheme* which is a funded *scheme* within the meaning of that term under Section 2(1) of the Pensions Act, 1990 and its funded status is such that, in the opinion of the *actuary,* its resources are inadequate to provide for the liabilities of the *scheme in* respect of the benefits payable as a first priority on wind-up under subparagraph (a) (i) of Section 48 (1) of the Pensions Act, 1990, the *actuary* may take account of the funded status of the *scheme* in arriving at the *actuarial value.*

[s. 12(17) 1995; s. 17(17) 1996]

217. Following the payment of the amount described in paragraph 215, the *trustees* will be discharged from any obligation to make any further payments in connection with the *order.*

[s. 12(2) 1995; s. 17(2) 1996]

218. If the *order* is made in favour of a specified person, for the benefit of a *dependent member of the family,* no further benefit is payable following the death of *the dependent member of the family. The order,* therefore, ceases to have any effect (see Part 6 of these notes in relation to calculation of *member spouse's retirement benefit* under the *scheme).*

Withdrawal from Reckonable Service of Member Spouse

219. If the *member spouse* is an *active member* of the *scheme* at the date of the *order* and subsequently withdraws from *reckonable service* prior to commencement of his/her *retirement benefit, the designated benefit* is calculated based on the *rules in force.*

[Art. 39 1997]

220. In most cases, the *designated benefit* will, therefore, represent a proportion of the *member spouse's deferred retirement benefit* entitlements under the *scheme,* including such periodic increases during deferment (if any) as are provided under the *rules in force.* In these circumstances, the principles governing the payment of the *designated benefit,* when it ultimately becomes payable at the time of commencement of the *member spouse's retirement benefit,* are the same as those applying where the *member spouse* retires from *reckonable service* (as set out in paragraphs 205 to 218).

[Art. 39 1997]

221. If part, or all, of the *member spouse's retirement benefit* on termination of *reckonable service* is represented by a refund of his/her contributions, the corresponding *designated benefit* will be a proportion of such refund. In these circumstances the part of the *designated benefit* which relates to the refund of contributions will be paid to the person specified in the *order* at the same time as the remaining part of the refund of contributions is paid to the *member spouse.*

[s. 12(8) 1995; s. 17(8) 1996]

222. The *member spouse* may on, or following, termination of *reckonable service* choose to have a transfer payment applied on his/her behalf under another *scheme* in lieu of retaining any deferred *retirement benefit* in the *scheme.* In such circumstances, the *trustees* may choose to transfer the then value of the *designated benefit* in accordance with the provisions of paragraphs 277 and 278.

[s. 12(12) 1995; s. 17(12) 1996]

223. If, after the making of an *order, the member spouse* ceases to be an *active member* of the *scheme, the trustees* must notify the registrar or clerk of the *Court,* and the *non-member spouse,* of the cessation within a period of 12 months following the cessation.

Death of Member Spouse prior to Commencement of Designated Benefit –
[s. 12(7) 1995; s. 17(7) 1996]

224. Where an *order* is made in relation to *retirement benefit* and the *member spouse* dies prior to commencement of the *designated benefit* and prior to a *transfer amount* being applied (i.e. while either an *active member* of the *scheme* in question or prior to the commencement of his/her deferred *retirement benefit* if *reckonable service* has terminated), an amount is payable to the person in whose favour the *order* is made.

[s. 12(7) 1995; s. 17(7) 1996; Art. 40(1)(a) 1997]

225. If the *order* is made in favour of the *non-member spouse,* the amount is calculated as the *transfer amount* which would otherwise have been available to that *spouse* immediately prior to the *member spouse's* death. Such *transfer amount* is calculated using the procedures set out in paragraphs 266 to 269 (assuming that the *member spouse* had a normal life expectancy).

[s. 12(7) 1995; s. 17(7) 1996; Art. 40(1)(b) 1997]

226. If the *order* is made in favour of a specified person, for the benefit of a *dependent member of the family,* the amount is calculated as the *actuarial value,* as at the date of *the member spouse's* death, of the *designated benefit* which the specified person would otherwise have expected to receive, for so long only as the person for whose benefit the *order* is made would have remained *a dependent member of the family.*

[Art. 40(2) 1997]

227. The amount in paragraph 225 or 226 should be calculated on a basis which an *actuary* has approved as being consistent with the appropriate guidelines issued by the Society of Actuaries in Ireland. Where the *scheme* is an *occupational pension scheme* which is a funded *scheme* within the meaning of that term under Section 2(1) of the Pensions Act, 1990 and its funded status is such that the *actuary* would have considered it necessary to reduce the transfer value which would have been paid in respect of the *member spouse* (to reflect the inadequacy of the funding) had he/she applied for a transfer value immediately prior to his/her death, the funded status may similarly be reflected in the calculation of the amount arising under the *order.*

[s. 12(7) 1995; s. 17(7) 1996]

228. *The legislation* requires the *trustees* to provide for the payment of the amount referred to in paragraphs 225 and 226 within 3 months of the death of the *member spouse.*

[s. 12(17) 1995; s. 17(17) 1996]

229.   Following the payment of the amount in paragraph 225 or 226, the trustees will be discharged from any obligation to make any further payments in connection with the *order.*

Death of Non-Member Spouse Prior to Commencement of Designated Benefit – [s. 12(9) 1995; s. 17(9) 1996; Art. 41 1997]

230.   Where an *order* is made in relation to *retirement benefit* in favour of the *non-member spouse* and he/she dies prior to a *transfer amount* being applied, and prior to the commencement of the *designated benefit,* an amount must be paid to the personal representatives of the deceased *spouse. The legislation* requires the *trustees* to provide for the payment of such amount within 3 months of his/her death. The amount is calculated as the *transfer amount* which would otherwise have been available to the *non-member spouse,* immediately prior to his/her death, using the procedures set out in paragraphs 266 to 269 (assuming that the *member spouse* had a normal life expectancy).

[s. 12(17) 1995; s. 17(17) 1996]

231.   Following the payment of the amount described in the preceding paragraph, the *trustees* will be discharged from any obligation to make any further payments in connection with the *order.*

Death of Dependent Member of the Family Prior to Commencement of Designated Benefit – [s. 12(11) 1995; s. 17(11) 1996]

232.   Where an *order* is made in relation to *retirement benefit* for the benefit of a *dependent member of the family,* and that person dies prior to the commencement of payment of *the designated benefit, the order* ceases to have effect. (See Part 6 of these notes in relation to calculation of *member spouse's retirement benefit* under *the scheme).*

Defined Contribution Schemes – [s. 12(6) 1995; s. 17(6) 1996; Art. 3 1997]

233.   *Trustees* of a *defined contribution scheme* may generally give effect to an *order* in relation to *retirement benefit* by transferring an amount representing the then value of the *designated benefit* to another *scheme* without seeking the consent of the person in whose favour the *order* is made. The circumstances under which such a transfer may be made, are described in paragraphs 277 and 278.

234.   The *transfer amount* referred to in paragraph 233 must be applied to establish an independent benefit for the person in whose favour the *order is* made. The form of the independent benefit must be in accordance with the conditions set down by the Revenue Commissioners (see paragraphs 328 to 336).

235.   If the *designated benefit* arising from the *member spouse's* membership of a *defined contribution scheme* is retained in that *scheme* it will be necessary to establish administrative procedures so that the *accumulated value,* at any subsequent date, of the *relevant percentage* of the *earmarked contributions* may be identified. The *trustees* may also wish to allow the person specified in the *order* (rather than the *member spouse)* to exercise choice over the investment medium in which the *relevant percentage* of the *earmarked contributions* is invested. When the *member* *spouse's retirement benefit* ultimately becomes payable, the value of the *designated benefit* must be equal to the then *accumulated value* of the *relevant percentage* of the *earmarked contributions.*

[s. 12(14) 1995; s. 17(14) 1996; Art. 37 1997]

236. Where the rules in force include a rule which allows the member spouse to receive part of his/her *retirement benefit* in lump sum form, an equivalent option must be provided to the *non-member spouse* (or other beneficiary). If the *member spouse* elects to exchange part of his/her pension to provide benefits on his/her death after retirement to a third party, this option must not affect the calculation or payment of the *designated benefit.*

[s. 12(10) 1995; s. 12(14) 1995; s. 17(10) 1996; s. 17(14) 1996; Art. 35 1997; Art. 38 1997]

237. Thus, where a *transfer amount* has not been applied, the *designated benefit* which corresponds to the *member spouse's* retirement pension is payable for the lifetime of the *member spouse* subject to any minimum payment period or pension increases attaching to the *member spouse's* retirement pension. If the *order* is made in favour of the *non-member spouse* and he/she predeceases the *member spouse* following commencement of the *designated benefit,* an amount is payable to the personal representatives of the deceased *spouse* as explained in paragraph 215.

Death of Member Spouse Prior to Commencement of Designated Benefit – [s. 12(7) 1995; s. 17(7) 1996; Art. 40(1)(c) 1997]

238. Where an *order* is made in relation to *retirement benefit* and the *member spouse* dies prior to commencement of the *designated benefit* and prior to a *transfer amount* being applied (i.e. while either an *active member* of the *scheme* in question or prior to the commencement of his/her deferred *retirement benefit* if *reckonable service* has terminated), an amount is payable to the person in whose favour the *order* is made. The amount is calculated as the *accumulated value,* as at the date of death, of the *relevant percentage* of the *earmarked contributions* assuming the *member spouse* had withdrawn from *reckonable service* immediately prior to his/her death.

[s. 12(7) 1995; s. 17(7) 1996]

239. The amount in paragraph 238 must be paid within 3 months of the death of the *member spouse* to the person named in the *order.*

[s. 12(17) 1995; s. 17(17) 1996]

240. Following the payment of the amount described in the preceding paragraph, the *trustees* will be discharged from any obligation to make any further payments in connection with the *order.*

Death of Non-Member Spouse Prior to Commencement of Designated Benefit – [s. 12(9) 1995; s. 17(9) 1996; Art. 41 1997]

241. Where an *order* is made in relation to *retirement benefit* in favour of the *non-member spouse* and he/she dies prior to a *transfer amount* being applied, and prior to the commencement of the *designated benefit,* a payment must be made to the personal representatives of the deceased *spouse* within 3 months of his/her death. The payment is calculated as the *transfer amount* which would otherwise have been available to the *non-member spouse* immediately prior to his/her death using the procedures set out in paragraphs 270 to 272.

[s. 12(17) 1995; s. 17(17) 1996]

242. Following the payment of the amount described in the preceding paragraph, the *trustees* will be discharged from any obligation to make any further payments in connection with the *order.*

Death of Dependent Member of the Family Prior to Commencement of Designated Benefit – [s. 12(11) 1995; s. 17(11) 1996]

243. Where an *order* is made in relation to *retirement benefit* for the benefit of a *dependent member of the family,* and that person dies prior to the commencement of payment of the *designated benefit, the order* ceases to have effect. (See Part 6 of these notes in relation to calculation of *member spouse's retirement benefit* under *the scheme).*

PART 6

CALCULATION OF RESIDUAL BENEFITS FOLLOWING ORDER IN RELATION TO RETIREMENT BENEFIT

This Part of the notes sets out the procedure for reducing the member spouse's retirement benefit or contingent benefit tinder the scheme following the making of a pension adjustment order in relation to his/her retirement benefit.

General – [s. 12(15) 1995; s. 12(16) 1995; s. 17(15) 1996; s. 17(16) 1996]

250. Where an *order* is made in relation to *retirement benefit,* the *legislation* provides that benefits payable to, or in respect of, *the member spouse in* accordance with the *rules* of the *scheme* concerned are reduced. Paragraphs 251 to 254 deal with the procedure for determining the *member spouse's* residual *retirement benefit (i.e. retirement benefit* payable in accordance with the rules less the appropriate adjustment to take account of the *order).* Paragraph 255 deals with the procedure for reducing the amount of *contingent benefit* payable in respect of a *member spouse* to take account of benefit obligations under an *order in* relation to *retirement benefit* in the event of his/her death.

Retirement Benefit – Defined Benefit – s. 12(15) 1995; s. 17(15) 1996; Art 6 1997]

251. Where an order is made in relation to the member spouse's retirement *benefit, and retirement benefit* is calculated on a *defined benefit basis,* the residual *retirement benefit* payable to, or in respect of, the *member spouse* is calculated as the *retirement benefit* payable in accordance with the *rules* of the *scheme* less the corresponding amount of the *designated benefit.*

Example

A *member* joined a *scheme* on 1st January, 1990, at age 25. The *rules* provide for a retirement pension of 2/3rds of pensionable salary on retirement at *normal pensionable age* 65 together with a dependent's pension, payable on death following retirement, of 1/3rd of pensionable salary.

Following the granting of a decree on 1st January, 2010 an order is made in relation to the *member spouse's* retirement benefit, in favour of the non-member spouse, which specifies:

Relevant period:	1st January, 1990 to 1st January, 2010
Relevant percentage:	50%

On the member spouse's retirement at normal pensionable age his pensionable salary is £100,000. The designated benefit which corresponds with the member spouse's retirement pension, is calculated as follows:

A =	2/3rds of £100,000	= £66,667
B =	1st January, 1990 to 1st January, 2010	= 20 years
C =	1st January, 1990 to 1st January, 2030	= 40 years
p =	50%	

Designated Benefit (retirement pension)

$$= £66,667 \times \frac{20}{40} \times 50\% \qquad = £16,667$$

Residual retirement pension, payable to *member spouse*

$$= £66,667 - £16,667 \qquad = £50,000$$

Using the same procedure, the *designated benefit* payable to *non-member spouse* following the member spouse's death in retirement amounts to £8,333 p.a. and the residual dependant's pension, payable in accordance with the rules, amounts to £25,000 p.a.

[s. 12(15) 1995; s. 17(15) 1996; Art. 26 1997]

252. In terms of calculating the residual *retirement benefit* payable to the *member spouse* **during his/her lifetime,** the principle in paragraph 251 applies regardless of whether the *designated benefit* is paid from the *scheme,* has been transferred to another *scheme* or (if the *order* is made in favour of the *non-member spouse*) has been paid as a lump sum following the death of the *non-member spouse*. The residual *retirement benefit*, if any, payable following the death of the *member spouse* may, however, be affected by the nature of payment made under the *order* (see paragraph 253 and attaching example).

Example

Details are as in the example in paragraph 251 except that the *trustees* applied a transfer amount of £75,000 to another *scheme* following a request from the *non-member spouse* shortly after the order was made on 1st January, 2010.

In these circumstances, the member spouse's residual retirement pension is calculated as:

Retirement pension under scheme rules	:	£66,667
LESS		
Designated Benefit that would have been payable, ignoring transfer	:	£16,667
Residual retirement pension	:	£50,000

(i.e. same as example in paragraph 251)

253. If *the order* has ceased to have effect, the *retirement benefit* payable to, or in respect of, *the member spouse* is calculated as the *retirement benefit* payable in accordance with the *rules of the scheme.* The circumstances under which the *order* could cease to have effect are:–

(1) If the *order* is made in favour of a specified person, for the benefit of *dependent member of the family* on the death or cessation of *dependency of* that *dependent member of the family;*

(2) If *the order* is made in favour of the *non-member spouse* (and he/she did not elect for *a transfer amount* in lieu of receiving designated *benefit)* following the death of both the *member spouse,* and the *non-member spouse* after the commencement of the *designated benefit.* **[s. 12(11)-95; s. 17(11) 1996]**

Example

Details as in the example in paragraph 251. Following the *member spouse's* death the *non-member spouse* receives the designated benefit which corresponds with the dependant's pension, i.e. £8,333 p.a. and the balance, i.e. £25,000 p.a. is payable in accordance with the scheme rules.

Following the subsequent death of the *non-member spouse*, the full amount of the dependent's pension, i.e. £33,333 p.a. is payable in accordance with the *scheme rules.*

If, however, the *non-member spouse* had elected to apply a transfer amount in lieu of receiving *designated benefit* (e.g. as in paragraph 252) the actuarial value of the designated portion of the dependant's pension would have been included in such transfer amount, and the payment of residual benefits in respect of the *member spouse* would be unaffected by the death of the *non-member spouse.*

Retirement Benefit – Defined Contribution – [s. 12(15) 1995; s. 17(15) 1996; Art. 27 1997]

254. Where an *order* is made in relation to the *member spouse's retirement benefit, and retirement benefit* is calculated on a *defined contribution basis, the* residual *retirement benefit* payable to, or in respect of, the *member spouse is* calculated by applying the *accumulated value* of contributions made for the purposes of *retirement benefit,* less the *accumulated value* of the *relevant percentage of earmarked* *contributions,* in accordance with the *rules* of the *scheme*. If the *order* has ceased to have effect, the *retirement benefit* payable to, or in respect of, the *member spouse* is calculated as the *retirement benefit* payable in accordance with the *rules* of the *scheme*.

Contingent Benefit – [s. 12(16) 1995; s. 17(16) 1996; Art. 28 1997]

255. Where an *order* is made in relation to *retirement benefit* and the *member spouse* dies prior to commencement of the *designated benefit,* the amount of any *contingent benefit* payable in accordance with the *rules* of the same *scheme is* reduced by the amount described in paragraphs 225, 226, or 238 as appropriate. For this purpose a *retirement benefit* arising under a *Section 235 retirement annuity contract (or trust scheme)* and a *contingent benefit* arising under a *Section 235A policy (or trust scheme)* for the same *member* are not regarded as benefits arising under the *rules* of the same *scheme.*

256. The reduction in *contingent benefit* referred to in paragraph 255 should be calculated on a basis which an *actuary* has approved as being consistent with the appropriate guidelines issued by the Society of Actuaries in Ireland.

PART 7

TRANSFER AMOUNTS

This Part of the notes sets out the circumstances in which the nonmember spouse or the trustees may initiate a transfer amount, and the basis for calculating and the procedure which must be followed in relation to transfer amounts.

General – [s. 12(4) 1995; s. 17(4) 1996]

260. If an *order* has been made in relation to the *member spouse's retirement benefit* in favour of the *non-member spouse, the legislation* enables the *non-member spouse* to opt for an independent benefit instead of receiving the *designated benefit* from the *scheme* (i.e. a proportion of each instalment of the *retirement benefit* payable to, or in respect of, the *member spouse* as it falls due). Paragraphs 262 to 276 deal with the procedures and methodology involved where the *non-member spouse* chooses to exercise this option. The *legislation* provides no such option where the *order* is made in favour of a specified person for the benefit of a *dependent member of the family.*

[s. 12(6) 1995; s. 12(8) 1995; s. 17(6) 1996; s. 17(8) 1996]

261. Regardless of whether the *order* is made in favour of *the non-member spouse* or a specified person for the benefit of a *dependent member of the family, the legislation* enables the *trustees,* in certain circumstances, to establish a separate arrangement for the person in whose favour the *order* is made without obtaining the consent of that person. Paragraphs 277 to 283 describe the procedures which must be followed in implementing such a transfer.

Transfer Following Request From Non-Member Spouse

Application – [s. 12(4) 1995]

262. At the time of the making of the *order,* or at any time prior to the commencement of the *designated bene*fit, *the non-member spouse* may make an application to the trustees requesting that a *transfer amount* be applied for his/her benefit in lieu of receiving payment of the *designated benefit* from the *scheme*

[s. 12(5) 1995; s. 17(5) 1996; Art. 30; Art. 34(4)(a) 1997]

263. The application must be made in writing, must relate to the full *designated benefit* payable from the *scheme,* and must be accompanied by whatever information is reasonably required by the trustees. Where the *trustees* had initiated a transfer (see paragraphs 277 and 278) within 30 days prior to the receipt of a valid application from the *non-member spouse,* they must make the transfer on the basis of the *non-member spouse's* application.

[s. 12(5) 1995; s. 17(5) 1996; Art. 30 1997]

264. Where the *trustees* of a *scheme* receive a valid application for a *transfer amount* from the *non-member spouse,* they must apply the *transfer amount* concerned as directed in the application within 3 months of the date of receipt of the application.

265. If no such application has been received by the *trustees* when payment of *the designated benefit* is due to commence (i.e. when the *trustees* become aware that the *member spouse's retirement benefit* is due to commence) they may choose (but are not obliged) to offer the transfer option to the *non-member spouse.*

Calculation of Transfer Amount – Defined Benefit – [s. 12(4) 1995; s. 17(4) 1996; Art. 31(1) 1997]

266. The *transfer amount* in respect of the *designated benefit,* or part of the *designated benefit* which has been determined on a *defined benefit basis,* is the *actuarial value,* as at the date of the application for *a transfer amount,* of the *designated benefit* (or part thereof).

[Art. 31(2) 1997]

267. If the *member spouse* is an *active member* of the *scheme* in question at the date of receipt of the application for a *transfer amount,* the calculation in paragraph 266 should be determined by reference to the *designated benefit* which would have arisen had the *member spouse's reckonable service* terminated of his/her own free will on the date of receipt of the application. In particular, if under the *rules in force, a member whose reckonable service* terminated had no entitlement to a benefit in respect of a specified period of *reckonable service (e.g.* pre-1991 *reckonable service) the designated benefit* for the purposes of calculating the *transfer amount* would similarly exclude any such period of *reckonable service.*

[Art. 31(3) 1997]

268. The *transfer amount* should be calculated on a basis which an *actuary has* approved as being consistent with the appropriate guidelines issued by the Society of Actuaries in Ireland.

[Art. 31(3) 1997]

269. Where the *scheme* is an *occupational pension scheme,* which is a funded *scheme* within the meaning of that term under Section 2(1) of the Pensions Act, 1990 and its funded status is such that the *actuary* would have considered it necessary to reduce the transfer value which would have been paid in respect of *a member* who had applied for a transfer value at the date of receipt of the application for a *transfer amount,* the funded status may similarly be reflected in arriving at the *transfer amount* arising under the *order.*

Calculation of Transfer Amount – Defined Contribution – [s. 12(4) 1995; s. 17(4) 1996; Art. 32(1) 1997]

270. *The transfer amount* in respect of a *designated benefit,* or part of a *designated benefit,* which has been determined on a *defined contribution basis* is the *accumulated value* of the *relevant percentage* of the *earmarked contributions.*

[Art. 32(2) 1997]

271. If the *member spouse* is an *active member* of the *scheme* in question at the date of receipt of the application for a *transfer amount,* the calculation in paragraph 270 should be determined by reference to the *accumulated value* which would have arisen if the *member spouse's reckonable service* had terminated of his/her own free will on the date of receipt of the application and his/her entitlement had been calculated under the *rules in force.* Thus, for example, if the *member spouse* was a *member* of an *occupational pension scheme* and the *rules in force* specified that, on termination of *reckonable service,* he/she would not be entitled to the benefit of contributions made by the sponsoring employer prior to 1991 for the purposes of *retirement benefit, the transfer amount* is calculated on an equivalent basis.

[Art. 32(3) 1997]

272. The *accumulated value* must be determined on a date not later than 3 months following the date on which the *trustees receive* an application for a *transfer amount.*

Establishment of Independent Benefit – [s. 12(5) 1995; s. 17(5) 1996]

273. There are three different methods provided for in the *legislation* whereby an independent benefit may be established for the *non-member spouse* by the application of the *transfer amount.*

[s. 12(5) 1995; s. 17(5) 1996; Art 33(2) 1997]

274. If the *trustees* of the *scheme* and the *non-member spouse* so agree, the *transfer amount* may be applied to provide a separate benefit for, or in respect of, the *non-member spouse* in that *scheme. The trustees* must ensure that the benefit or benefits to be provided for, or in respect of, the *non-member spouse* are of an *actuarial value* equivalent to the *transfer amount* but the benefits may be in such form as the *trustees and non-member spouse* agree provided only that they conform to Revenue requirements. (See paragraphs 328 and 329). The *trustees* must also inform the *non-member spouse* in writing of the benefits to be provided as soon as practicable after the *transfer amount* has been applied.

[s. 12(5) 1995; s. 17(5) 1996; Art. 33(3) 1997]

275.   Subject to the agreement of the *trustees* of any other *occupational pension scheme* of which he/she is a *member, the ion-member spouse* in whose favour the *order* is made may alternatively elect to have the *transfer amount* paid to that other *scheme. The trustees* of the receiving *scheme* must ensure that the benefit or benefits to be provided for, or in respect of, the *non-member spouse* are of an *actuarial value* equivalent to the *transfer amount* received but the benefits may be in such form as the *trustees* and the *non-member spouse* agree provided only that they conform to Revenue requirements. (See paragraph 330). The *trustees* of the receiving *scheme* must also inform the *non-member spouse* in writing of the benefits to be provided as soon as practicable after the *transfer amount* has been applied. This option is not available where the *member spouse* is a *member* of a *Section 235 retirement annuity contract* or a *trust scheme.*

[s. 12(5) 1995; s. 17(5) 1996]

276.   As an alternative to the options described in paragraphs 274 and 275, the *non-member spouse* may elect to have the *transfer amount* applied to an insurance policy or contract provided that this is approved by the Revenue Commissioners and that the insurance company which offers the policy or contract is willing to accept the *transfer amount. The trustees* of the paying *scheme* must ensure that the *transfer amount* is paid directly to the insurance company and must inform the insurance company of the maximum amount which may be received in lump sum form on retirement (see paragraph 332).

Transfer Initiated by Trustees – [s. 12(6) 1995; s. 12(g) 1995; s. 17(6) 1996; s. 17(g) 1996; Art. 34(1) 1997]

277.   In certain circumstances the *trustees* of the *scheme* of which the *member spouse* is a *member,* may choose to give effect to the *order* by applying a *transfer* amount (representing the value of the *designated benefit* which would otherwise be paid) to another *scheme* or approved insurance policy without requiring the consent of the person in whose favour the *order* is made. The circumstances under which such a transfer may be made are:-

    (1) where the *designated benefit* arises from the *member spouse's* membership of a *defined contribution scheme* and the *transfer amount* represents *the accumulated value* of the *relevant percentage* of all of the *earmarked contributions* (i.e. none of the contributions made by the sponsoring employer in respect of the *member spouse for* the purposes of *retirement benefit* are excluded as provided for in paragraph 271);

    (2) where the *member spouse* ceases to be a *member* of the *scheme* following his/her termination of *reckonable service* (i.e. he/she decides to transfer the value of the residual *retirement benefit* to another *scheme* or approved insurance policy or contract).

278.   Where the *trustees* initiate a transfer in the circumstances described in paragraph 277, the following conditions must be observed:-

(1) Written notice must be given to the person in whose favour the *order is* made at least 30 days before the proposed transfer; **[Art. 34(4) 1997]**

(2) There must be no outstanding application from the *non-member spouse* to have the *designated benefit* transferred to another *scheme* or approved insurance policy or contract that is willing and capable of receiving the *transfer amount;* **[Art. 34(4) 1997]**

(3) The *trustees* must be satisfied that the benefits that will be provided in the receiving *scheme* are of an *actuarial value* equivalent to the *transfer amount* (after allowing for reasonable charges, fees and costs); **[Art. 34(4) 1997]**

(4) Where the *scheme* is an *occupational pension scheme* which is a funded *scheme* within the meaning of that term under Section 2(1) of the Pensions Act, 1990, the *actuarial value* of the *transfer amount* shall not be reduced to reflect an inadequate funded status (i.e. as provided for in paragraph 269); **[Art. 34(3) 1997]**

(5) Where the *transfer amount* is applied to provide an independent benefit in the same *scheme, the trustees* of that *scheme* must ensure that the benefits are in such form as they and the person in whose favour the *order* is made agree, provided that the benefits conform with Revenue requirements; **[Art. 34(5) 1997]**

(6) Where the *transfer amount* is applied to provide an independent benefit in a separate *occupational pension scheme, the trustees* of the receiving *scheme* must ensure that the benefits are in such form as they and the person in whose favour the *order* is made agree, provided that the benefits conform with Revenue requirements; **[Art. 34(6) 1997]**

(7) Where the *transfer amount* is applied to an insurance policy or contract *the trustees* of the paying *scheme* must ensure that the *transfer amount is* paid directly to the insurance company and must inform the insurance company of the maximum amount which may be received in lump sum form on retirement. (See paragraph 332); **[Art. 34(7) 1997]**

(8) The person in whose favour the *order* is made, and the registrar or clerk of the *Court,* must subsequently be notified of the *transfer amount and* of the *occupational pension scheme* or insurance policy or contract to which the *transfer amount* has been applied; **[s. 12(13) 1997]**

(9) For the benefits to be established under another *occupational pension* scheme, unless the transfer is being made from a previous *occupational pension scheme* relating to the same *relevant employment* the person in whose favour the *order* is made must be a *member* of that *scheme* and the *scheme* from which the transfer is made must be an *occupational pension scheme* or a *buy-out bond.*

Order Made for Benefit of a Dependent Member of the Family – [s. 12(6) 1995; s. 12(8) 1995; s. 17(6) 1996; s. 17(8) 1996]

279. If the *order* is in favour of a person for the benefit of a *dependent member of the family*, a transfer may not be made unless initiated by the *trustees* in the circumstances and subject to the conditions specified in paragraphs 277 and 278.

[Art. 34(3) 1997]

280. If the *order* is made in favour of a person for the benefit of a *dependent member of the family, the transfer amount* in respect of the *designated benefit,* or part of the *designated benefit* which has been determined on a *defined benefit basis* is the *actuarial value* of the *designated benefit* which the specified person would otherwise have expected to receive, for so long only as the person for whose benefit the *order* is made would have remained a *dependent member of the family.*

281. The transfer amount should be calculated on a basis which an actuary has approved as being consistent with the appropriate guidelines issued by the Society of Actuaries in Ireland.

[Art. 34(2) 1997]

282. If the *order* is made in favour of a person for the benefit of a *dependent member of the family, the transfer amount* in respect of the *designated benefit,* or part of the *designated benefit,* which is calculated on a *defined contribution basis* will be *the accumulated value,* as at the date the benefit is transferred, of the *relevant percentage* of the *earmarked contributions.* Where the *member spouse* is an *active member* of the *scheme* when calculating the *transfer amount,* it is not permissible to exclude the contributions made by the sponsoring employer in respect of the *member spouse* for the purposes of *retirement benefit* as provided for in paragraph 271.

283. There are three different methods provided for in the *legislation* whereby an independent benefit may be established for the *dependent member of the family* by the application of the *transfer amount.* These are as described in paragraphs 274 to 276.

Discharge of Trustees Responsibilities – [s. 12(17) 1995; s. 17(1 7) 1996]

284. Where the *trustees* apply a *transfer amount* in accordance with the *legislation* (either at the request of the *non-member spouse* if the *order* is made in his/her favour or on their own initiative) they are discharged from any further obligation to make payments in connection with the *order.*

PART 8

CONTINGENT BENEFITS

This Part of the notes sets out the conditions governing the calculation and payment of contingent benefit from a scheme following a pension adjustment order in relation to the member spouse's contingent benefit and the procedure for reducing the member spouse's contingent benefit under the scheme.

General – [s. 12(3) 1995; s. 17(3) 1996]

290. Following the granting of a *decree the Court* may, on application by *either spouse* or by a person for the benefit of a *dependent member of the family,* make an *order* in relation to *contingent benefit* that is payable (or which, but for the *decree,* would have been payable) under a *scheme* of which either *spouse* is a *member.* This type of *order* may be made in addition to any *order* in relation to *retirement benefit.*

[s. 12(3) 1995; s. 17(3) 1996]

291. Paragraphs 75 to 77 deal with the criteria governing the application for *an order.* Most importantly, an application for an *order* in relation to *contingent benefit* must be made within 12 months following the granting of the *decree.*

[Art. 50 1997]

292. Paragraph 61 sets out the information that the *trustees* must provide in relation to *contingent benefit,* if directed by the *Court.* As the *order* may apply to part but not all of the *contingent benefit* (e.g. it may relate to the lump sum death benefit but not to the dependant's pension) it will be necessary for the *trustees to* separately identify each element of the *contingent benefit* by reference to the corresponding *scheme* rule or policy or contract number.

293. Paragraph 80 sets out the information that will be set out in the *order. In* particular, this will inform the *trustees* of the percentage of either the total or a specified element of the *contingent benefit* that must be payable to the person(s) named in the *order.*

[s. 12(20) 1995; s. 17(20) 1996]

294. The order, provided that the *Court* so directs the *trustees,* will override any discretionary powers regarding payment of death benefits which the *trustees* are empowered to exercise under the *rules* of the *scheme.* Subject to paragraph 255 any residual *contingent benefit* will be paid in accordance with the *rules* of the *scheme.*

Duration of Order – [s. 12(19) 1995; s. 17(19) 1996]

295. An *order* made in relation to *contingent benefit* will cease to have effect: –

(1) on the death of the person in whose favour the *order* was made;

(2) if the *order* was made in favour of the *non-member spouse, the* remarriage of that *spouse;*

(3) if the *order* was made for the benefit of a *dependent member of the family,* the cessation of the beneficiary's *dependency.*

296. In any of the circumstances outlined in paragraph 295, an *order* may continue to apply to other persons. For example, if the *order* is made in favour of *the non-member spouse* and also for the benefit of a *dependent member of the family* and the *non-member spouse* remarries, it would continue to have effect insofar as it related to the *dependent member of the family* for so long as he/she remained dependent.

[s. 12(1) 1995; s. 12(12) 1995; s. 17(1) 1996; s. 17(12) 1996]

297. *The legislation* defines a *contingent benefit* as a benefit payable under a *scheme* if the *member spouse* dies while in *relevant employment* and before attaining any *normal pensionable age* provided for under the *rules* of the *scheme*. Hence, an *order* in relation to *contingent benefit* ceases to have effect when the *member spouse's relevant employment* terminates. In these circumstances, the *trustees* must notify the registrar or clerk of the *Court,* and the *non-member spouse* (within a period of 12 months following such termination).

Relevant Employment – **[s. 12(1) 1995; s. 17(1) 1996; Art. 3 1997]**

298. A *member* is regarded as being in *relevant employment* if he/she is in any employment (or any period treated as employment) or any period of self-employment to which a *scheme* applies. Where under the *rules* of a *scheme* a "death-in-service benefit" is provided on the death of the *member* following termination of employment (e.g. in the case of a *member* who retires prior to *normal pensionable age*, death benefits continue to be provided until *normal pensionable age*) such a period shall be treated as a period of *relevant employment.*

299. A *scheme* is regarded as applying to an employment where an employee is, or is capable of becoming, a *member* of that *scheme*. A *scheme* is regarded as no longer applying to an employment where:

(1) the *scheme* is wound up and not replaced by another *scheme;*

(2) the *scheme* is "frozen" (i.e. benefits for existing *members* are no longer accruing, and no new *members* are being included) and not replaced;

(3) an employee has declined to join, or has opted to terminate his/her membership of, the *scheme,*

(4) in the case of a self-employed person, he is no longer contributing to either a *Section 235 retirement annuity contract or trust scheme,* or a *Section 235A policy.*

[Art. 44 1997]

300. If a *member's* employment is interrupted due to a period of temporary absence, the *member's relevant employment* is not treated as terminated and, hence, an *order* in relation to *contingent benefit* continues to have effect. For this purpose, temporary absence means a period of absence:–

(1) on account of the *member's* pregnancy or childbirth;

(2) in furtherance of a trade dispute;

(3) where under the *scheme's* temporary absence rule, the *member's* employment is not treated as terminated;

(4) of less than one month.

Termination of Relevant Employment – [Art. 43 1997]

301.   If:–

(1) in the case of a *scheme* with more than one participating employer (including an industry-wide *scheme) a member's* employment ceases and within a period of one month (or such longer period as the trustees decide) following such cessation he/she becomes employed by another employer participating in the same *scheme,*

or

(2) in the case of a change in ownership of the employer, or of the employer's business, a *member's* employment ceases and within a period of one month (or such longer period as the *trustees* decide) following such cessation he/she becomes employed by the new employer and resumes membership of the same *scheme,*

his/her *relevant employment* is not treated as terminated and, hence, an *order in relation* to *contingent benefit* continues to have effect.

Death of Member Spouse – [s. 12(3) 1995; s. 17(3) 1996; Art. 46 1997]

302.   Where, on the death of the *member spouse, a contingent benefit* is payable under the *rules* of the *scheme,* the percentage of the *contingent benefit* specified in *the order* must be paid to the person named in the *order.*

303.   The *contingent benefit* must be calculated as at the date of the *member spouse's* death (e.g. if *contingent benefit* under the *rules* of the *scheme* is based on the *member's* salary at death, it must be similarly calculated for the purposes of determining the percentage specified in the *order).* It must also be based on the *rules* of the *scheme* as at the date of the *decree.* In particular, the *legislation* specifies that an order relates to any *contingent benefit* that is payable or which, but for the *decree,* would have been payable.

304.   A *scheme* may, therefore, have to continue to provide (and, if appropriate, insure) part, or all, of a *contingent benefit* which, had it not been for the *order,* would have lapsed. For example, if the *rules* of the *scheme* include a cohabitation requirement in the case of a *spouse's* benefit, the *trustees* must nonetheless pay a percentage of that benefit to a separated *spouse* if so specified in the *order.* Similarly, if the *rules* of the *scheme* provide that a *spouse's* benefit will not be payable if the *non-member spouse* cohabits with any other person, the *trustees* must nonetheless pay a percentage of the benefit to a cohabiting *spouse* if so specified in the *order.*

Example

The *rules* of a *member spouse's scheme* provide for a lump sum death benefit of 4 times salary at date of death to be paid in the event of death during, *relevant employment.*

An *order* made in relation to the *member spouse's contingent benefit* in favour of the non-member spouse, which specifies:

Contingent Benefit:	Lump sum of 4 times salary at date of death
Percentage of *contingent benefit* to be paid to *non-member spouse*:	50%

The member spouse dies during the relevant employment. Her salary at the date of death is £50,000. The amount of benefit paid in accordance with the order is calculated as:–

$$4 \times £50,000 \times 50\% = £100,000$$

305. Any alteration in *contingent benefit* which takes effect after the date of the *decree,* (whether such alteration represents an increase or reduction in the benefit scale, or the addition or deletion of a specified element of *contingent benefit)* is not taken into account for the purposes of determining the percentage of the *contingent benefit* specified in the *order.*

306. Where a *member spouse* is allowed, under the *rules* of the *scheme, to* exercise a choice in the rate or scale *of contingent benefit* to be provided in respect of him/her, the percentage of the *contingent benefit* specified in the *order is* calculated based on the rate or scale in force as at the date of the *decree.*

[s. 12(7) 1995; s. 17(7) 1996]

307. If a separate *order* (in relation to the *member spouse's retirement benefit)* has been served on the *trustees,* in the event of the *member spouse's* death before payment of the *designated benefit* has commenced, a *transfer amount* (as outlined in paragraphs 225, 226 or 238) must also be paid to the person in whose favour this separate *order* has been made.

[s. 12(16) 1995; s. 17(16) 1996]

308. Any residual *contingent benefit* (having deducted any lump sum or dependant's pension payments arising under paragraphs 302 or any payment arising under paragraph 307) is payable in accordance with the *rules* of the *scheme.* Where, prior to the death of the *member spouse, a transfer amount* had already been paid by the *trustees* in accordance with the provisions of paragraphs 230, 241, 262 or 277, such amount is not deducted when determining any residual *contingent benefit* payable on the subsequent death of the *member spouse.*

Example

Details are as set out in the example in paragraph 304, except that a separate order has been made, in favour of the non-member spouse, in relation to the *member spouse's retirement benefit*. The amount payable on the member spouse's retirement benefit. the amount payable on the member spouse's death under the order in relation to retirement benefit is calculated as £75,000.

The residual *contingent benefit* is calculated as follows:

Death benefits payable under *scheme* rules:	£200,000 (i.e. 4 x £50,000)
Amount payable under *order* in relation to *contingent benefit*:	£100,000 (see paragraph 304)
Amount payable under *order* in relation to *retirement benefit*:	£75,000
Residual *contingent benefit*:	£25,000

(payable in accordance with *rules* of the *scheme*).

309.   If an *order* in relation to *contingent benefit* ceases to have effect (e.g. because of the remarriage of the *non-member spouse* or due to the ending of *dependency* if the *order* is made for the benefit of a *dependent member of the family) the contingent benefit* will be payable in accordance with the *rules* of the *scheme. The order may,* however, continue to apply to any other person specified in the *order* and the provisions of paragraph 307 may also apply.

Example

Details are as in the example in paragraph 308, except that the *non-member spouse* had remarried at the date of the member spouse's death.

The residual *contingent benefit* is calculated as follows:

Death benefits payable under *scheme* rules:	£200,000 (i.e. x £50,000)
Amount payable under order in relation to *retirement benefit*:	£75,000
Residual *contingent benefit*:	£125,000

(payable in accordance with *rules* of the *scheme*).

Payment of Contingent Benefit – [s. 12(14) 1995; s. 17(14) 1996]

310. If, following the *member spouse's* death, a dependant's pension becomes payable under the *order,* this will be payable in accordance with the *rules* of the *scheme* (other than as indicated in paragraph 304). Thus if:–

(1) the *rules* of the *scheme* at the date of the *decree* provide for guaranteed increases in the *contingent benefit* payable in pension form, or

(2) the *rules* of the *scheme* at the date of the *decree* permit, and the appropriate person or persons exercise a discretion to grant a cost of living increase in the *contingent benefit* payable in pension form to all, or a certain category of, pensioners,

and the *contingent benefit* payable in respect of the *member spouse* is increased as a result, the same increase must be applied to the dependant's pension payable under the *order.*

311. The *legislation* does not specify the period within which a lump sum *contingent benefit* payable under an *order* in relation to *contingent benefit* must be paid. Hence, any period specified in the *rules* of the *scheme* would apply. Where no such period is specified, the *trustees* should endeavour to make the payment to the person specified in the *order* within 3 months of the death of the *member spouse.*

INDEX